W9-BYF-569

An Invitation to Be Faithful

There's something else going on: It is love. I wish I
could prove to you that it would work right now, but
love does not necessarily "work." I wish I could
convince you, make it self-evident, so you could not
deny it. But I can only invite you to do what Jesus did,
somehow to not run around our humanity but enter
into it and feel it. I invite you into the pain and joy of
being human.

Jesus invites us to participate not in this
world's power, but in its powerlessness. For Christians
it is the absolutely necessary beginning point. Logic of
the world will never understand that. But look gently,
quietly at how life and energy are communicated
between people. Look how people are changed. It
always starts with powerlessness. Power, as Napoleon
said in retrospect, really does not change things; it only
rearranges them. Change is finally and fully brought
about by the life of the Spirit. I invite you to that life,
and to everything that follows from it.

from *Days of Renewal*

RADICAL GRACE

Daily Meditations
by
Richard Rohr

Edited by John Feister

ST. ANTHONY MESSENGER PRESS
Cincinnati, Ohio

To four grace-filled women:

Cathy Bookser-Feister
Patti Dailey Garrity
Sr. Pat Brockman, O.S.U.
Christiana Spahn

Scripture citations are the author's paraphrase except where noted from *The Jerusalem Bible (JB)*, copyright ©1966 by Darton Longman & Todd, Ltd. and Doubleday, a division of Bantam Doubleday Dell or *The New American Bible With Revised New Testament (NAB)*, copyright ©1986 by the Confraternity of Christian Doctrine, and used by permission. All rights reserved. Excerpts from the English translation of *The Liturgy of the Hours* ©1974, International Committee on English in the Liturgy, Inc. All rights reserved. Excerpts from *The Enneagram: Naming Our Illusions* and *Enneagram II: Tool for Conversion*, copyright ©1988 by Credence Cassettes, are used with permission. Material from the article "Recipes of a Gourmet Pray-er: Art and Betty Winter Interview Richard Rohr" (*U.S. Catholic*, May 1983), is reprinted with permission from *U.S. Catholic*, published by Claretian Publications, 205 West Monroe St., Chicago, IL 60606. Material from the following issues of *The Catholic Agitatior* is reprinted with permission from the Los Angeles Catholic Worker: "Creative Dissent" (January 1987); "Finding a Place for Prayer: A Talk About Prayer With Richard Rohr" (January 1990). Material from the following issues of *Sojourners* is reprinted with permission from *Sojourners*, P.O. Box 29272, Washington, D.C. 20017: "Building Family: God's Strategy for the Reluctant Church" (January 1979); "Reflections on Marriage and Celibacy" (May 1979); "The Energy of Promise" (November 1979); "Baptism of Joy" (December 1979); "All of Life Together Is a Stage" (February 1981); "Authors of Life Together: Inner Authority in Community" (March 1981); "A Life Pure and Simple: A Franciscan Reflects on the Saint" (December 1981); "The Holiness of Human Sexuality" (October 1982); "Why Does Psychology Always Win? The Process of Conversion From Self-actualization to Self-transcendence" (November 1991).

Cover design by Candle Light Studios
Book design by Julie Lonneman

ISBN-13: 978-0-86716-257-8
ISBN-10: 0-86716-257-0

Copyright ©1995, Richard Rohr and John Feister
All rights reserved

Published by St. Anthony Messenger Press
28 W. Liberty St.
Cincinnati, Ohio 45202
www.SAMPBooks.org

Printed in the U.S.A.
08 09 10 11 12 12 11 10 9 8

Contents

Acknowledgments

This book is the product of many minds, hands and hearts. The authors would like to thank Pat McCloskey, O.F.M., for the idea, and Lisa Biedenbach, Tom Bruce, Diane Houdek and others at St. Anthony Messenger Press for encouraging us to pursue it and skillfully guiding us through to completion. Special thanks go to Margaret Warminski. She quickly and accurately transcribed piles of audiocassettes and articles, creating the pool from which these meditations were drawn and edited. We thank Wanda Biddle for her transcription work at the project's outset.

For providing audiocassettes from their library we thank the New Jerusalem Community, especially Walt and Joan Bassett. Joe Nangle, O.F.M., at Sojourners Community was kind enough to review a draft and give comments, as was Cathy Bookser-Feister, who lent a keen eye for inclusive language. Gregory Norbet's gift of music, especially expressed in his recording *Mountains of My Soul*, kept deep waters stirring when this book seemed too big to complete. Finally we thank Ed Stieritz and the staff of Marydale Retreat Center, Covington, Kentucky, who provided quiet nourishing space during two critical phases of the book's creation.

Preface

The meditations in this collection are arranged according to the
seasons the Church celebrates, but we encourage readers to use
this book in any way they find most helpful. Some will use it as a
"day-by day" book of meditations; others will browse and find
favorites. Either method would be true to our purpose: to provide
a volume of thoughtful passages from Father Richard Rohr's two
decades of public preaching and writing.

 If you listen to Richard Rohr's audiocassettes, you'll realize
these meditations were not taken verbatim. The tools of good
speaking—repetition, inflection, timing and other techniques—
seldom make for good reading. You'll find here tightened
phrasing, some condensing, occasional construction of a
meditation from several sources. Richard contributed new
wordings or new material to almost all the meditations once they
were assembled. In many instances, Richard contributed material
which has been published throughout his many outlets. (He is a
prolific person!)

 Where it was necessary, especially in the earlier talks,
non-inclusive language was updated to conform to the Richard
Rohr of the 1990's, not the 1970's. The ways we talk about God
and each other have evolved considerably during the past twenty
years. There is a sensitivity in the later meditations to feminine
metaphors for God, but the relationship between father and son
as a metaphor for understanding God remains a central theme
for Richard and was left alone.

You'll find many more days in this book than there are in any one year. That is because some seasons fluctuate in duration from one year to the next. For example, Advent only rarely requires four full weeks: Christmas usually comes before the end of week four. In this book you'll find the longest possible Advent and the longest possible Christmas season. The same applies to the periods of Ordinary Time before Lent and after Pentecost, which also fluctuate in duration.

In each case enough meditations are included here to make it through the longest possible season, so this book will be useful over time. If you're using the book for day-by-day meditation, skip ahead whenever necessary to follow the liturgical calendar. The calendar on page 398 will help you keep your bearings. If you're browsing, think of the extra meditations as a bonus.

Although the meditations are arranged according to the Church's liturgical calendar, no attempt was made to link meditations with the Lectionary's Scripture passages for each day, only to stike the spirit of the season.

At the back of the book, you will find an index giving the title of each meditation. The Bibliography lists audiocassette and print sources, with their publication dates.

The title for this book comes from a concept Richard first spoke about in the 1970's, recorded in *The Spiritual Family and the Natural Family.* To this day it is used as the name of the newsletter of the Center for Action and Contemplation. It reflects a deep yearing within Richard. See Day 99, "Catholic Radicals," and Day 403, "Radical Grace," for more on this.

May this collection inspire you, challenge you and open you up, as it certainly has done for me.

—John Feister

Introduction

Public speaking is always a risk, especially when you dare to speak for God, but writing it down is just foolhardy! My friends accuse me of not having an untaped thought, but now I fear my rambling meditations are now also "written in stone"—just in time to be stoned with them.

A communications expert recently told me that only twelve percent of what is communicated is done by the naked choice of word itself. Thirty-six percent of the meaning is communicated by gesture, inflection, emphasis, repetition and tone, while a full 52 percent comes from precisely the setting and context in which the word is spoken. Live preaching and tapes are "hotter" media than books. You have time to cover your tracks, hold your audience with you through the hard parts, undo an overemphasis, and make up for poor logic or grammar with your own excited conviction.

On paper things have to follow, make sense and inherently hold the interest of the reader. If this collection does any of this, it is largely due to John Feister, who cajoled me into this project, lovingly listened to years of tapes, kept me believing that it might do some good and edited my informal manner into occasional eloquence. A friend wrote me recently that "a man must dream a long time before he acts in grandeur, and dreaming is nurtured in darkness." This book is the fruit of my own struggle with darkness, but surely John's, too. We both hope we are acting without too much grandeur.

Many people on the road say to me, "I have watched you

grow up." And I usually answer, "I hope it is true, although I really need to grow *down*." I see in my career four clear stages during which these words were spoken: (1) evangelistic, (2) relational, (3) social gospel and (4) contemplative.

I began with my first set of tapes, *The Great Themes of Scripture*, published by St. Anthony Messenger Press in 1973. It was the golden period of the New Jerusalem Community: I was young, unapologetic, enthusiastic, in love with God and possibilities. Perhaps it was "first naïveté," but lives were changed and I expected them to be. The power of a newfound gospel was exhilarating both for me and for many who first fell in love with the man Jesus. I sometimes wish I could return to simple evangelism. It was the most fun and often the most effective.

By the later 70's, we had moved into complex consciousness, where contradictions are no longer hidden by the newness of things. The vision didn't always work so easily. That was my relational period: I tried to patch up the breaks with endless talks on relationship, family, sexuality, healing, journaling, dreams, management, leadership, personality types, enneagram, group dynamics, law and freedom, forms of prayer, ego and shadow, left brain and right brain—and finally what felt like no brain.

Only God knows how we tried at New Jerusalem! And it often did a lot of good. It increased our self-knowledge, drove us into the bottomless mystery of being human together and often enough called us back to God and community. We knew that was all we had, although we sure wanted to hide in our heads where there was at least a semblance of control. That's the trouble with complex consciousness: You want to stay there, fixing and understanding, instead of merely passing through to enlightenment. It was good and even necessary, but not the whole path.

By 1980 I had started giving retreats in Third World countries and could not forget what I had seen, felt and suffered. God's agenda was much larger than America, much larger than the Catholic Church, and certainly much larger than one fine community in Cincinnati. I began to speak, often out of anger and frustration, on issues of justice, social concerns and peacemaking. Many were not amused, "even among the elect." They must have thought, "For false Christs and false prophets will arise" (Matthew 24:24). "Why can't Richard leave well enough alone, without dragging in all of Asia and Latin America with him? Besides, it doesn't feel like 'good news' anymore."

During this time, I continued to see that we were victims of an all-embracing and self-serving myth. The only way back to a true gospel was to read from the underside of history, to stand in solidarity with the lambs who are slain, the crucified Jesus in every age. My only regret was that I had not made this social gospel obvious in my earliest teaching. The many who rejected me during these years of awakening have left a deep imprint within me: Religion is not always the same as gospel—in fact sometimes they are mortal enemies.

By the mid-1980's the need for integration between outer and inner was so great that the Franciscans gave me a contemplative/sabbatical year to try to put it all together. That led me to a rediscovery of our own contemplative tradition and I found rich lodging in what Thomas Merton called "the palace of nowhere, where all the many things are one." Prayer is the only place spacious enough for all truth.

Since that time, I have moved to New Mexico and established the Center for Action and Contemplation, where many of us are working for an integration of prayer with an engaged life in this world. Not coincidentally, the contemplative path has been paralleled by a reappreciation of issues of gender, feminism and masculine spirituality. These taboos and fascinations are at the spiritual heart of most issues of justice and prayer. When you touch Spirit, you find embodiment. When you stay with embodiment, you will invariably touch soul, which opens you again to Spirit.

I would encourage you to read these daily meditations

knowing the likely contexts in which they were first spoken: evangelistic, relational, social gospel and contemplative. (You can check dates in the Bibliography.) Some may not speak to you now; some might be just what you need for your own next step. If one gets in the way of your own enlightenment, if it needlessly pulls you back into complex consciousness, then "shake the dust from your feet" (Matthew 10:14), and go on to the next. If you find resistance in yourself, if you do not agree with what I say, impute the blame to this weak instrument but never to the gospel, which is still power and life and eventually light. The messenger is weak, but the message is unfailing. I hope some of it seeps through.

I would be fooling myself if I thought I were either a scholar or a saint. I am just a Franciscan. Our calling is to bring the riches of the gospel to the masses and to bring it, as Francis said, "without gloss."

Richard Rohr, O.F.M.
Center for Action and Contemplation
Albuquerque, New Mexico
March 1993

Part I:

ADVENT THROUGH PENTECOST

ADVENT

First Sunday of Advent   Day 1

Come, Lord Jesus

"Come, Lord Jesus." The Christian Bible ends with this great
invitation for Jesus to be with us, the acknowledgment that what
is coming is not fully here (Revelation 22:17). "Come, Lord
Jesus" means that all of Christian history has to live out of a kind
of chosen non-fulfillment.

Yet we demand that our anxiety be taken away. We say,
"Why didn't you do that for me?" We tend to get disappointed
because reality does not fulfill our expectations—or more likely
somebody doesn't: our spouse, our children, our community.
We're refusing to say, Come, Lord Jesus.

So we refuse to live with openness, with freedom, with
surrender. We demand of ourselves and one another what the
Word of God told us not to demand and not even to expect.

To demand total life now is not to live in hope or faith. The
only life promised to us in this world is the "mystery of faith"—
which is life and death all mixed together, the paschal mystery:
Christ has died, Christ is risen, Christ will *always* come again.

from *Preparing for Christmas With Richard Rohr*

Recognize the Lord

We, like Bethlehem, are too tiny to imagine the greatness within us:

> You Bethlehem-Ephrathah, too small to be among the clans of Judah, from you shall come forth for me one who is to rule my people Israel. (Micah 5:1-2, *NAB*)

Wholeness of God is to be found everywhere, but it is only apparent as every part learns to love every other part. I suspect that those who by grace can recognize the Lord within their own puny souls will be the same who will freely and intelligently affirm the Lord's presence in the body of Jesus and the body of the universe.

"But who am I that the mother of my Lord should come to me?" Elizabeth says. Perhaps if I can recognize and trust this little graciousness, this hidden wholeness, this child in the womb, then my spirit will be prepared for the greater visitation, the revelation of the Son of God. Yet I am always aware that God is not just an experience of mine. More rightly, I am an experience in the mind and heart of God. This is very difficult for us self-centered moderns to comprehend. But if we dare to trust this holy mystery, we participate in a Presence that is at once overwhelming gift and precious surprise—not really demanded or necessary, but actually not difficult to believe at all!

So we Christians prepare to make festival. God goes ahead enfleshing spirit and inspiriting flesh, while for those of us who have learned, like Elizabeth, to trust these holy visitations, our life leaps within us for joy!

from *Sojourners*, "Baptism of Joy"

Mary's Action Beyond Fear

Upon receiving the sacred word, Mary does not contemplate, she *acts* immediately: She "went as quickly as she could to a town in the hill country" (Luke 1:39, *JB*). There is no mention of planning, companionship, means of travel or encountered difficulties. Like Abraham and winged Mercury, she moved *with* the action, *toward* the action of her cousin's need. The events themselves will be her guide and teacher. She does not need to figure it out and plan accordingly; the plan will be given by God through life's encounters. Reality is her teacher. That is why she could hear angels. And that is why she could hear Elizabeth.

Decisive action beyond our fears gives us a sense of our own power and the power of God within us. Mary offers no refusal or false humility to Elizabeth's "loud cry": "Of all women you are the most blessed.... Yes, blessed is she who believed that the promise made her by the Lord would be fulfilled" (Luke 1:42, 45, *JB*).

Mary is a woman who is profoundly self-possessed. She can hold her power comfortably because she knows it is from Beyond. It is hers to hold and offer, to proudly acclaim in the Magnificat. This woman knows her boundaries, her Center and her gift. Her dignity is not earned or attained. It *is.*

from *Radical Grace*, "A Masculine Magnificat"

Thy Kingdom Come,
My Kingdom Go

All false religion proceeds in a certain sense from one illusion: People say, "Thy Kingdom come" out of one side of their mouth, but they don't, out of the other side of their mouth, say, "My kingdom go." It happens when we try to have both of those kingdoms reign, when we say that the Lord is the lord of our lives, but in fact we're the lord of our own lives. When Jesus is not the Lord of our lives, we will most assuredly lord it over one another. That attitude has resulted in the domination, competition and unbelievable success agenda of much of Western civilization: Christians have sought to lord it over one another while saying they were submitted to the lordship of Jesus Christ.

We just can't keep saying, "Thy Kingdom come," when it's obvious we're preoccupied with our own individual or nationalistic kingdoms. Look at Spain, France, England: These were the Christian nations. Were they in love with the Kingdom of God or, as many Americans, with their own turf?

As a preacher, I know all I need do is touch that sacred cow to find people's real lordship. While they're saying, "Come, Lord Jesus," the golden calf they're bowed down before, more often than not, is their own agenda and the agenda of their nation-state. You can't say, "Come, Lord Jesus" and live that way! God doesn't care about national boundaries!

from *Preparing for Christmas With Richard Rohr*

Submitting to the Lordship of Christ

The Church is like John the Baptist; it's like the body of Jesus. The body of Jesus had to die for the coming of the Kingdom; John the Baptist had to point beyond himself to the Kingdom. The Church is not an end in itself; the Church is a means. The Kingdom is the end. And whenever we make the means into the end, we have created an idol. It is the major sin in the Bible—maybe the only one.

from *Preparing for Christmas With Richard Rohr*

Love Is Like a Mirror

The mirror, as Zen masters say, is without ego and without mind. If a face comes in front of it, it reflects a face. If a table comes by, it reflects a table. It shows a crooked object to be crooked and a straight object to be straight. Everything is revealed as it really is There is no discriminating mind or self-consciousness on the part of the mirror.

If something comes, the mirror reflects it; if it moves on, the mirror lets it move on. The mirror is always empty of itself and therefore able to receive the other. The mirror has no preconditions for entry, no preconditions for acceptance. It receives and reflects back what is there, nothing more or nothing less. The mirror is the perfect lover and the perfect contemplative. It does not evaluate, judge or act. It takes the advice of the philosopher Wittgenstein: "Don't think, just look."

If we are to see as God sees, we must first become mirrors. We must become no-thing so that we can receive some-thing. That is probably the only way that love is ever going to happen. To love demands a complete transformation of consciousness, a transformation that has been the goal of all religious founders, saints, mystics and gurus since we began to talk about love. And the transformation of consciousness is this: We must be liberated from ourselves.

We really need to be saved from the tyranny of our own judgments, opinions and feelings about everything, the "undisciplined squads of emotions" that T.S. Eliot criticizes in his poetry. We must stop believing our false subjectivity that chooses to objectify everybody and everything else in the world— including God and our own soul. (Which is the likely reason why most Western individualists hate themselves. We treat our own souls as objects to be dissected, judged and perfected.)

from "Image and Likeness: The Restoration of the Divine Image"

Saturday of the First Week of Advent   **Day 7**

Commit Yourself to Joy

Zephaniah, addressing a slum of Northern Kingdom refugees in Jerusalem (Zephaniah 3:14-18), and Paul, writing to the Philippians from his chains (Philippians 4:4-7), counsel an unprecedented joy to their listeners. They are calling us to wholeness and holiness. They have gone far beyond our existential states and happy feelings to an objective source, a bottomless well where joy is drawn and received in obedience. They know that joy is finally a decision. They are no longer preoccupied with creating a fault-free environment that will ensure their own happiness, but they know that joy is finally in entering into another, the Other, an objective Presence, love itself, the Lord. Joy is the Lord.

What freedom when we no longer have to wait upon ourselves to be in love! We are led beyond loving just ourselves, our own adequacy and our own personal responses. We are, instead, commanded to recognize joy—to trust it and believe it. We are daringly *commanded* to love God and thereby assured of an unfailing reservoir of true and profound joy in the Other.

Undoubtedly this is the "baptism of the Holy Spirit and fire" that John the Baptizer announces in the gospel. It is a baptism not created, like mere water baptism, but a baptism that can only be waited for, longed for, believed in and therefore received. We see that the people listening to John "were filled with expectation" (Luke 3:15, *NAB*). They were predisposed and ready for joy to reveal itself. The seers and listeners, the contemplatives of every age, will be prepared to recognize joy and to recognize its possibility everywhere.

I have committed myself to joy. I have come to realize that those who make space for joy, those who prefer nothing to joy, those who desire the utter reality, will most assuredly have it.

We must not be afraid to announce it to refugees, slum dwellers, saddened prisoners, angry prophets. Now and then we must even announce it to ourselves. In this prison of now, in this cynical and sophisticated age, Christians must believe in joy.

from *Sojourners*, "Baptism of Joy"

Hardened Silos of Self

St. Bonaventure and St. Thomas Aquinas both said that being and goodness are the same thing. In fact, if we can get back to the level of pure being, we experience profound goodness. That's the contemplative stance. That's the perspective of the Kingdom. That's the Original Blessing. Jesus recognized the Kingdom because he lived out of that contemplative center.

Many other forms of prayer we've been taught require thinking thoughts or saying and reading words. I'm not saying they're bad; they're obviously good. But we can do all of the above, think thoughts about Jesus and Mary, read the psalms or recite memorized prayers without transforming our consciousness. We do it in the old system. The ego is still in charge. It may not be conscious, but we think, "I'm the center of the world. I have my feelings. I have my opinions and I, in this hardened silo, will now think about Jesus."

Guess what? Nothing will change.

The egg hasn't been cracked. The illusion is intact. When we talk about contemplative prayer, we're not talking about thinking about Jesus inside your old system, but about a transformation of consciousness where you move to a new place beyond over-identification with the ego, beyond identification with the privatized, separate self. That's a true and lasting revolution.

from *Preparing for Christmas With Richard Rohr*

Prayer and Justice

We've got to know the true source of our truth. In my attempts to dismantle the false system of our American political system, am I just fighting for my Richard Rohr truth, or am I really in touch with the great truth that Jesus calls the reign of God? I've got to know that it's not just what I do but why I do it and where it comes from. I think the sequence of Jesus' words about himself is significant. He is first *Way*, and only then *Truth*, which is finally *Life* (see John 14:6).

Without prayer, we social activists end up as ideologues. We're trapped in our heads, our opinions, our righteous selves. Maybe we'll be doing the right thing, but from an egocentric place, not a place of unitive consciousness, the place where all things are one. In other words, we'll be doing our own agenda instead of God's. As soon as we fail, you'll see the difference. That's why failure, rejection and humiliation are so important for us. They are the only things that tell us whether we're operating out of the center place, the place of prayer, or whether we're basically doing our own thing and calling it God's thing. When people are doing God's thing, they have freedom—they can laugh at themselves, they can take humiliation and non-success because their own reputation is not at stake. The mature believer will probably look more like a holy fool than a do-gooder or a "saint."

from Catholic Agitator, "Finding a Place for Prayer"

Don't Name Darkness Light

We're not waiting for the darkness to go away, brothers and sisters. I've certainly worked long enough in ministry to know it won't go away.

We wish it would go away, especially in some of the great social issues. We wish world hunger would be eliminated. We wish we'd stop creating all these arms and killing people. But one has to surrender at a certain point and admit that the darkness is here. How do we deal with that? We've got to find the freedom within our spirits and within our communities to at least recognize that darkness and learn how to live in relationship to it.

In other words, don't name darkness light! Don't name darkness good. I think many of our people have been seduced into doing that. The way out is to simply stop calling it OK. When we refuse to name darkness, we will be trapped by it. That's dangerous and false innocence. When we can *name* the darkness, we can learn how to live so that the darkness does not overcome us.

The problem of the liberation of the First World countries is that the edges between darkness and light in middle-class society have become very, very vague. When nothing is forbidden, nothing is required. We are close to that today. I believe it is what Thomas Merton predicted as "organized despair."

from *Preparing for Christmas With Richard Rohr*

Women in Jail

I'm a jail chaplain in Albuquerque. I'm delighted by the way I can preach to those guys in the jail. They don't have all of our sophistication, and they're not lost in worlds of words whereby everything is made vague. It's very clear to them what death is, very clear to them what's destroying people and how it's destroying people. There simply isn't a lot of self-protection in the psyche because their situation is forcing them to face reality.

One of my three Sunday Masses there is for women. These women feel so bad about themselves. For some reason, men are *supposed* to go to jail; men are bad, you know. But women aren't supposed to be bad; women are good. Women have children. Women are wise. These women in prison carry an extra dose of guilt. They're constantly asking me, "Why am I here? What'd I do?" Their children are at home, and they're in jail. And how do they tell their children they're in jail and their mother's a bad person or an evil person?

To be any kind of minister for them, I have to dig into places that you and I don't often look. "Religion" isn't enough; these women have to scratch their way back to faith—faith in themselves and faith in a God who seems to have abandoned them. It's not just their own mistakes that tell them they are bad, the structure of their reality also condemns them.

By necessity much of the system is based on the self-interest of the dominant class. The examples I love to use are the Fifth and Sixth Commandments. A theologian once asked, "Why were there no exceptions to the Sixth Commandment, 'Thou shalt not commit adultery,' while we find ways around the Fifth Commandment, 'Thou shall not kill'?" Because the governments, the powers that be always wanted to have their excuses for why they could kill. And we gave them their justifications for capital punishment and "just" war. I call it institutionalized darkness.

Paul uses the pre-psychological language of his time to describe the same: "For it is not against human enemies that we have to struggle, but against the Sovereignties and Powers who originate the darkness of this world, the spiritual army of evil in the heavens" (Ephesians 6:12, JB). Whether we speak of "the world," principalities and powers or structural sin, we are in each case trying to describe the overarching power that the system itself has in driving us toward evil. Such corporate evil can only be countered by corporate good—individualism alone will never survive.

The women and men in jail need a positive community to stand against the negative community of the system. Now we call it a support group; we need to call it the Church.

from *Preparing for Christmas With Richard Rohr*

Thursday of the Second Week of Advent   Day 12

The Tenth Commandment

I've never in my years as a Catholic Christian heard a sermon on the Tenth Commandment. We can't possibly preach on "Thou shalt not covet thy neighbor's goods" because Western society is based on that. It's called capitalism. Mass advertising tells us we need things none of us need. It sows confusion about what's important for life. The level of need has moved to such a level of illusion and sophistication that what were once ultimate luxuries have become necessities. In our culture, people cannot feel good about themselves unless next year's vacation is more luxurious than last year's, unless everything is upgraded—while most of God's people on this earth starve.

The affluent West has made happiness impossible. We've created a pseudo-happiness, a pseudo-success, a pseudo-security that will never satisfy the human heart. Most of God's people are forced to learn to find happiness and freedom at a much more simple level. The gospel says that's where happiness is always to be found.

That is about as traditional, old-fashioned, conservative a gospel as there is, and it will never change. We have to keep saying it: There *is* a Tenth Commandment.

from *Preparing for Christmas With Richard Rohr*

Friday of the Second Week of Advent   Day 13

Managing Life

"It comes like a gentle dew" (Isaiah 45:8). Isn't that what so many of your Christmas cards are going to say and what the readings from the Old Testament say during Advent? Grace comes when you stop being preoccupied and stop thinking that by your own meddling, managing and manufacturing you can create it.

We're trained to be managers, to organize life, to make things happen. That's what's built our culture, and it's not all bad. But if you transfer that to the spiritual life, it's pure heresy. It doesn't work.

You can't manage and maneuver and manipulate spiritual energy. It's a matter of letting go. It's a matter of getting the self out of the way, and becoming smaller, as John the Baptist said. It's a matter of the great *kenosis*, as Paul talks about in Philippians 2:6-11, the emptying of the self so that there's room for another.

It's very hard for us not to fix and manage life and to wait upon it, "like a gentle dew."

Are we to be passive? No; very much the opposite. When Buddha asked a question similar to the one Jesus asked, "Who do people say that I am?" his disciples all gave reasons—"Oh, you're this, you're that." The Buddha replied, "I am awake." To be awake is to be vigilant and active.

Many of the Advent readings call us to the single, most difficult thing: to be awake.

from *Preparing for Christmas With Richard Rohr*

Saturday of the Second Week of Advent   Day 14

Men and Women Together

St. Paul says, "There can be neither male nor female, for you are all one in Christ Jesus" (Galatians 3:28). The new humanity that we are pointed toward is not neuter, unisex or oversexed, all of which make love impossible. In Christ we are whole, one, in union, integrated. The self becomes *wholly holy*. That is the final product of the Spirit making all things one. It is the consummate achievement of God in Christ who reconciles all things within himself (Colossians 1:20) and invites us into the ongoing reconciliation of all things (Ephesians 1:3-14).

Men must be converted to the feminine, women to the masculine. Maybe that is why God made sexual attraction so compelling. If we are converted to the non-self, *everything* changes. Thereby we approach authentic religious conversion toward the utter not-me: God. From the whole—and center—position, we see through eyes other than our own half-blinded ones. We see the other side of things and forgiveness becomes possible. We see that the enemy is not enemy but spiritual helpmate. Once we have met and accepted our inner opposite, there is nothing more to defend and nothing more to be afraid of.

from *Radical Grace*, "Masculine Spirituality"

Third Sunday of Advent   Day 15

Advent Prayer

O Wisdom, O holy Word of God, you govern all creation with your strong yet tender care: Come. O Sacred Lord of ancient Israel, you showed yourself to Moses in the burning bush and you gave the holy law on Mount Sinai: Come. O Flower of Jesse's stem, you have been raised up as a sign for all peoples; kings stand silent in your presence; the nations bow down in worship before you: Come. O Key of David, O royal Power of Israel, you [not the systems of this world] control at your will the gate of heaven: Come break down the prison walls of death. O Radiant Dawn, splendor of eternal light, sun of justice: Come shine on those who dwell in darkness and the shadow of death. O, King of all the nations, the only joy of every human heart; O Keystone of the mighty arch of humankind: Come and save these creatures you fashioned from the dust. O, Emmanuel, God-With-Us, king and lawgiver, desire of the nations, Savior of all people: Come and set us free.

The Spirit and the bride say, "Come." Amen. Lord Jesus, come soon! Lord Jesus, come and free us from the prisons of death. We ask for it together as his people. And we ask for it in Jesus' name. Amen.

from *Preparing for Christmas With Richard Rohr*

Monday of the Third Week of Advent   Day 16

The Three P's

In the Sermon on the Mount, Jesus says there are three basic obstacles to the coming of the Kingdom. These are the three P's: power, prestige and possessions. Nine-tenths of his teaching can be aligned under one of those three categories.

I'm all for sexual morality, but Jesus does not say that's the issue. In fact, he says the prostitutes are getting into the Kingdom of God before some of us who have made bedfellows with power, prestige and possessions (see Matthew 21:31-32). Those three numb the heart and deaden the spirit, says Jesus.

Read Luke's Gospel. Read the Sermon on the Mount. Read Matthew's Gospel and tell me if Jesus is not saying that power, prestige and possessions are the barriers to truth and are the barriers to the Kingdom.

I'm not pointing to bishops and popes, I'm pointing to us as the Church. The Church has been comfortable with power, prestige and possessions for centuries and has not called that heresy. You can't see your own sin.

from *Preparing for Christmas With Richard Rohr*

Self-hatred

When I started working with young people in the early 70's I spent a lot of time trying to convince teenagers that they were good. They all seemed endlessly, bottomlessly to hate themselves. Later, I was working with the New Jerusalem Community and I found it wasn't just teenagers but adults, too. They endlessly hate themselves, doubt themselves and have to spend most of their energy to feel good about themselves.

I'm convinced that much guilt, or negative self-image, or whatever we want to call it, happens because we have allowed our Christian people to accept the wrong agenda. Christians today feel at home in a world that Jesus told us never to be at home in. Even worse, they're at home in a world in which girls become anorexic, boys think they must be on the starting football lineup, and all the rest compare themselves to the rich, the well-known, the image makers.

Competition is simply our name for domination. Whenever you create a society that has to define itself by power and success, there will have to be those who are the powerless and the non-successful. And that's the vast majority of the people in our society. People in our society are set up to lose.

from *Preparing for Christmas With Richard Rohr*

Let Reality Get at Me

Many of our people create for themselves a permanently maintained happiness in the midst of so much public suffering. That state is based on an illusion about the nature of reality. It can only work if we block ourselves from a certain degree of that reality. That's what's meant by *denial*.

The Christian, though, is always saying, "Come, Lord Jesus." In other words, "Let reality get at me, the full reality, the Cosmic Christ, all that is."

The Incarnation is the refusal of all denial. It is God saying yes to the muddy, the messy, the partial, the powerlessness of it all.

from *Preparing for Christmas With Richard Rohr*

Base Communities

We have a lot to learn from people like Quakers and Mennonites. They're well practiced in being a minority. They don't need to have crowds around them to believe in the truth. They gather in little groupings and share the word of God. Thank God this is also happening now, again, in the Catholic Church, in the base communities.

Out of the people who don't consider themselves experts or

theologians comes a special gospel wisdom. It surpasses the wisdom that we ever came to by thinking that white, materially secure celibate males were the group who could best interpret the word of God. Whatever gave us the idea that a select group of overeducated people would best understand what God was saying to all people?

The poor and uneducated are reclaiming the word of God. The word of God is being reclaimed by women, by people of color and by people who still understand community and family relationships, by people who look at life from the side of the victims instead of the victors.

The word of God is being reclaimed by those who haven't been beneficiaries of the system. And we're finding that the word of God is being read with a vitality, with a truth, with a freedom that is frightening and makes some of us wonder if we've ever understood it before.

When we see what the gospel demands of our lives, we may not even want to understand it.

from *Preparing for Christmas With Richard Rohr*

God Is the Only One We Can Surrender To

God is the only one we can surrender to without losing ourselves. It's a paradox. I can't prove it to you, and it sure doesn't feel like that, but I promise you it's true.

When Jesus says those who lose their life will find their life and those who let go of their life will discover their life, obviously he's talking about life in a different way than you and I experience it. We think life is the thing that we've got to protect. He's saying, No, the true self needs no protection: It just *is*. What we are usually protecting is the repetitive illusions and addictive feelings of the false self.

God is the only one we can surrender to without losing ourselves. The Christian people, the brothers and sisters of God's Son, Jesus, are those who are called to that life of surrender.

from *Preparing for Christmas With Richard Rohr*

Saturday of the Third Week of Advent   Day 21

Crossing a Line

The Scriptures very clearly have a "bias toward action." Simply put, the word of God tells us that if you don't do it, you in fact have not heard it and do not believe it (see Matthew 21:28-32; James 1:22-25).

The only way that we become convinced of our own sense of empowerment and the power of the Spirit and the truth of the Gospel is by crossing a line—a line of decision, testing, risking, doing and owning the consequences.

It has a certain degree of non-sensical-ness, of unprovability, to it: That's why we call it faith. When we cross that line, we act in a new way based on what we believe the Kingdom values are. Walking is probably a lot more important than talking, even if we walk the wrong way for a while.

from *Preparing for Christmas With Richard Rohr*

Loving the Lover

Sit by the stream, on the edge. Don't let the ego try to fix, control, categorize or ensure any of your experience. The ego wants to ensure that things are significant, that events make us important. Our activities become little righteousness trips, and we stand on our certitude.

"I've done 'this much' in my life," we say. "I was faithful to my husband. I raised my children; I sent them to a Catholic school. I paid my bills." But these are often self-serving kinds of duty and responsibility. Much religion is using God to bolster our own self-image. True religion is not attached to self-image, but to God.

Christian life has little to do with me doing anything right. It has everything to do with falling in love with a Lover who does everything right. What I love is that Lover and not my own accomplishments.

from *Preparing for Christmas With Richard Rohr*

I Am Utter Absurdity and Paradox

People are odd creatures: We are at the same time very good *and* very sinful. These qualities do not cancel each other out. Faith is to live and to hold onto that paradox. Those with room for those two seemingly contradictory truths to coexist are the ones who can recognize the Kingdom of God.

The absurdity of human reality will not shock them: They've already faced it inside themselves. The enemy is not out there, the enemy is us. And when they see the paradox, they stop fighting the world. They stop hating and avoiding the world. They're free to live that threshold existence that we call the Kingdom.

Why call it threshold? Because the threshold is between the house and the outside. We live on the boundary, on the narrow road that leads to life (Matthew 7:13-14), in between two undeniable truths. Can you live in that in-between? To care yet not care at all? Those who can will be free to welcome the Kingdom. They are free to pass through because they don't have any turf—whether possessions, identity, reputation or self-image—to protect or maintain. The threshold experience is always getting slammed in the face—with *paradox*.

from *Preparing for Christmas With Richard Rohr*

Tuesday of the Fourth Week of Advent   Day 24

John the Baptist: Wild Wise Man

For many reasons we have chosen St. John the Baptist as the patron of our Center for Action and Contemplation. Our feast day is celebrated on June 24, as the sun (reminiscent of John 3:30) agrees to decrease. John the Baptist is the prophet who rejects the system without apology, eats the harsh food of that choice and wears the clothes of rejection. Like our native peoples here in New Mexico, he goes on his vision quest into the desert where he faces his aloneness, boredom and naked self. He returns with a message, a clarity, a surety of heart that reveals a totally surrendered man. First he listens long and self-forgetfully; then he speaks, acts and accepts the consequences. Surely he is the ultimate wild man! Or is it wise man? He is both.

Always pointing beyond himself, ready to get out of the way, finally beheaded by the powers that be, John represents the kind of liberation and the kind of prophecy that we need in our affluent culture. He is not just free from the system, he is amazingly free from himself. These are the only prophets God can use, the only prophets we can trust.

John is seen by his contemporaries and by Jesus himself as a return and image of Elijah the Prophet. Elijah, of course, is the contemplative on Mount Horeb who met the Holy One "not in the earthquake, not in the fire, but in the sound of a gentle breeze" (1 Kings 19:11-13). He has fled to the prayer of the mountain from the hostility of king and queen, who see him as "the troubler of Israel" (1 Kings 18:17), who makes clear their idolatries.

Who wants to be a troubler? Who would dare to think of himself as a prophet? What did we come out to the desert to see? John the Baptist seems to tell us that it is the only place bare enough, empty enough to mirror our own motives and disguises. The desert is the prophet to the prophet. We had to come here, we had to come to the quiet, we have to trust men like John to begin to trust our own action and contemplation. Trouble us, John! You're our pointing-patron-prophet. We're not wild yet.

from *Radical Grace*, "Masculine Spirituality"

Remember Everything

Jerusalem, take off your robe of mourning and misery;
put on the splendor of glory from God forever:
Wrapped in the cloak of justice from God,
bear on your head the mitre that displays the glory of the
    eternal name.
For God will show all the earth your splendor:
you will be named by God forever the peace of justice, the glory
    of God's worship.
Up Jerusalem! stand upon the heights;
look to the east and see your children
Gathered from the east and the west at the word of the Holy
    One,
rejoicing that they are remembered by God. (Baruch 5:1-5, NAB)

Our remembrance that God remembers us will be the highway
into the future, the straight path of the Lord promised by John the
Baptizer (Luke 3:4). Memory is the basis of both pain and
rejoicing: We cannot have one without the other.

Do not be too quick to heal all of those memories, unless that
means also feeling them deeply and taking them all into your
salvation history. God calls us to suffer the whole of reality, to
remember the good along with the bad. Perhaps that is the course
of the journey toward new sight and new hope. Memory creates
a readiness for salvation, an emptiness to receive love and a
fullness to enjoy it.

Strangely enough, it seems so much easier to remember the
hurts, the failures and the rejections. In a seeming love of freedom
God has allowed us to be very vulnerable to evil. And until we have
learned how to see, evil comes to us easily and holds us in its grasp.

Yet only in an experience and a remembering of the good do
we have the power to stand against death. As Baruch tells
Jerusalem, you must "rejoice that you are remembered by God."

In that remembrance we have new sight, and the evil can be
absorbed and blotted out.

from *Sojourners*, "The Energy of Promise"

Good Friends Help Us to Remember

It takes a prophet of sorts, one who has traveled the highway
before and remembers everything, to guide us beyond our blind,
selective remembering. Choose your friends carefully and listen
to those who speak truth to you, who help you remember all
things, "so that you may value the things that really matter, up to
the very day of Christ" (Philippians 1:10).

Ask the Lord for companions (sometimes Jesus alone!) who
will walk the highway of remembering with you, mentors in the
Spirit who can help you fill in the valleys and level the mountains
and hills, making the winding ways straight and the rough ways
smooth. People are going to support groups for those spiritual
friends because we have too often failed them in the churches.
When the soul is ready, the teacher will be found.

from *Sojourners*, "The Energy of Promise"

Those at the Edge Hold the Secret

Those at the edge, ironically, always hold the secret for the conversion of every age and culture. They always hold the projected and denied parts of our soul, the parts of ourselves that we are ashamed of, that we hate and deny—that we're afraid of in ourselves. Only as the People of God receive the stranger and the leper, those who don't play our game, do we discover not only the hidden and hated parts of our own souls, but the Lord Jesus himself. That's how we say, "Come, Lord Jesus." In letting go, we make room for the Other. The Church is always converted when the outcasts are reinvited into the temple.

from *Preparing for Christmas With Richard Rohr*

Welcome the Stranger

How much we still live in the systems of this world, how much we are still influenced by the life-styles of the rich and famous, by people who talk right, dress right, have a job that's impressive! A lot of us figure out each other's social status right away: Now we know what box another fits in. "He's educated, lives in the right part of town—I can trust him. Good. My kind of person! He played the system the same way I did, calls reward the same thing I call reward, calls success...."

In doing this we avoid conversion. And that's why already in the Old Testament the word of God challenges the Jewish people to recognize and welcome the stranger at the gate. Always the Jewish people were told to welcome the stranger. That tradition continues through to the Letter to the Hebrews in the New Testament where the author says that many have received angels unawares (Hebrews 13:2). We've inherited the constant tradition of the angel, the messenger of God hidden in the stranger—the one who is strange, the one who is not like our folks, not like us.

Tonight Jesus enters Bethlehem as stranger, as refugee, as outsider. Can we make room in our overstuffed inn?

from *Preparing for Christmas With Richard Rohr*

Christmas Day   Day 29

The Feast of the Word Becoming Flesh

In Jesus, God achieved the perfect synthesis of divine and human. God gave humanity the vision of the whole, and assured us that we could be at home within that vision. The incarnation of Jesus demonstrates that God meets us where we are. It assures us that we do not have to leave the world or relinquish our humanity in order to know God, but simply that we must turn from evil. In the birth of the God-man, we have been "consecrated in truth," so we are sent into the world to continue the saving pattern of embodiment.

We tend to fear incarnation precisely because it makes religion so real, so particular, so worldly. We prefer to keep religion on the level of word, yet the Jesus-pattern is word-becoming-flesh. The great lie is that redemption can happen apart from incarnation. Annie Dillard called it "the scandal of particularity." For the Christian, power is always hidden in powerlessness, just as God was hidden in a poor baby.

We may want the spiritual without the fleshly; we may want the cosmic without the concrete. But if the Word is ever to be loved and shared, we must risk embodiment, which is always concrete and ordinary. There God is both perfectly hidden and perfectly revealed.

from *New Covenant*, "The Incarnation"

Seduced Into Solidarity

Pope John Paul II says many good things in his encyclical *Laborem Exercens.* He says the best name today for agape love, for perfect Christian love, is *solidarity.* We thought solidarity was being nice and affirming, but ultimately it's to stay in there with brokenness and let it lead you where it will, and to be willing to pay the price. It led Jesus to the cross.

I think solidarity with pain, with weakness, even with the signs of death in society might be the best name for love in the world today, especially for masculine love, a side of love expressed by both men and women. None of us would choose to be nailed to the cross, or freely take the side of the victims in society. Circumstances will unwittingly trap us there and finally there will be no noble way out.

We're not converted willingly; we're converted in spite of ourselves. Step by step, God seduces and draws us into solidarity.

from A Man's Approach to God

The Journey of John the Beloved

That first journey from cultural masculine (what culture tells us it is to be a man) into the feminine I call the Journey of John the Beloved Disciple. He was secure enough in his masculinity and comfortable enough with the community of the twelve male apostles to put his head on the breast of Jesus and not be ashamed or afraid. Most of us would consider that emotionally, if not socially, impossible. We are so homophobic! We're so afraid, either from within or without, of what everyone will think if a man ever shows affection for another man.

Yet none of us would deny the affection shown in John's Gospel. In fact, he sort of boasts about it: "I was the one who had my head on the breast of Jesus at the Last Supper, while all the other guys were there." That's a very different culture than you and I grew up in. We can't imagine being that way. That's why John is the patron saint of men's journey into their feminine selves, which is really the necessary gateway into a man's soul.

from *A Man's Approach to God*

Preferential Option for the Poor

There's a phrase that has become common in the world of theology today: the preferential option for the poor. It means God is biased toward the poor, toward those who live in unjust situations. Some people think this is some strange new theology. We Franciscans are aware that Francis always believed that; it's certainly eight hundred years old. And yet if you go back and read the Sermon on the Mount, it's obvious that it's two thousand years old. In fact, if you read Exodus, it's thirty-two hundred years old! God always takes the side of the poor and the voiceless.

from *Breathing Under Water: Spirituality and the 12 Steps*

Go to Jail

The outcast, the poor, the little ones always come before the Church and before each one of us holding a gift. It's the gift of those things we hate: insecurity, disability, a not-so-smart mind, a sexual problem or addiction. We shun anyone who isn't like us, who hasn't succeeded in our system—like people in jail.

We *need* the corporal works of mercy. Go to jail, we are told. Why? We thought to help others or to be a "good" Christian, but those aren't the reasons. We need to go to jail to get converted ourselves. We must go to the edges and discover what the questions really are, what true success is, and we must face our own failure.

I was able to live with my illusions as long as I stayed out of the jail. I mistakenly thought prisoners were the bad people.

from *Breathing Under Water: Spirituality and the 12 Steps*

Allowing the Word of God to Speak

It is good Franciscan theology that love precedes knowledge. We truly know only that which we love. When we stand back analyzing and coolly calculating, we will never really *know*. It is only in stepping out and giving ourselves to a person that a person can speak to us. Love precedes understanding.

Take that leap of faith, of love, of self-gift wherein you allow God to speak to you. I cannot prove to you with any kind of logic or by any bit of philosophy, for example, that this is the word of God, that God exists or that Jesus is Lord. But I call you to step out, trust, love. Say, "Lord, if you are in fact the Lord, then show yourself in my life and speak to my heart."

from *The Great Themes of Scripture*

Sons and Daughters of God

Christians are told at Baptism we are sons and daughters of God. It takes the rest of our lives to believe our Baptism. We don't have to earn our place; we already have it. Let us agree to that: We are of the divine nature, we are children of God.

Where else did we come from? What was once inside of God, is now outside of God and that is us. Christianity doesn't make that happen. Christianity simply announces it, and we are the lucky ones who have heard it. We are the announcers of the Good News, we proclaim that all are the sons and daughters of God.

But there's a problem: What we have done in this functional Church is turn everything around. People are spending their whole lives trying to earn what they already have, trying to be worthy of God. You don't *get* worthy; you *are* worthy. The only thing that initially separates you from God is the belief that you *are* separate!

from *A Man's Approach to God*

The Way God Loves

Marriage Encounter teaches spouses how to fight with each other.
They hold one another's hands, look one another in the eye and
yell at each other. Through it all, they're not to let go of the other's
hands. Married folks tell me that this is the hardest thing in the
world to do. Because what you want to do when she or he is really
hurting you is push away. You don't want to touch or look at one
another.

But the given is union: We're together. Don't question that.
Wife and husband are one. They are committed to one another
and mustn't pull away from it. As long as they keep holding
hands, they can call each other whatever they want. That is a
fantastic image of the way God loves us: God won't let go of our
hands.

from A Man's Approach to God

Mary, Mother of God

Mary symbolizes the people of God, the Church, the symbol of
humanity in need of God. The medievals had a great sense of this.
They used to picture Mary in their art as the woman with a giant
cape. Beneath the cape were all the people of God. She summed

up the meaning of their Christianity in her person, in her "yes."

She is the symbol of God's final victory in humanity. In her bodily Assumption we know that all of our humanity is free, redeemable and of unmeasurable dignity. It happened in her in accelerated and perfect fashion so we could look at her and say, yes. She is one of us and she is what we will be. We now know that the resurrection Jesus has promised will also be given to us in spirit and in body.

We are redeemed totally. We are not just set free in our spirits; in our bodies, too, we share in the redemption and freedom of the Lord. That is what Marian celebrations are all about.

from The Great Themes of Scripture

Christmas Season Weekday   Day 38

Beginning to Live

Love alone of all things is sufficient unto itself. It is its own end, its own merit, its own satisfaction. It seeks no cause beyond itself and needs no fruit outside of itself. Its fruit is its use. I love simply because I am love. That is my deepest identity, what I am created in and for.

For me to love others "in God" is to love them for their own sake and not for what they do for me or because I am psychologically healed and capable. Our transformed consciousness sees another person as another self, as one who also is loved by Christ with me and not an object separate from myself on which I generously bestow my Christian favors.

If I have not yet loved or if love wears me out, is it partly because other people are seen as tasks or threats instead of extensions of my own suffering and loneliness? Yet are they not in truth extensions of the suffering and loneliness of God?

When I live out of this truth of the love-that-I-am, I will at last begin to live.

from "Image and Likeness: The Restoration of the Divine Image"

Christmas Season Weekday   Day 39

The Boy and the Old Man

I believe in every man there are two basic archetypes, and they are most simple: the boy and the old man. In many of our lives, one or the other dominates. The ideal is when the two become friends.

The ideal is if they both love and respect one another at the end of life, and that is for me the Grand Father. The boy inspires the blossoming of things; the old man presides over the harvest. The boy hopes and expects, is optimistic. I remember feeling that way: "It is still coming, it's out there, wherever it is." In my twenties it was still going to come. Now in my late forties "it" seems to have already happened, and "it" deserves both tears and humor.

It has been said that the young man who will not weep is a savage and the old man who will not laugh is a fool. Spirituality teaches us to do both.

The boy hopes and expects; the old man holds, knows and loves. The boy is ready to be surprised and ready to meet something new. The old man holds the past with serenity and forgiveness. Both must honor the other, both at the beginning and the end of our journey.

from *A Man's Approach to God*

Christmas Season Weekday   Day 40

History Makers

Kingdom people are history makers. People who are still living in the false self, in the false world of illusion, are history stoppers. They just keep repeating. They're conformists, fearful people, the nice respectable proper thinkers of every age who think collectively and have no power to break through.

"Woe to you when the world speaks well of you," Jesus says (Luke 6:26). He seems to know that unhealthiness will usually be called healthy and normal.

Kingdom reality is seeing life in a new way: Things are not what they seem. It's not what you think. Only one thing is absolute. All else is relative and passing. The system is the way people think when they *don't* think.

Kingdom thinking will never be commonly accepted. The system is very seductive and blinding.

from *Preparing for Christmas With Richard Rohr*

Addictions

Fear is an addiction for a lot of people. They don't know how to motivate themselves without being afraid of something. They don't know how not to worry. When you're living an inauthentic life, you're going to worry because your subconscious, your spirit, knows your life has no truth. That is why we're creating so many fearful people.

The more illusory stuff we have to protect, the more fearful we will be. There's almost a correlation between the fears that people have and the false lives that they live. Beneath all the layers of behavior, it is fear that brings more people into counseling than any other emotion. The counselor's role is to help people identify what is behind their fear. Real lives start then.

from *Preparing for Christmas With Richard Rohr*

Beyond Money, Sex and Power

Take away money, sex and power, and most men on this earth do not know how to motivate themselves. They don't know how to make decisions about what they want to do with life, where they want to go, who they want to be. This is why we don't have a lot of male spirituality or spiritual men: because most Western men don't know how to draw their life from within. They need something outside to kick them, to reward them, to promote them, to secure them, to get themselves going. That is the opposite of a spiritual person. Spirituality is precisely a source of energy from within, called spirit, which is beyond money, sex and power.

from A Man's Approach to God

To Whom Else Shall We Go?

Faith is a gift. There's no way you can prove to yourself that God exists, that Jesus is Lord, that Jesus is truly present and giving himself to us in Eucharist. Those are gifts from God. Have we ever asked for them? Have we ever said, "Lord, let me know that you are Lord"? We get what we expect from God. It must have been in sadness that Jesus replied to the Twelve, " 'Do you also want to leave?' Simon Peter answered him, 'Master, to whom shall we go? You have the words of eternal life' " (John 6:67-68, *NAB*).

We, too, come to this: "Lord, we're not certain what our lives mean. We're not certain at this point that they're going anywhere. Sometimes you're not so real to us. Sometimes we don't experience any joy with you. But Lord, to whom else shall we go? We have seen your glory and we have seen your action in our lives. You've loved us and led us this far, so we stand on that goodness." That's a real act of faith.

Faith isn't so much to believe that God *is* as to believe that God is *for you*. That is the good news.

from The Great Themes of Scripture

A Free Banquet

Jesus preaches a new kind of justice, a new kind of righteousness: to trust in the infallible love of God. Jesus calls the people to an eternal banquet feast, the banquet feast of God's love. God is feeding his people and there is no end to the wine and food of God's love. The promise made to Isaiah is now fulfilled. The people of Israel are called to the banquet feast.

Yet the people do not want to come. They want to organize a party with a proper guest list. It seems so simple to come to the banquet table unearned, yet for the class-conscious, that is very difficult. What is right at hand—their land, their status, their spouse—seems good enough for them. So Jesus says to go out and beg the people to come in. Tell them to come to my feast. And still it is not half full. Few can accept something unearned. So he finally says to go out and bring in the harlots, bring in the drunkards, the lame and the sick and force them to come in. Someone has to believe my good news!

Jesus taught in parables such as this, parables that make little or no sense to the practical justice of humans. If you are into worthiness, competition and rewards, the gospel won't make much sense.

from *The Great Themes of Scripture*

Incarnational Theology

Every time Catholics celebrate Eucharist, we take something of this earth, of this world, bread and wine, and we say—daringly, unbelievably—it's God. I don't know any other religion that ever does that. Most of the world's religions—Hinduism, Buddhism and many forms of Protestantism—are always trying to get you up into transcendental holy thinking: ideas, explanations and principles, visions. The Catholic worldview is always saying, "Get into history, get into the flesh, get into the bread and wine, get into the material." Get into this world and this world will still be the mediation point of the spiritual.

That's our greatest strength. The fancy word for that is incarnational Christianity. The most popular feast is not Easter. You'd have no doubt about it if you have ever been to Europe, or any countries where Catholicism held the strongest sway. The big feast is Christmas, the feast of the Incarnation, the proclamation that God became flesh in a little baby. Easter's redemption is just the logical conclusion.

from *Why Be Catholic?*

The Look of Love

I remember a summer that I could have lived on the look of love. You know it if you've experienced it. Somehow things that could be a pain or a burden are a joy because you know you're loved. You know your life has a meaning, you know someone loves you. It isn't that the person has to be there, it's just that someone out there thinks you're lovable. Just thinking about that and knowing it makes the rest easy to take.

The look of love is what each person lives for! It's so unnecessary and such a gift, which is why it's so redemptive and so freeing. Why me? Why none of those other neat guys, those other people? Why did she choose me? It's an experience of election, of choice, of unworthiness!

We can live on that look of love from God for a lifetime. With it, we can bear the unbearable, and it will be a joy. The burden becomes light, and sweet!

from *The Great Themes of Scripture*

The Meaning of Life

Humans are called not to make something of themselves but to submit to creation and to re-creation from another. Yahweh alone is our support, our rock, our deliverer. A person's life cannot be made secure by what one owns, but by who one is.

The central Old Testament themes of election and of the *anawim*—a Hebrew word meaning "the poor little ones"—show a continual refinement of what Jesus finds most attractive in human persons, and, therefore, the core meaning of humanness. It can be summed up in four terms: littleness, longing, openness and surrender.

from *The Great Themes of Scripture*

Put Into My Heart the Right Questions

Before you open the Gospels, ask each time, What is the question that Jesus is trying to answer? Then say, Lord, put in my heart those questions. Make me ask the right questions. Jesus answers people who are asking the right questions. If the Gospel is not an answer to the world anymore, it's perhaps because the world is not asking the right questions. The world is saying, How can I be making $40,000 by the time I'm forty? Our country is obsessed with that question. Yet Jesus says it's a false question. He in fact says it's an utter lie, and it's all going to pass away.

Unless you move deeper into asking his questions, you will always get the wrong answer—especially wrong because it will look religious.

from *On Pilgrimage With Father Richard Rohr*

Spiritual Consumerism

Soul knowledge sends you in the opposite direction from consumerism. It's not addition that makes one holy but subtraction: stripping the illusions, letting go of the pretense, exposing the false self, breaking open the heart and the understanding, not taking my private self too seriously.

In a certain sense we are on the utterly wrong track. We are climbing while Jesus is descending, and I think in that we reflect the pride and the arrogance of Western civilization, always trying to accomplish, perform and achieve. We transferred all that to Christianity and became spiritual consumers. The ego is still in charge. When the self takes itself that seriously, there's no room left for God.

All we can really do is get ourselves out of the way, and *we* can't even do that.

from *Why Be Catholic?*

Demons

How do you keep the heart free? How do you keep from turning bitter? How do you deal with the demons? Maybe you've seen paintings of St. Anthony the Abbot (who lived in the third and fourth centuries) in the desert. There are all these little devils trying to get at him. It's a wonderful image of spiritual warfare.

The real demons that get at us, though, are very subtle. The hearts of most Christians are destroyed by things like cynicism. It grows over them for maybe a ten-year period and they don't even know it's there. After a while it has suffocated their hearts.

We "harden into hell," as Gerald Vann said. We take on an unforgiving attitude and don't even know we have done it.

from *Why Be Catholic?*

The Freedom of Mother Teresa

We were raised with a philosophy of progress like no generation in history. We can change everything. All of our technological advertisements tell us that next year will be better. That has affected our soul. It has made impossible the mystery of acceptance, the mystery of Mary's "Let it be."

Mother Teresa talks about acceptance. At first you can say, She's just being a martyr, you know, she's fatalistic, she's surrendering too quickly. But when you see the peace, the freedom and joy on her face and eyes and in her actions, it's like meeting a different species of human being. It's like meeting a person from Mars.

No one talks about acceptance or surrender anymore. It's "Change it, make it the way we want it to be. Fix things. Manage the moment. Improve reality." But in the middle of that you have Mary's "Let it be."

from *Letting Go: A Spirituality of Subtraction*

Love Also Wounds

Jesus' whole spirituality was a growing and an opening up to the Spirit. He was a Spirit-led and Spirit-taught man. When do we see the big change in Jesus' life? In the moment of his baptism in the Spirit. What is this experience of his baptism? When he comes to know that he is Son. "This is my son, the beloved, my favor rests on him."

When Jesus comes to know himself in relation to a loving Father as a loving Son, when he comes to know the election of the Father, God's favor "rests on him." In that moment, Jesus' whole mission changes. For thirty years he has waited and listened for that revelation, that knowledge that he is the elect of God, the chosen of God.

The pattern is exactly the same for every Christian. Conversion awaits that moment when you know the election of God—just as Israel did—when you know your sonship or daughterhood, when you come to hear the Lord speak your name, when you know that you are absolutely created. There has never been another with eyes like your eyes, with your smile and your personality. You are unique, and God speaks your name uniquely. When you finally hear that unique pronouncing of your name, that is your first opening to the gift of the Spirit. Now that's what Baptism should be.

In eagles' nests that are built on high cliffs, the little eaglets just want to keep eating off Mom and Dad who keep bringing the food. At a certain point the mother or father eagle quite simply comes along and pushes them out of the nest, so they will fall off the cliff. They are pretty high up, but they just let them fall, screaming and squawking, and when they almost hit the ground, magnificently, the father eagle will come underneath and catch them. He sends them through it again until they learn to fly.

Masculine spirituality says that you finally must go out of the nest. If a father is simply a nurturer and doesn't also challenge, or wound, I don't know if the sons and daughters will have a very strong sense of themselves. I have always struggled with this essential relationship between the Father and Jesus. The Father was also wounder, demanding that Jesus be wounded, and through his wounds we were healed, and in a certain sense he was, too. It is the struggle with the wound and even against the wound that makes us whole—and holy.

from *The Great Themes of Scripture* and *A Man's Approach to God*

Monday of the First Week in Ordinary Time   Day 53

Respect One Another

We could all learn something from the rule of reverence for married folks found in 1 Peter 3:7 (JB): "Husbands must always treat their wives with consideration in their life together, respecting a woman as one who, though she may be the weaker partner"—he was a man of his times—"is equally an heir to the life of grace. This will stop anything from coming in the way of your prayers."

It's hard to respect one another and to communicate reverence. But we only believe in our worth through the eyes of people who treat us with respect. The word *re-spect* means to look at *again*. Married partners owe that to one another. Don't let your relationship enter into a lot of negative humor, quick sarcasm and put-downs—the stupid way the world talks at cocktail parties.

God has called us to a life of reverence and respect. Through our reverence we become messengers of God for one another. We look at one another again through new eyes.

from *The Spiritual Family and the Natural Family*

Marriage and Celibacy: Gifts for the Community

Jesus says in Matthew 19:12, "There are some of you who are celibate for the sake of the Kingdom. Let anyone accept this who can."

Deep within the Catholic tradition, we've taken that passage and concluded celibacy is better than marriage. But Jesus isn't saying that. I don't think that's what the Church wants to say. Jesus is saying the celibate is simply a gift in the midst of the Body of Christ, like the married people are a gift. The celibate people are a gift to tell us of what ultimately matters and what's ultimately real. The final state of affairs is community, not coupling.

Healthy celibates give us that pledge, that calling power. Their lives tell us God's love is sufficient. The Body of Christ, for its wholeness, must have celibates within its midst to tell us that Jesus' love is enough, that the Kingdom can be primary and can be *now*.

That's why unhappy celibates—complaining, materialistic, soft—are such an uncertain trumpet. They've lost their power for the Body of Christ. In that state they actually do more harm than good.

from The Spiritual Family and the Natural Family

Pray With Your Spouse

Paul gives us a teaching where he carries the new agenda of Jesus a little further. He says in 1 Corinthians 7:5 (JB), "Do not refuse each other except by mutual consent and then only for an agreed time, to leave yourselves free for prayer." Can you imagine if I were a parish priest and I got up and preached on that text? I would be laughed at.

Paul is convinced of the supreme importance of shared faith. He says there's no way you can go together in a new common life, a new love, unless together you have a new vision of something good, real, powerful happening between the two of you, that you share even in the context of prayer. It's another way of stating the absolute primacy of the Kingdom. He says the all-important thing is freedom to pray together.

Francis had a rule of discernment for the friars very similar to that. It roughly said you can do anything as long as it does not interfere with the spirit of prayer and devotion. That's a very simple rule of thumb. If you're still free to pray with a brother and sister whom you are in relationship with, you're probably free. But when you've lost the spirit of dialogue with the Lord, you've probably lost your freedom.

from *The Spiritual Family and the Natural Family*

Learning Family Love

Jesus says anyone who prefers father or mother, son or daughter to him is not worthy of him. He says the natural family is only the beginning, and he was saying that to a culture that had much stronger family units than we do. He was calling them into the new community, into the spiritual family.

"'Who are my mother and my brothers?' And looking round at those sitting in a circle about him, he said: 'Here are my mother and my brothers. Anyone who does the will of God, that person is my brother and sister and mother'" (Mark 3:34-35, JB). Against all cultural expectations, Jesus radically redefines the nature of family: right relationship instead of right blood.

All spiritual growth takes place in the context of the healing, the restoring and the recreating of the family relationships in their original ideal sense. Paradoxically, people are most scarred and people are most freed in relation to fathers, mothers, sisters and brothers. We are wounded, imprinted and hopefully blessed in our natural families. We are both hurt and healed in the spiritual family, which is the work of a lifetime. Yet the second can only hope to match the desires that are created in the first. The love that heals will usually feel like mothering, fathering, sisterhood, brotherhood.

from *The Spiritual Family and the Natural Family*

Search and Surrender

We can only play the prophet within the admitted and chosen realm of mystery. Who could have foreseen the miracle of Vatican II in the humdrum of 1958? Could reason or futurism have concluded the cultural shift that took place somewhere in the mid-1960's? Who would have predicted the seeming reactionary era of the 1980's—both in Church and state? Is there any possibility that this maddening rhythm is actually a part of the Holy Mystery? Oh, I want us to use our minds, our will, our spiritual intuition to plot and plan for what we think must be God's future and God's plan. But I can only trust that seeing and foreseeing in those who have first surrendered to the Holy Mystery. Otherwise we will have only more of what we already have too much of: willfulness and ego-centered determination calling itself the new age of the Spirit.

Have no doubt, brothers and sisters of the faith, that cannot be the best of the American Church or any Church. In that house there is too much of the privatized, eccentric self to ever perceive the true Master of the house. True surrender must precede the search. It is surrender that finally generates the search. I do not trust the search without surrender. As Yahweh said to Job, "Where were you when I laid the earth's foundations?... Have you ever in your life given orders to the morning or sent the dawn to its post?" (Job 38:4, 12, JB). Is Yahweh talking to Job or to us?

from "The Future of the American Church"

Sacramental Marriages

We have to baptize marriage just as we baptize individuals. We must be free to say we have come to serve, to lay down our life, to take up the cross. God promises us in the sacrament of matrimony that God will be known in our togetherness.

I don't know that any other religion has ever dared to say that. That's very fleshly, earthy and sensual. But thank God the Church has made matrimony a sacrament. The relationship of a man and woman, in a true life of surrender, is an encounter with Christ. That is the basis for our spirituality of marriage. You don't have to run off to a monastery. You don't have to practice asceticism. Christ is encountered in your concrete love for one another.

But we have to learn how to love the way God loves. Your moments of encounter, your moments of sharing, your moments of physical nakedness and psychic nakedness must also somehow be moments of nakedness to God, moments of prayer and freedom. In your intimate moments with one another you're entering into the great mystery, into who God is for you and what God asks of you.

from The Spiritual Family and the Natural Family

Choices About Today

"And he instructed them to take nothing for the journey."
(Mark 6:8)

In his most radical proclamation of the Kingdom, the Lord tells us that today's choices have to be such that tomorrow is still open. Most people are not free to hear the gospel because it would take too much backtracking and undoing.

So many of our people have put all their roots into this world. They're good people who come to days of recollection and buy meditation books like this one and ask, "How do we extract ourselves?" We've made so many choices in the past that have completely determined our tomorrows, and so tomorrow is not open for new questions. The old answers have us in a leghold.

We must ask: Is tomorrow open to ask the radical questions that Jesus asked about success, security, power, possessions and love?

from *Preparing for Christmas With Richard Rohr*

Religious Dropouts

I am convinced that most of the saints were religious dropouts from societies that were going nowhere. Faith called them to drop out and believe in something else. Jesus' announcement of the reign of God was telling us that culture as we've created it is on a track toward self-destruction and emptiness. He told us we can get off the train at the next stop and re-center our lives in truth and objectivity. All we have to give up is the utterly false understanding that we have of ourselves from civil society. For some reason that liberation seems to be the most difficult thing in the world!

Finding God and losing the self are the same thing. That is why faith is never *our* thing; we don't really come to it naturally or choose it of ourselves. Faith is always God's thing. It seems to be the only way that the Lord can draw us into a new viewpoint, a new point from which to view the Life that is larger than life. That life is love.

from "Image and Likeness: The Restoration of the Divine Image"

Tuesday of the Second Week in Ordinary Time   Day 61

Building the City of God

In America we don't have anything even close to Europe's great cities with fountains, cathedrals, promenades and parks. I know we've only had two hundred years to work at it, but the point is, Americans don't dream of building a great city. The American dream is having one's own house.

In America, we have moved from the great Catholic consciousness of the community, of building the city of God, a great people, to taking care of our houses, protecting our neighborhoods, so that handicapped people and people of other skin colors don't move into it and kill property values. We have got to call this what it is: narcissism.

There's a world bigger than our families. The only way we can ultimately protect our family is to create and protect the entire human family.

from *A Man's Approach to God*

Called by Name

Once you know that you and the Father are one, you can take some risks. You don't need to be the perfect little boy or girl all the time, you don't need to be the pleaser of the system, because your Father has named you. Isn't that what happened to Jesus in the desert? At thirty years of age, he heard his name and he went out from that point with great determination and self-assurance.

The place within is your soul. It is where you have heard your name spoken, that spiritual name, that sense of yourself. That place within is where you have heard yourself believed in and affirmed, that place where God has given the divine name and self to you, that place where all your names are as one.

from *A Man's Approach to God*

Retreats and Confronts

For every retreat we should make sure there is at least one confront. We all should take retreats, but for some people retreats are an entire way of life. Every few months, they come out for retreat. It's obvious with a lot of these people that they aren't involved in ministry, with serving anybody else. They're navel gazing. In the name of searching for God, they are actually running from God. There is no more effective way to run from God than to be overly religious, to be involved in pious and holy things for their own sake.

A good balance between masculine and feminine energy is to balance your life between retreats and confronts. Make sure you do pull back and reflect in your solitude or in your prayers, but make sure also that there is some engagement, involvement, incarnation, some activity.

from A Man's Approach to God

Near Occasions of Grace

We want to plant ourselves in near occasions of grace, yet we spend all our life avoiding near occasions of sin. Can there be situations that we allow ourselves to enter which will force us to reevaluate everything? That is certainly what the Third World did for me. That's what joining the Franciscans as a young man did for me, that's what New Jerusalem did for me. You have to find those situations and contexts and ways of looking out at the world, so you will feel and think differently about reality. It won't come just from sermons and books. We are converted through new circumstances. Grace best gets at us when our guard is down.

from *A Man's Approach to God*

The Gift of Prayer Within Us

A Hasidic Jew said, to be able to experience ourselves as givers of energy, we have somehow to know ourselves as God (here you find a thin line between truth and illusion!). We have to know who we belong to, we have to believe in the divine indwelling, we have to trust our souls. The Hasidic Jew said something beautiful: "When I pray I'm God." Prayer itself is God. It's not an activity to get God to like me, or to talk to God. It's not something that I do for God; prayer is God in me loving God outside of me, and God outside of me loving God in me. The Spirit is the gift of prayer within us (see Romans 8:26-27).

A lot of us feel unhappy with our prayer lives. I always tell this to people on retreats: I don't really care where you are in the stages of prayer, just ask yourself, Do you *desire* to pray? As long as the desire to pray is there the Spirit is still alive in you. When there isn't even the desire, then you are in trouble.

from *A Man's Approach to God*

The Gift of Guilt

Steps 4, 5 and 6 of The Twelve Steps:

[We]

4. Made a searching and fearless moral inventory of ourselves.

5. Admitted to God, to ourselves and to another human being the exact nature of our wrongs.

6. Were entirely ready to have God remove all these defects of character.

The story of the woman caught in adultery is a perfect example of Jesus giving people the "gift of guilt," something our sophisticated, liberal society would not imagine possible or desirable. He said two things to her: (1) "I do not condemn you" (shame is not the answer) and (2) "Go and sin no more" (take ownership of yourself and change).

In this he teaches the same lesson as steps 4 and 5 and 6 of the Twelve-Step program. Be entirely ready to have God remove all of these defects of character, which means we've got to own all those defects of character. We've somehow got to find the freedom and the readiness to want to do this. The world teaches us denial, rationalization and blame.

But Jesus gives the gift of guilt (ownership and responsibility), while taking away shame. Shame is quite simply fear of the contempt of others. We all carry it. We're afraid of being looked down upon. We're afraid of being thought of as nothing. We're afraid of being hated for who we are.

Jesus never shamed people. But he did encourage them to take full responsibility for their mistakes. That's the narrow and healthy road that the gospel and Twelve-Step programs make possible.

from *Breathing Under Water: Spirituality and the 12 Steps*

The Spirituality of A.A.

The spirituality of Alcoholics Anonymous will go down in history as the significant and authentic American contribution to the history of spirituality. It is genuinely a spirituality. What's so exciting about it for me as a Christian is to see the Twelve Steps and the Twelve Traditions stating clearly what we've been saying so feebly in theological language. Religious jargon has become so overused and mystified that it doesn't have much punch anymore. Words like "love" and "conversion" connote so many things that their message no longer is clear. They often obscure instead of reveal, mystify instead of name.

Twelve-Step language is clearing away the mystification that religion is so prone to. Mystification is the religious form of repression and denial. The Twelve Steps call it "stinking thinking." They have no time for it.

from *Breathing Under Water: Spirituality and the 12 Steps*

You Must Be Like Children

Jesus said, "Unless you change and become like little children you will never enter the Kingdom of heaven" (Matthew 18:3). You can't even recognize the Kingdom of heaven, he says, except through childlike eyes. I think a very legitimate interpretation of that is that all of us grew up in families where not all our needs were met—families that carried degrees of darkness, and even abuse. Every one of us has been sinned against.

That's really the doctrine of Original Sin: All of us carry the wound. We pass down that wound from father to child, from mother to child. Someday, each of us has to walk back through our family of origin to rename our fears and security needs, re-feel repressed emotions, re-own, relive and re-feel the things we were never allowed to feel and never allowed to think. And that is, in truth, becoming a little child, because you feel like a damned fool when you do it. Yet without reliving and reclaiming the child's journey, you will nurse your wounded child forever.

from *Breathing Under Water: Spirituality and the 12 Steps*

The Place of Healing

Why do many languages use the word *spirit* to describe liquor? What if, next time I have Mass with you, when I hold up the chalice I say, "liquor of Christ"? Wouldn't that shock you all? Isn't it strange that the very thing that has caused so much pain in some of your lives, alcohol, would be the very thing that we use for the sacrament? Is it mere irony or coincidence—or providence? The blood of Christ, the wine of Christ, the liquor of Christ.

The place of the wound is the place of the healing. The place of the break is the place of the greatest strength. That's why Jesus himself, even in his resurrected body, reappears with the wounds still in his hands, in his side, in his feet. They do not disappear as you might expect.

What's the problem for Thomas? He can't deal with the wounds. Jesus tells him, Put your finger in. Deal with pain. Deal with the fact that I'm still broken.

No, you're resurrected, you're not supposed to have a hole in your side, says Thomas.

"Thomas, put your finger in my hands. Put it in my side. Now, believe" (John 20:27). I don't think you can begin to believe until you put your finger in your own wounds, the wounds of one another and the wounds of Christ.

from *Breathing Under Water: Spirituality and the 12 Steps*

Thursday of the Third Week in Ordinary Time   Day 70

Negative Energy

There's a tendency toward deception in the dysfunctional family. There is a kind of endless crisis orientation, marked by anxiety. I've seen it in myself at times. Sometimes I can't get motivated unless I have something to be anxious about. Apparently, a lot of us were never taught or encouraged to get the positive juices going, so we don't even know how to do it.

When we need something to worry about, to be angry or upset about, we begin on a negative foundation. And if we begin negatively, we're probably going to end negatively. It's no wonder that so many of us, against our best intentions, have become negative people, operating out of various kinds of toxic energy. Those energies are often taken on by entire families. For some of us it's the only kind of response we have modeled for us early in life. We were told what we did wrong, what we should not feel, what we should be afraid of. We were not told how to see and feel the good, how to trust life instead of death.

from *Breathing Under Water: Spirituality and the 12 Steps*

Friday of the Third Week in Ordinary Time   Day 71

The Hole in the Soul

Do you realize with what difficulty surrender will come to a fixing, managing mentality? There's nothing in that psyche prepared to understand the spiritual wisdom of surrender. All of the great world religions teach surrender. Yet most of us, until we go through the hole in our soul—our weak spot in the middle—just don't think surrender is necessary. At least that's how it is for those of us in First World countries. The poor, on the other hand, seem to understand limitation at a very early age.

The Third World faces its limitation through a breakdown in the social-economic system. But we have to face our limitations, it seems, in the interior world. That's our liberation theology. We must recognize our own poor man, our own abused woman, the oppressed part of ourselves that we hate, that we deny, that we're afraid of. That's the hole in our soul. It's the way *through*, maybe the only way, says the crucified Jesus.

from *Breathing Under Water: Spirituality and the 12 Steps*

Irish Wisdom

Once after I gave a retreat in Ireland, three older women came up afterward and said, "Oh, Father, what you were saying is what we believed years ago, but we threw it out with the Second Vatican Council."

They told me about the fallen priest. He was the priest who'd had some terrible moral failure, as if all of us didn't. The fallen priest was, of course, looked down upon and whisked away to some monastery on the coast of Ireland so the good Irish people wouldn't imagine that their priest sinned or drank. Yet the three women told me, excitedly, "You know what? We don't know if the priests knew this, but we old Irish people always went to the fallen ones for the cure."

Now, *there's* Irish wisdom.

from Breathing Under Water: Spirituality and the 12 Steps

Honor the Sabbath

We see in the Third Commandment a very basic understanding of the relationship between God and humanity. The Hebrews said, on the seventh day, the Sabbath, they would rest. Everything would stop. "This is the day the Lord has made. Let us rejoice in God and be glad," sings the psalmist.

The Lord says: "I have to teach these people that I'm their power, that I'm their lover and that I'm their life. So just one day a week, a seventh of your time, stop proving yourselves, stop achieving, stop accomplishing. Stop doing anything that is task oriented. Let me do the saving, the loving, the liberating." That was the meaning of the sabbath rest: to wait upon the Lord, to rest in the Lord. And in order to allow the Lord to prove himself, they would not sow their fields every seventh year.

We find out that it is not we who are doing the loving. Someone is loving through us.

from The Great Themes of Scripture

Monday of the Fourth Week in Ordinary Time   Day 74

God Loves You

Read the praise prayers of St. Francis from beginning to end. All St. Francis needs to do is praise God. That takes care of everything else. Because he's letting God be God. He praises God for this, he praises God for that. Every situation, even though immediately it might look unhappy or difficult or absurd or impossible, he praises God. That becomes the transparency through which God is able to act through us and in us, when we trust God that much, when we believe that God is always loving us.

There is no time, no place, no situation in which God is not loving you. There is no way God is not loving you. We have to be the continual "yes" for the love to come through. And then our lives become no more coincidence, but continuous providence!

from The Great Themes of Scripture

Gospel Power

God speaks the true word of power, but we cannot believe it. We trust in our power, which we think will change the world. But what has it done? Look at our own government. Look at the world! How little culture, how little real civilization the world has achieved. How little humanity! Conservatives tend to mistrust powerlessness, while liberals tend to mistrust power. Jesus puts them both together in an utterly new way that satisfies neither group.

We have never had the courage to take the word of the Lord seriously. We are afraid of both gospel power and gospel powerlessness. We've experienced just enough Christianity, someone once said, to forever inoculate ourselves from wanting the real thing.

from The Great Themes of Scripture

God Has No Grandchildren

Judges 2:10 (JB) says: "When that generation too had been gathered to its fathers, another generation followed it which knew neither Yahweh nor the deeds that he had done for the sake of Israel." They had forgotten.

We must become *children* of God. Every generation has to be converted anew. Each generation has to be called into God's life to know the fidelity of God, to step out, and to base their life on the word of God.

It's not enough to say that my mother was Catholic, my father was Christian. Until you come to that moment in your life when you choose the God you will serve, you have not begun to experience conversion. The reason that the word of the Lord does not speak to our people is because, most simply, they have never been converted. Many church-goers are in fact baptized pagans. Our parents' faith is not ours until we walk the journey ourselves. God has no grandchildren.

from *The Great Themes of Scripture*

Thursday of the Fourth Week in Ordinary Time   Day 77

Faith Is Faith Is Faith

Knowledge of God cannot be proven, processed, reasoned, justified or legitimated. This God-knowing and God-energy always risks being misunderstood (as God also risks) and risks being misinterpreted (as God puts up with) and even risks being not appreciated (as God also feels).

To live in faith—which is to live with God—one has to risk looking and feeling like nothing—nothing that can be possessed, bargained for, developed, controlled, sold, bought, measured, merited, applauded, or even rightly communicated. Faith, finally, is beyond the world of power, function and purpose.

I must say it or I would deny the entire history of faith from Abraham to Jesus to Francis of Assisi to our own Donny Flowers and Erwin Wolke: Faith is beyond any reasonable and objective process that even good people can devise. There is no community program or structure, no matter how perfect or how much we own it or invest in it, that will ever make biblical faith unnecessary. Faith is faith is faith. And God can only be known by faith (see Romans 3-5). I wonder why religious people so easily forget that?

Faith is finally to stand in nothingness, with nothing to prove and nothing to protect, knowing itself in an ever-alive charity that urges us to surrender, to let go, to give away, to hand over, to forgive, to walk across, to take no offense, to trust another, to lose oneself—while being quite sure that we are going to find ourselves afterward.

A consumer-oriented, functional and materialistic age finds faith almost impossible. We want religion, but we surely do not want faith. Because if faith is nothing, the faithful person is a nobody. In our shallow culture, trust is called naïveté. Forgiveness always looks like being soft and conceding to the enemy—even speaking the truth will not win you any votes or look patriotic on the evening news. Faith is nothing in this age and culture. Faith always has been nothing.

from "Image and Likeness: The Restoration of the Divine Image"

Masks of God

The Latin word for mask is *persona*, from which comes our word for the individual human. The word seems to indicate that the individual manifestation is no more than a mask of a larger reality. It first referred to the large theatrical masks which the Greek actors used to "speak through" (*per-sonare*) to magnify their voices. Eventually *persona* was used by Christian philosophers and theologians to define the individual as separate from the group. Each person was a mask of God. Each person was one breathing and sounding through the mask, one image of a much larger truth.

I come to know my personhood only in the infinite respect of the I-thou relationship, which finally only God can show me: subject to subject, gaze to gaze, one who refuses to treat me as an object. In one sense, love is *always* between equals. God's love for us is so perfect, we know ourselves to be respected as equals and lovers. It takes a lifetime to absorb that!

from "Image and Likeness: The Restoration of the Divine Image"

Wrestling With an Angel

Our faith is not in words. Our faith is in a person. Our faith is in God, who is revealing the divine self to us in Christ and in the lives of the Body of Christ. The word calls us into a personal dialogue, not a slavish idealization of words, not a rigid love affair with ideas. That is fundamentalism.

The Scriptures call us into a personal struggle like Jacob's. He wrestled with the angel of Yahweh (Genesis 32:24-31). In that personal involvement, in our personal wrestling match with the mystery of God, we come to faith. Faith is not just another competing ideology. It is more a process than a conclusion, more a way of relating than a way of explaining, more a wrestling match than a classroom lesson.

from *The Great Themes of Scripture*

Outstaring the Darkness

The faith-filled people in the Bible heard the word of God just as you and I must hear it. Perhaps they didn't hear audible voices, perhaps they didn't see visions any more than you and I do. But somehow they knew the call of God. They received the word of God. They experienced and received the gifts of God. And they rarely doubted their gift.

For the Hebrew people, history was always the time between promise and fulfillment. The faithful one was the one who outstared the darkness—the void—and knew that somehow, some way, out of all of this absurdity and aimlessness, the word of the Lord would be fulfilled.

from *The Great Themes of Scripture*

Monday of the Fifth Week in Ordinary Time   Day 81

The Promised Land

The Good News is always pointing to the future, to someplace new, to the promised land. It never points backward, except to validate the call to faith in God's future. This is the irony of Christian history: Much of it has been looking backward to the good old days of faith and miracles, back to "when God was God," when the great prophets lived.

How did the word of God become this conservative thing, this disguised fear holding humanity down, holding us to the (usually recent) past? We clearly were not listening to the word of God.

The word always points us to the future and calls us out of our own idol-making and insecurities to the security and future God will create. Christianity, like Judaism, is essentially a forward-looking religion because it destroys our idols, character armor and defense mechanisms, and leads us to trust in God's future. Faith is the security to be insecure.

from *The Great Themes of Scripture*

The Promise of God

Our age has come to expect satisfaction. We have grown up in an absolutely unique period when having and possessing and accomplishing have been real options. We have the illusion of fulfillment and an even more dangerous illusion that we have a right to expect fulfillment—and fulfillment now—as long as we are clever enough, quick enough and pray or work hard enough for our goals.

We want to be energized by the bird in the hand; but the word of God and the history of those who have struggled with that word would seem to tell us that we are, in fact, energized much more by the bird in the bush. God's people are led forward by promises. Promises, with all their daring and risk, empower the hearts of people.

God's people are called through the enticement of the call itself, much more than through the direct vision of God's face, the certitude of God's answers or the unfailing presence of God's joy. The Lord is "Our Justice" not by fulfilling us but by calling us from where we are. God restores us not by making it happen but by promising us that it will. God tells us who we are by telling us who we are to become. Somehow that is enough. It works! At least it works for those who can learn how to believe: "Blessed is she who believed that the promise made her by the Lord would be fulfilled" (Luke 1:45).

from *Sojourners*, "The Energy of Promise"

Loving the Church

Nothing in this world is an end in itself, including Church, priests, bishops, popes, laws, Bible—nothing! Only God is an end; everything else is a means. Only God can save us, not the Church.

I say that out of a great love for the Church. God saves, and the Church is that beautiful gift given by God to preach that word which will set us free. But when we preach "Church" and raise up "Church," we are not necessarily proclaiming the Lord. We often are preaching ourselves. Jesus never preached Israel, he preached Yahweh. He preached the absolute transcendence of Yahweh and fidelity and obedience to Yahweh.

At the same time Jesus never put Israel down. He loved Israel. Insofar as Israel was true to the covenant and true to the prophets, Jesus was obedient to Israel, obedient to the priests, obedient to "the Church." But he wasn't afraid to keep knocking on the door. He kept inviting Israel to be true to itself. Jesus taught us to love the unlovely, exactly as it is.

If we simply love that which is worthy of love, we will never love at all. The Lord loved "the Church," Israel, exactly as it was. You cannot love the Church as it was fifty years ago. That's a cop-out. The only Church you must love is the Church today.

from *The Great Themes of Scripture*

Trust in God

A favorite saying is, "God helps those who help themselves." I think the phrase can be understood correctly, but in most practical situations it is pure heresy. Scripture clearly says God helps those who trust in God, not those who help themselves.

We need to be told that so strongly because of our entire "do it yourself" orientation. As educated people, as Americans, our orientation is to do it. It takes applying the brakes, turning off our own power and allowing Another. What the lordship of Jesus means is that first we come to him, first we put things into his hands. Our doing must proceed from our being. Our being is "hidden with Christ in God" (Colossians 3:3).

from *The Great Themes of Scripture*

Step Out in Silence

We must learn to trust God. Developing that trust is worth some particular attention, worth making time to stop and pray, and be quiet in God. That may be impractical, but the way of faith is not the way of efficiency. God has not called us to an efficient way of life. We are called to a way of faith. Much is a matter of listening and waiting.

At times we have to step into God's silence. We have to put

out the fleece as Gideon did (Judges 6:37-40). Then we step out and see if God backs us up. It can be a greater act of faith, to go ahead and act on our own best intuition and presume that the Lord is speaking to us. God works through trust. When moving forward is done out of a spirit of prayer, we can trust the Lord will be there, even if we are mistaken.

from The Great Themes of Scripture

Prophets in Your Hometowns

The prophets had one foot in Israel and one foot outside. So must you have one foot in your faith community and one foot in the world. Always we have to find our love, then give our love away. Sometimes it isn't easy to give or to see. We must love where we are called to love, and sometimes that means loving people and institutions that really turn us off.

The prophets always loved Israel; they were always faithful to her. They believed that the Lord was using Israel to proclaim his presence and love to the world. They didn't feel they were better than Israel. They knew they had to speak a word of truth to that nation. Although they suffered at the hands of the world, they suffered even more at the hands of Israel.

from The Great Themes of Scripture

Catholic Identity

Most of us over forty today were given a strong sense of Catholic identity. Catholicism was a total world, a total way of thinking and feeling. Someone said you could just as easily stop being Catholic as you could stop being black, brown, yellow, red or white. You couldn't change it. "Holy Mother Church" is still our mother. You can't change mothers. You can't kill your mother. Maturity usually means accepting that Mom was a good enough mother and not a perfect one.

But most people who have been formed since Vatican II have never had that experience. Except in rare instances, they were never given a strong sense of Catholic identity. So they don't have a strong sense of loyalty to Catholicism. Neither, however, do they have a big need to fight the Church. I don't know which is worse. Is it worse to have a mother to rebel against or not to have a mother at all?

Those of my generation are putting all their time into reforming structures and models of authority. The younger set, however, have an entirely different set of problems: no Christian or Catholic identity, a poor sense of healthy boundaries and almost no sense of the sacred.

from *Why Be Catholic?*

Three Fundamental Questions

The first question that the gospel sets out to answer for us is Who are you? That's the question of spirituality. And of course we're told right at the beginning, on our baptismal day, "You are a beloved."

All our life we hope to raise up our eyes and see someone looking at us and speaking that answer to our basic spiritual question. Hopefully our parents looked into our eyes, told us we were beautiful and kissed us endlessly. All of our lives we hope for that to be repeated and for someone to tell us what our soul of souls and our heart of hearts knows: I'm special, I'm good, I'm a beloved somewhere. We long for it to be repeated because we know it's the truth, the only truth, for which we were created.

The second question the gospel asks is one of sexuality: Can we love? Whatever this life is, whatever this identity is that I'm finding inside of myself, I'm never going to be totally sure of it until it's received by another. I don't know I have power within until I can hand over that power to another. In that eternal learning how to hand it over and to have it received, we answer the real questions of sexuality: Can I be a loving, intimate person? Can I walk through those doors of fear into intimacy? Can I reveal my true soul to at least one person? Can I take the big risk and somehow discover who I am in another's eyes?

Finally, the gospel helps us ask: Can I create? Everyone must be creative. We'll never discover that place of passion within until we find our creative place, that place where we can create life in another, in the world, in our backyard.

Love is of one piece. We either love everybody or we do not really love. So after we talk about spirituality and after we talk about sexuality, finally we have to talk about service. We can't love our family and hate our enemies. We either love all things (to be "in love") or we don't really love anything.

from *The Passion of God and the Passion Within*

Love Thyself

There's no way you can love until you forgive yourself for not being perfect, for not being the saint you thought you were going to be. To use Franciscan imagery, until you've leapt across the chasm and embraced the leper, until you've recognized that really the leper is not on the other side of the chasm but the leper is, first of all, the leper within, you won't really know your passion, or be capable of com-passion.

Compassion comes from a spacious place where a lot of things are put together and coexist, where we recognize, forgive and make friends with the enemy within. There's nothing you hate, there's nothing you fear over there in other people that you haven't met and forgiven in your own soul. The passionate struggle with your own shadow becomes compassion for the struggles of our neighbor.

from *The Passion of God and the Passion Within*

Hope's Lovely Daughters

Augustine said that if we discover hope, hope will have two lovely daughters: anger and courage. But many of us, like good German Catholic boys raised in Kansas, were told that anger was a bad emotion.

Nothing would happen on this earth if people didn't get angry. Nothing would change. Anger is often good and necessary.

Anger, like hope, is a part of the passion of God. It's part of God's feeling for what is not and should be, and *could* be if only someone would be willing to carry God's feeling. Anger is often a form of grieving for the good things that have been allowed to die.

Hope leads us, after the anger, to courage. *Courage* literally means an action of the heart. With courage we finally trust some of those fierce feelings, our sense of that wild God. Then we can lay our life down in servanthood for the places where things aren't right, where God's people are being told lies and being oppressed.

The problem with passion isn't that we desire too much, in spite of what the moralists used to tell us. The real problem is that we don't desire enough! We are the desiring of God.

from *The Passion of God and the Passion Within*

Spirit Versus Sin

Sin is to claim the self as an independent possession or as a private right. Sin is always a type of self-absorption, which is a lie about the nature of reality; whereas the Spirit, who teaches all truth, celebrates and reconciles that which is fragmented. The Spirit of God makes all things one by reminding them that they are first one—more one than many fragmented parts of a larger whole.

What looks like discovery is really recognition. What appears to be exploration is much more homecoming. The Spirit unites; sin always separates. The work of God is total and full reconciliation. In other words, our only real badness consists in the repression of our goodness, which is the Spirit given and promised. And that is indeed bad.

Empirically, this badness shows itself in hardness, non-listening, the refusal to feel, self-hatred in its many disguises and superficiality in general. This is the great sin of nonbelief, which aborts the human soul a thousand times a day: We refuse to believe who the Son has told us we are—sons and daughters of the living God. We hate ourselves mercilessly, and in many ways our preoccupation with sins has kept us from the recognition of this great sin. It is the unforgivable and unrecognized sin against the Holy Spirit, because it is unrecognized disbelief in what God has done.

from *Sojourners*, "The Holiness of Human Sexuality"

Falling in Love

Somewhere each day we have to fall in love, with someone, something, some moment, event, phrase. Somehow each day we must allow the softening of the heart. Otherwise our hearts will move inevitably toward hardness. We will move toward cynicism, bitterness, fear and despair. That's where most of the world is trapped and doesn't even know it.

The world's been in love with death so long that it calls death life. It tries to conjure up life by making itself falsely excited, by creating parties where there's no reason to celebrate.

We have to create and discover the parties of the heart, the place where we know we can enjoy, the place where we can give of ourselves. If you're not involved in giving your thoughts, your emotions, "for-giving," you will be involved only in taking. Yet the only way to experience joy is to give yourself to reality. Joy comes after you go that extra mile and offer yourself first-thing every day.

Ask the Lord to give you the grace to fall in love. Then you'll see rightly, because only when we are in love do we understand. Only when we've given ourselves to reality can we in fact receive reality. That is the endless mystery of the Trinity that is expressed in every facet of this world: Perfect giving equals perfect receiving.

from *The Passion of God and the Passion Within*

Go to the Edges

Whatever your life situation might be, find some way to be in immediate contact with the little ones, the nobodies. Get in touch with the people who are of no account, who haven't made it into the great American midstream. Maybe they don't talk "right" and smell "right." They may not seem to be part of the "in" group.

If we of the middle-class Church have found ourselves scandalized by our own brokenness and imperfection, it's because we have separated ourselves from the broken character of almost all of reality.

When a severely disabled person confronts us, we're scandalized and afraid. Everything in our being says, Oh, it shouldn't be that way, let's change it. But we can't change it. The only thing we know how to do is to draw apart, to pull away in fear, anger and disappointment with God. But God gives us each other. Those who are disabled can remind the rest of us who we are. We live under an illusion, thinking we're not handicapped or retarded, thinking we've got it together.

We're afraid of those who seem weak because they come with the faces of the crucified Jesus. We push them to the edge of society. The elderly we shove aside because they remind us that we, too, one day will be old. We ignore little children, thinking they don't know anything yet and have nothing to teach us. We shun disabled people, who remind us that our bodies are also one step away, any moment, from crippledness. People with mental disabilities painfully remind us we really aren't very smart. Refugees bring forth the fear within each of us of not having a place to lay our head. Gays and lesbians remind us that we all are both masculine and feminine. Prisoners remind us we also are imprisoned and trapped.

There is a reason we push all these people far away and far

apart: They represent everything we fear and everything we deny about ourselves. Yet to be touched by these people is to discover the deepest recesses of our own life.

from *The Passion of God and the Passion Within*

Suffering

When I was young, I wanted to suffer for God. I pictured myself being the great and glorious martyr. There's something so romantic about laying down your life. I guess every young person might see themselves that way. But there is nothing glorious about the moment of suffering when you're in the middle of it. You swear it's meaningless. You swear it has nothing to do with goodness or holiness.

The very essence of the desert experience is that you want to get out. A lack of purpose, of meaning—that's what causes us to suffer. When you find a pattern in your suffering, a direction, you can accept it and go with it. The great suffering, the suffering of Jesus, is when that pattern is not given.

from *The Great Themes of Scripture*

Left-brain Christianity

Westerners don't naturally understand the inner world. When I went to Africa and Asia, I saw people who do. We have achieved a great control over the outer world. That's how we produced the scientific and industrial revolution. The left-brain-oriented Western mind is victorious in the outer world but almost infantile in the inner world.

Western Christianity has paid a price for that. I don't mean this to sound cynical or unfair, but let me say it in a way to shock, to make us feel the truth of it: The Western Church really isn't that spiritual. It doesn't understand spirituality. Buying and selling in the Temple makes more sense to us.

from *Why Be Catholic?*

Two Pastorals

We Americans are very aware of the pastorals our U.S. bishops have written on war and peace and on the economy. (When you think of it, it's unbelievable that it took us two thousand years to begin seriously to address these problems!)

Because of the European mind, the Western Church, so bellicose and warlike, had no mind to deal with Jesus' teachings on nonviolence. It just ignored them: It wasn't culturally ready.

We created the just war theory, but it was used much more to legitimize war than to form mature Christians.

The same is true with economics. You can't go more than two or three paragraphs in any of the Synoptic Gospels without Jesus addressing the question of materialism and money. It's constant, and he is absolute as he can be: You cannot serve God and money, period. If you think you can play both games, you're fooling yourself. Yet we were convinced we could. The people thought they could get as wealthy as they wanted and still become spiritual people. "Impossible!" Jesus says.

The U.S. bishops' pastorals are two examples of Catholicism's strength at this point in history. For all of our evident weakness, for all the ways we've experienced darkness or hurt in the Catholic Church, there is some tremendous spiritual power at work in the Church now that we're daring to address even the cultural demons of war and greed. That tells me the Spirit is very alive in the Church. I frankly don't know any other Church that's trying so hard to evangelize *culture*, not just individuals.

from *Why Be Catholic?*

Stories, Songs and Saints

We grew up with a whole set of words and language, the words that first touched our souls. They were sacred words with deep connotations, and overnight those words were changed. Not just from Latin to English. But all of a sudden the theological language of the *Baltimore Catechism* seemed not to apply anymore. We haven't recovered from that decades later.

We lost our sacred words, and we haven't found new sacred words that have the punch those words had for many of us when we were little Catholic boys and girls. Those words were the ones our mothers and fathers told us. But I believe words, in the long run, don't really form the Catholic worldview. The underlying "myth" or ethos, the underlying imagination formed by stories, songs and saints, forms a worldview that is largely indestructible.

The Catholic "myth" is even deeper than the Catholic words. If you are a part of this deeper symbolic universe, the words can change and cause only minor disruption.

from *Why Be Catholic?*

Thursday of the Seventh Week in Ordinary Time   Day 98

Universal Faith

There is nothing we can do, in the end, except adore. There is nothing we can do except love in some way just as we've been loved. Great souls don't move up into the head, with all kinds of principles, laws, explanations, Bible quotes, ways to get saved, sacramental regulations. That's not great Catholicism. Great Catholicism has entered into the union underneath it all. That's what makes it universal.

That catholicity encourages me so comfortably and even lovingly to be a Catholic. I've probably seen more of the garbage of Catholicism than most, but I've also experienced the grace of God, good parenting, good early experiences of religious life, good celebrations of the sacraments and a good Catholic education (which is not the same as Catholic propaganda).

I can't thank God enough for our universal worldview. Yet how can we pass this on to the next generation? I know I was given that richness and depth, I was born just in time to get the best of the "old Church." Good Franciscans and good teachers entered my life at the right time. People of love and wisdom have touched me along the way, so the Catholic worldview made sense to me. What breaks my heart is the huge number of our people (not just young people) who have received nothing but crumbs. They have legalism, function, structure and institutional expectations, but they do not have that rich and profound Catholic worldview that allows you and prepares you to dialogue with everything.

It saddens me that most Catholics are more Roman than catholic. Most Catholics have not been given a good, universal set of glasses with which to examine God and the world.

from *Why Be Catholic?*

Friday of the Seventh Week in Ordinary Time   Day 99

Catholic Radicals

We want to take this occasion to clarify and announce the proud and necessary meaning of *radical Catholics*, to which we allude in our title and which we now find essential in this secular and post-Christian age. First, the word itself is the clue. *Radix* is the Latin word for "root." A *radical* is one who moves beyond the liberal and conservative branches of an institution and goes back to a fundamental questioning. The dictionary says that a radical is one "who goes back to the root, the source, the fundamentals."

This is very different from a modernist or liberal who wants to update or accommodate to the present situation. There is a place for such reform, but that is not the primary concern of a true radical. Neither is a radical the same as a traditionalist or conservative, who usually does not go back far enough. A radical Catholic will at different times look like both of these types, yet is neither of them at all.

The questions and concerns of radicals would undercut all self-interest, ideology and institution. In this case, they ask: "What does our humanity demand of us? What does love ask of us? What did Jesus present as essential and all-embracing? What is God doing on earth?" John Paul II asks just such questions in *On Social Concerns* and finds himself speaking for truly radical Catholics. Striking at the root of the tree, he does not ask us to "change" as much as to "CHANGE!" That is why the priests and the presidents and other men of power have thus far been unable to admit that this encyclical even exists. It lets no one off the hook!

from *Radical Grace*, *"On Social Concern:*
Pope John Paul II's Radical Manifesto to All Christians"

The 'Immoral' Minority

We should not want to be the moral majority but the "immoral" minority. It's from the minority perspective that we ask the right questions and the Church gets purified. The

Spirit works best underground.

Christianity does not really flourish in the majority position. Where Catholics think of themselves as the majority, real faith is often very anemic. We aren't forced to ask the hard questions about faith.

from *Why Be Catholic?*

Eighth Sunday in Ordinary Time   Day 101

Fingers Pointing to the Moon

Thomas Merton liked to repeat an insight from Zen Masters: All of these religious gifts that are given to us are no more than fingers pointing to the moon. Religion endlessly gets involved with the fingers—defining them, proclaiming them, protecting them, fighting about which finger is better, which finger is going to save you, instead of paying attention to the moon. Everything, in the light of the Kingdom of God, is a means, a finger. It's the moon, the goal, that matters, and the goal is God.

Pope, institutional Church, Bible, sacraments, priesthood, all of these things that we spend ninety percent of our time worrying about, those are the fingers pointing to the moon. But it's the moon we must see.

from *Letting Go: A Spirituality of Subtraction*

Do You Have a Little Time to Talk?

You've never seen a people with as little time as Westerners. Yet we have kitchens filled with time- and work-saving objects. Go to the poor Third World countries and ask, "Do you have a little time to talk?" "The rest of my life," they'll say, and sit down and share themselves with you for the afternoon.

We should have more time than anybody, but we don't have any time at all. We've defined freedom falsely as an outer thing, in terms of time, space and options. Americans think they're free if they have more options. In fact we're paralyzed by them. With so many choices, we don't have to surrender to any one of them. There's always another door to open. We are pushed around by our options and kept busy fixing our time-saving appliances.

from *Letting Go: A Spirituality of Subtraction*

This Moment Is as Perfect as It Can Be

Gospel people don't need to hang on to anything. For them, the ego is out of the way. They'll make a difference in the world precisely because they don't need to. They don't need to be first, they don't need to be important, they don't need to be number one. They don't need to be rich, secure, popular, so they can do what God has told them to do. They can be obedient, God can move through them with power. That's why spirituality is always about letting go.

We all occasionally see how incapable we are. I was reminded of this on a muggy July afternoon, sitting at a stoplight in downtown Cincinnati. It seemed interminable. After a few moments, I became mad at everybody around me: the car in front of me, the car behind me, the car on each side of me. I began thinking vicious, unkind things about all kinds of people whom I hadn't seen in months.

Some other part of me asked a question: "Where is this coming from? Richard, you're a spiritual teacher and you're supposed to be wise and you're supposed to be free, but you are so unfree and you are so trapped in yourself that you can't even accept a little red light."

The Lord gave me a little mantra that I've used ever since: "This moment is as perfect as it can be." I've had to repeat it many times (and most times not wanting to). This moment is as perfect as it can be. Everything is right here, right now. And if I can't rejoice now, I can't know joy at all. Is my joy based on circumstances, or is my joy based on something within that no one can take from me or give to me?

from *Letting Go: A Spirituality of Subtraction*

India's Inner Freedom

It's no accident the First Commandment is a directive not to set up idols. Religion can make an idol of itself. That's exactly what Jesus' proclamation of the Kingdom tells us not to do. We are not to make absolutes of things, including our own explanations, self-understandings, self-importance. That even applies to our self-image, including our image of ourself as good, holy or righteous.

Whenever the doctrine of the Kingdom is not proclaimed in the way Jesus proclaimed it, religion creates idols. Bede Griffiths, the English Benedictine, founded an ashram (school of prayer) in India where he's been for thirty years. When he went there he said something shocking, maybe exaggerated, but certainly with a level of truth to it. He said, "I don't think Western Christianity has the power to lead people to God anymore. All they keep doing is meeting themselves and calling it God."

Now that's scary and I hope it's not true, because here we are in the Western Church. But he went off to the East and said, "Here is a culture which can get people enough out of the way so that it's possible for God to enter in."

In India the Kingdom can more easily be proclaimed. There is not so much trust in the world. They have not put their trust in outer technology and in a philosophy of progress and achievement the way we have. Indians idealize the holy man, the holy woman, the person who is searching for truth in some kind of inner freedom, not in the kind of outer freedoms that Western societies proclaim.

from *Letting Go: A Spirituality of Subtraction*

Who Read the Book for Us?

J. L. McKenzie, S.J., said in his late seventies, the great thing about being an old man is you can finally say what you know is the truth.

I can't wait! I finally can say what I really know is the truth instead of always saying things I know other people want me to say!

McKenzie was a great Scripture scholar who wrote the *Dictionary of the Bible* single-handedly. He said we should just admit that much of Western civilization, and the gospel of the Kingdom that Jesus proclaimed, have made terrible bedfellows. We have prostituted the teaching of Jesus from the very beginning, and used it to serve our own purposes, to protect European societies and invariably the society at the top.

Again and again the gospel was read from the side of what protected the privileges of the clergy, what protected the privileges of the wealthy, instead of really reading it in all of its daring truth which isn't saying either of those things. The gospel is not creating a clergy class of people who have all spiritual wisdom and truth to keep the laity eternally dependent on them for salvation.

Who was interpreting the Gospels? Clergy. Certain passages never seem to occur to us. Those of us who came out of Catholic schools basically knew only several Scripture quotes. "Thou art Peter and upon this rock I shall build my Church" was one of them. Fine quote, I believe it has great meaning and power. But does it occur to you, that would be a quote that hierarchs would notice? For a lady who's raising eight children and learning how to survive, that probably would not be the first Gospel quote that would jump out at her. Maybe it would be the widow's mite. Maybe it would be something about forgiveness. It might be one of hundreds but probably not "Thou art Peter and upon this rock I shall build my Church."

from *Letting Go: A Spirituality of Subtraction*

Friday of the Eighth Week in Ordinary Time Day 106

Consuming Jesus

How can we understand this present moment of history when the Lord seems to be taking away the priesthood and, therefore, the Eucharist all over the world? It's obvious the Lord's saying, Hey, there's something else that has to be learned here by this people. That's the only way we can understand this moment of history when we've been praying and praying for vocations. Either the Lord does not answer our prayers or the Lord has a better idea.

Often, the liturgy falls flat. We keep handing out the bread and the cup, this is my body, given for you, this is my blood, poured out for you, and yet we don't see a surrendered people who are also pouring out their lives and surrendering their body and blood! And these are sometimes the very people who, every day, are eating of the bread and drinking of the cup and living self-centered and self-protective lives.

Is this a breakthrough sacrament or, in fact, an ego disguise to keep us from doing what it's talking about?

The ritual can become a substitute for the reality. Do we keep performing the ritual of body broken and blood poured out, all the while domesticating it into a consumer object, a devotional practice to maintain our positive self-image? Does it make me feel good about myself in the morning instead of defining my action for the day? If I *consume* Jesus, I will probably consume and use all other things as self-objects. If I *meet* Jesus and make room for him, I will know how to meet and make room for all other persons and events.

from *Letting Go: A Spirituality of Subtraction*

Saturday of the Eighth Week in Ordinary Time   Day 107

Be Nice, or Be Faithful?

"Do not suppose that I have come to bring peace to the earth: it is not peace I have come to bring, but a sword" (Matthew 10:34, JB). This isn't a Christianity of niceness, of pretty words and feel-good experiences. I'll bet a good seventy to eighty percent of all the thousands of sermons I've ever heard have basically been about being nice. That's how domestic the gospel has become: how to be nice in this world and live a nice life. The word *nice* isn't found anywhere in the Bible, to my knowledge.

There's nothing more dangerous to true religious thinking than conventionalism, being like everybody else in our neighborhoods or cities. There's no depth or power to that. The masses are never going to be ready for the word of surrender, of going beyond the self. They will settle for civil religion and cultural Christianity. It's easier to be nice than to be faithful.

from *Letting Go: A Spirituality of Subtraction*

Take Up Your Cross

The phrase "Take up your cross" has been softened by usage. We've all heard it since we've been kids; we don't get the punch of it anymore. The cross is not simply enduring your hangnail for the day for the love of Jesus, or putting up with the inconvenience that your air conditioner doesn't work. That's what it's become in affluent societies. The "cross" in the New Testament is precisely the suffering that comes into our lives by the choices we make for the Kingdom. In that sense it is always optional and voluntary.

In other words, maybe I can't take this defense-industry job, which would allow my family to live with greater security and greater comfort. My conscience says no. I do not want to build weapons for the rest of my life. I have to pay the price for that.

We recognize the absolute and everything else becomes relative, including the economic and political systems. We proclaim that God is Lord, and therefore everything else is not lord.

That's where the Kingdom proclamation relativizes all of reality. If Jesus is Lord, then America is not lord. The Pentagon is not lord. The gross national product and economic development are not lord. Whiteness, neighborhood, culture, gender and denomination—all are not lord.

I constantly meet good Catholics whose actual doctrine is the lordship of American institutions. They say, Don't knock the free enterprise system. Don't knock capitalism. Don't knock the military-industrial complex.

Our religious doctrines have often been allowed to become the smokescreen for our real doctrine: our privileged position. Christ is too often a cover for our de facto allegiance to Caesar.

from *Letting Go: A Spirituality of Subtraction*

The Limits of Liberalism

We've reached the limits of liberalism.

Liberalism is basically a philosophy that proclaims the rights and the freedoms and the growth and the development of the individual. My rights, my career, my wholeness, my options. Vatican II really affirmed that agenda, protecting the person, the growth and freedom of the individual Christian. And we had to run with it for twenty-five years. We tasted its fruits, thank God, and I don't want to go back on any of those. But we've reached the limits of it. It finally moves to a place where all that we have are individuals seeking their own growth, their own happiness, their own development. Most cultures since the beginning of time would not share this worldview.

There's little possibility there for the common good, for opening myself to what's good for the whole parish, the whole diocese, the whole people. The common good is what's good for the world, not just what's good for America or good for Christianity. One wonders if our people have forgotten how to think that way. It was once the centerpiece of Catholic vision and morality.

from Letting Go: A Spirituality of Subtraction

Mardi Gras!

Some groups of radical disciples wear us out because they are so serious. Everything is so moralistic, heavy and a value judgment of good, better, best, right, wrong: "The Scriptures say, Don't do this; you must do that." Maybe I tire of this quickly because I was raised Catholic. Too much moralizing really becomes laborious, self-serving and finally, part of the problem. The mature Christian usually is a "holy fool."

We really aren't a heavy Church, a fact that has often scandalized other denominations. There is time to be on the front line, then you can take some time in the back enjoying the good and the beautiful, poetry, love, friends, laughter. That's action and contemplation, fasting and feasting—and knowing how and when to do them both. It is the most mature form of Christianity, and also the rarest.

from Why Be Catholic?

LENT

Waking Up

In the New Testament, whenever Jesus eats with or encounters the rich he always, without exception, challenges them to come beyond where they are. Yet he never accuses them of malice. He instead shows them their blindness.

Always the judgment is blindness: The rich man just can't see the plight of Lazarus (Luke 16:19-31). The rich man is not evil, he didn't cause the poor man at his gate to be poor. He simply wasn't aware. He couldn't see. That spiritual blindness is the primary sin.

Spirituality is about waking up. Eastern religions know this. The word *Buddha* means "the awakened one." Spirituality has come upon hard times in the West, where legalism so often took over that we didn't need spirituality. We lost the spiritual disciplines and tools to know how to remain awake. We lost the disciplines that show us what's happening, what human relationships mean, the effects of what we do to one another in our relationships.

The Church must continually be taught by the poor. Those who are oppressed and kicked around, who are not beneficiaries of the system, always hold for us the greatest breakthrough-truth and the greatest wisdom. In mythology they are imaged as blind beggars who in fact are true seers.

The same is true inside ourselves. That part of ourself that we most hate, that we are most afraid of and most reject, is the poor, oppressed woman or man within. That hated person within holds our greatest gift. We must hold out a preferential option for our own poverty. Our poverty has the key; it offers the breakthrough moment for us to wake up. It's the hole in the soul, that place where we are radically broken, where we are powerless and therefore open.

from *Breathing Under Water: Spirituality and the 12 Steps*

Thursday After Ash Wednesday   Day 112

Taking Responsibility

The dysfunctional family relies upon denial. There is an endless need to control everything and everyone. Children in these families grow up with a kind of chaotic emotional life coming from anywhere, coming from nowhere, coming from points beyond. They don't know where it came from, but they grow up in the middle of it.

To survive that, people try to control their world, other people and their own feelings. And after practicing that for four or five years, they really don't know any other way to live. Is that anybody's fault? No. But until that individual takes responsibility and stops blaming his mother or her father and says, "This is my life, I am an alcoholic, my life is powerless and has become unmanageable," nothing new is going to happen. The other members of the family who are codependent on the addict must make their own break with the unhealthy process. The conservative personality usually wants to shame or blame somebody; the liberal says no one should ever be blamed (except perhaps the conservatives!). We are all afraid of the radical self-responsibility of the Twelve Steps. No blame, no denial, no toxic shame, just the honest statement, "I am a _____."

from *Breathing Under Water: Spirituality and the 12 Steps*

Friday After Ash Wednesday   Day 113

Being Alive

What we lack in an addictive society and an addictive family is a sense of being truly alive. So we look for pseudo-ways to feel alive. They never work, as you know, but for some reason they seem better than doing nothing. We use nicotine, caffeine, or just stick food in our mouths to have some kind of sensation. Some of us pour liquor down our throats, or overstimulate ourselves through gambling or destructive sexual activity.

These behaviors are a testimony to a lack of spirituality. One who is spiritually alive has an excess of strength, an honest sense of interior creativity and interior imagination. They can say, "I have more than enough. There's enough of me that I can give some of it away."

When we find the spirit of Jesus inside of us, more than we asked for, expected or earned, *then* we understand grace. And grace is the perennial threat to addiction.

from *Breathing Under Water: Spirituality and the 12 Steps*

Solitude

The most simple spiritual discipline is some degree of solitude and silence. But it's the hardest, because none of us want to be with someone we don't love. To be with our own thoughts and feelings, to stop the addictive prayer wheels and just feel what we're really feeling, think what we're really thinking, is probably the most courageous act most of us will ever do.

There's probably no way out of our addictive society—and our addictive, dysfunctional families—apart from some significant and chosen degree of silence and solitude.

I go to agrarian societies, places in Africa or the Philippines, and there I see non-addicted people. I see people who lead quiet, simple lives, understimulated, with a few basic truths that they hold onto all their life. Think of how many things stimulate us daily: radio, television, billboards, conversations. We've got to slow down the chatter, the stimulation; we've got to feel many feelings which have been pent up and denied for decades. We've become overloaded, which is why we're afraid to do it.

We won't have the courage to go into that terrifying place of the soul without a great love, without the light and love of the Lord. Such silence is the most spacious and empowering technique in the world, yet it's not a technique at all. It's precisely the refusal of all technique.

from *Breathing Under Water: Spirituality and the 12 Steps*

Grace

God's love is total, unconditional, absolute and forever. The state of grace—God's attitude toward us—is eternal. We are the ones who change.

Sometimes we are able to believe that God loves us unconditionally, absolutely and forever. That's grace! And sometimes because we get down on ourselves, and carry guilt and fear and burdens, we are not able to believe that God loves us. Biblically, that's the greatest sin: not to believe the good news, not to accept the unconditional love of God. When we no longer believe God loves us, we can no longer love ourselves. We have to allow God to continually fill us. Then we find in our own lives the power to give love away.

from *The Great Themes of Scripture*

There Is No Promised Land

Moses's story contains one of the ironies of history: Moses did not get to the land of Israel. He saw it from the distance, as he looked over the River Jordan. It seemed that he did die, before the crossing over, so the biblical writers later looked for a theological significance for that. We were told that he failed in faith in the desert, that God punished him.

No doubt, though, Moses was already experiencing his Promised Land in the journey. Walking, leading the people, was already a real joy for him, a full life for him. We don't have to see his fate as some great divine punishment on the part of God. The journey was already the promise fulfilled. In this world there is no promised land. He didn't have to cross over the Jordan: He had fulfillment in the desert.

Sometimes I don't want to see another teenager, and I wonder how I ever got into this, and I'd love to go running off to some Trappist monastery. What we love the most often gives us the greatest pain. What we love in our work often brings us the greatest heartaches. No doubt this was true for Moses, too. His moments of religious experience, his moments in Sinai, were no doubt his greatest religious fulfillment. Yet for all the heartaches his people gave him, I'll bet he wouldn't have traded the journey itself for anything. I know I wouldn't.

from *The Great Themes of Scripture*

Tuesday of the First Week of Lent   Day 117

The Commandment

In the final chapters of the Book of Joshua we hear Joshua's last words to the people. He sets a vocation before the people and asks them once again to choose the Lord. He says, "Stand firm...and fulfill all that is written...never turning aside from it to right or left" (23:6, *JB*). Then he says to obey the commandments, which we immediately think refers to the Ten Commandments.

The commandment, in fact, is to trust the one God. That is

the commandment they are called to live by. It is in that relationship that they find their power. "Do not utter the names of [other] gods. Do not swear by them" (23:7, JB).

To our world God says: Do not put your trust in gods that cannot save—your looks, intelligence, money, your home. Do not put your trust in your children, wife, husband, your high position. They cannot save you. What is your money going to do for you? *God* is security, the rock of our salvation. No one has trusted in God and ever been put to shame.

from *The Great Themes of Scripture*

Wednesday of the First Week of Lent   Day 118

Sin

Liberation theology has largely come from the Third World. One of its first recognitions is that the real sin of the world is not, first of all, the little things that human beings do. Sin is, first of all, a total reality we get trapped in, "institutionalized evil." Pope John Paul II speaks of "structural sin." Even original sin is not a sin we committed, but one that was committed against us, in spite of ourselves. The classic sources of evil are the world, the flesh and the devil—in that order!

We became preoccupied with guilt. We had to know who was bad, who should feel shame. Many people were made to feel bad as children. The Church and the world have both used shame to control the people. It usually works, and it emphasizes the flesh (personal fault) instead of a social critique of the world.

But the original notion of sin is not to impute guilt; it's to

name reality. That's what I see the spirituality of Alcoholics
Anonymous doing, trying to name what's happening. What is
going on in our lives, in our society that is so blinding, so
addictive? What is trapping people from loving God and neighbor
and being truly alive? It's self-evident to me after twenty years of
ministry that most people are victims, not malicious.

from Breathing Under Water: Spirituality and the 12 Steps

Romans 7

Read Romans 7 sometime, live with the agony of Paul and see that
he's just like every one of us. Why do I do what I don't want to do?
I hate myself for doing it. And I don't understand myself, woe is
me. Paul says, "Who will rescue me from this body doomed to
death?" There you can feel a man almost tortured with
self-hatred, trying to get out of his body. Haven't all of us, at some
point in our lives, disliked the person we'd become?

Church people set out to be nice people. Yet, in our
moments of honesty, we know much of our soul is not of God:
We have negative, destructive, even violent and vengeful
thoughts toward other people.

Romans 7, thank God, is followed by Romans 8. St. Paul
leaps to the most ecstatic chapter in the New Testament: "This I
know, in Christ there is no condemnation" (8:1).

What allowed Paul to jump out of the immense self-hatred
of Romans 7 into immense hopefulness? Whatever it is—grace?
enlightenment? conversion? powerlessness? surrender?—it's the

most important thing to pray for: "Lead us not into temptation, deliver us from evil.... Thy kingdom come." God *will* answer that Our Father and deliver us from Romans 7 to Romans 8. Depend on it.

from *Breathing Under Water: Spirituality and the 12 Steps*

Confession

Confession is not just for the confessional. Sometimes, maybe even more often, it needs to be done with a wife, husband, child, friend—someone who has the power to recognize and receive the sinner.

What is not received is not redeemed: That's the principle of redemption, as far as I'm concerned. Redemption isn't experienced until the wound is received, until the hole in the soul—the weakness within that shows the way out—is recognized and somewhere looked at and named exactly for what it is.

In jail we try to talk without euphemisms and niceties: Don't say the money got stolen; say, I stole the money. Take responsibility. Your mother hurt you, your father didn't love you, we all know that. Now will you take personal responsibility for what *you* did?

The sense of personhood that comes from truthfulness is immense. It's the sacred no, the ability to say no to the false self. That gives one a sense of having boundaries, of knowing what is part of oneself and what isn't. Until a person can do that there is

an endless, amorphous kind of personality without dignity or
self-respect. Good morality provides good boundaries and good
identity.

from *Breathing Under Water: Spirituality and the 12 Steps*

Saturday of the First Week of Lent   Day 121

A Radical Call

We must somehow be a Church growing in resistance. Faith and
resistance must be reconnected in our hearts and in our corporate
decisions. Otherwise we are always drawn into passing fads and
cultural biases. I must admit that I have serious doubts whether
a large pluralistic Church, a Church with the imperialistic past of
the Roman Catholic Church, can easily be a sign of resistance.

We have such a tradition of civil religion and cultural
Catholicism that it is hard to imagine we could ever represent the
alternative consciousness. Numbers tend to move a group toward
the lowest common denominator, a gospel of minimals, with easy
"entrance exams" and a necessary pluralism. Even though we
have made great strides as a resistance Church with the two
pastorals of our bishops on war and the economy, it is obvious
that our leaders are still anxious to be seen as intelligent and
respectable dialogue partners within the system. They are
unwilling to condemn deterrence in fact and action; they are
unable to see from within what even John Paul II could see from
without: that "each of the two blocks [capitalism and
Communism] harbors in its own way a tendency toward
imperialism...or toward forms of new-colonialism" (*On Social*

Concerns, Sollicitudo Rei Socialis, #22).

If this most powerful nation does not call forth a Church which is most powerful in the ways of the Spirit, we will have surely missed our moment to radically proclaim the gospel. Precisely because of our universality and our tired tradition of supporting kings and dictators, it is ironically the Roman Catholic Church which is most prepared to move beyond self-serving patriotic religion. Our own government is aware of this movement of Catholicism. In the "Santa Fe Document" in 1980 to prepare for the Reagan Administration it was recommended that "United States foreign policy must begin to oppose liberation theology," as it is growing within the Roman Catholic Church. Further on they encouraged the growth of fundamentalist and charismatic style religion which could be depended upon to blindly support U.S. national interests. So much for those who say that theology and politics are not intrinsically linked! The politicians, unfortunately, seem to know that linkage better than most Church people.

from "The Future of the American Church"

Second Sunday of Lent   Day 122

The Transcendence of God

Worship means lifting our hands to a God who seems totally beyond us. Modern humanity has lost the call to worship because it's a blow to our pride and sophistication to worship God who is utter otherness. So instead of adoring God, much worship becomes an attempt to control or influence God.

Is adoration pushing God away from us? No! It's allowing God to make the voluntary move toward us—but from beyond us. Sometimes we want to pull God down here. But God is already totally here, by God's own action. In worshiping what seems like a totally transcendent God, we discover the opposite is also true: God is within us. Such faith comes hard to modern humankind: We don't know how to adore.

from *The Great Themes of Scripture*

Monday of the Second Week of Lent   Day 123

Spirituality of Subtraction

The notion of a spirituality of subtraction comes from Meister Eckhart, the medieval Dominican mystic. He said the spiritual life has much more to do with subtraction than it does with addition. Yet I think Christians today are involved in great part in a spirituality of *addition*.

The capitalist worldview is the only world most of us have ever known. We see reality, experiences, events, other people, things—in fact, everything—as objects for consumption. The nature of the capitalist mind is that things (and often people!) are there for me. Finally, even God becomes an object for our consumption.

Remember the bumper sticker "I found it"? The Holy One becomes "it," a pronoun, a thing. Even the Lord becomes a consumer object that I can privately possess. Now that is surely heresy in any religion.

You almost wonder if true spirituality is even possible in this culture. Everything gets turned around so that we're in the driver's seat: God, the Bible, the sacraments, the Church, people and prayer. Everything is there to foster my own ego and its need to feel good about itself.

from *Letting Go: A Spirituality of Subtraction*

Tuesday of the Second Week of Lent   Day 124

Discernment

It may be the last thing to occur to you, but even the desire to be a saint, to be the holiest or most generous person in your parish, the most observant priest—whatever—all of that is ego. It's not the love of God, it's the love of self.

Ego takes endless disguises, but basically it is the need to *control* reality and think well of oneself. Ego is dominating so many of the institutions of the Church (which should know better!). Ego has remained largely unquestioned and uncountered because we put all our emphasis on controlling the shadow or dark side of the personality. Jesus is clearly saying the shadow is *not* the problem, but power and pride are.

The ego, therefore, remains largely out of control. (If we do question ego, it is usually the rebellious egos of those at the bottom. And we at the top go on controlling.)

from *Letting Go: A Spirituality of Subtraction*

Back to Basics

(Written while touring Africa) These African mornings are almost perfect: clear blue sky with enough billowy clouds for contrast, fresh clean breeze carrying with it the sounds of different birds I have never heard before, temperature about the same as my body surface so I feel neither cold nor hot, and the glorious sun reigning primitive and early over these black-skinned nobles who are both civilized and Stone Age. Not only did humankind likely begin here in East Africa, but somehow it is still beginning here—maybe it will always be beginning here. God needed to keep one part of this world "back to basics," it seems. And here it is: spirituality, family, sex, food, celebration without occasion, life and death unashamedly.

These black-skinned folks, on whom most races project their deepest shadow, live their own shadow rather gracefully—much better, I should think, than the camouflaged and denied (but nevertheless operative) shadows of much of the "civilized" East and West. There is something honest here. Maybe their various degrees of nakedness even symbolize it.

from *St. Anthony Messenger*, "African Journal"

Freedom From Self

Conversion, the movement toward the Lord, is a process of disenchantment with the ego, recognizing how truly afraid and poor it is. The only way people can ever be freed from their fears is to be freed from themselves. There is almost a complete correlation between the amount of fear in our lives and the amount of attachment we have to ourselves. The person who is beyond fear has given up the need to control or possess. That one says, I am who I am in God's eyes—nothing more, nothing less. I don't need to impress you because I am who I am, and not who you think I am—or who *I* think I am.

That's what the Pauline theology of Baptism is saying: You have died, you're dead (Romans 6:3-5). In Christ you don't need the false self. You have faced the enemy once and for all and, guess what? It's you!

from Letting Go: A Spirituality of Subtraction

Do We Love Christ?

A man shocked me one day when he said, "You Christians don't love Christ. You hate Christ. You hate what Christ stands for." He continued, "You cover up your own hatred and fear of Christ by talking about how much you love Jesus. But if you love Jesus, why don't you love your enemies? If you love Jesus, why don't you really obey the gospel, most of which you ignore?"

I heard those words and I trembled inside, thinking, *My God, is that true of me?* Brothers and sisters, just open Mark's Gospel. Most of us haven't paid attention to nine-tenths of it. Most of the passages are just conveniently ignored by the institutional Church and by ourselves. In fact, I find we very often do the *exact opposite* of what Jesus teaches about, as if a bigger lie is easier to cover up. Christians and their bishops have been condoning and participating in war, greed and false security for centuries, while calling themselves the Body of Christ—or even the magisterium! Matthew 23 would seemingly make us unwilling to wear a long robe or tassels ever again! Strange, isn't it?

When was the last time you heard that someone was thrown out of the Church for not rejoicing and exalting when they were criticized? Did anybody ever think of it? Well, Jesus taught that (Matthew 5:11-13). How come we don't make that a matter for excommunication? The thought never entered our minds.

from *Letting Go: A Spirituality of Subtraction*

Saturday of the Second Week of Lent   Day 128

From Merton's Hermitage

I was offered the use of Thomas Merton's hermitage at Gethsemani for thirty days at the beginning of my contemplative sabbatical year. I wasn't sure then that I could live thirty days alone out in the woods of Kentucky. I'm an extrovert, always thinking with my mouth. Yet I really wanted to begin the year with thirty days of solitude. I'd always been a Merton fan, and I knew he could be my brother-guide.

To make a long and wonderful story very short, it was sweet and got sweeter and sweeter. Have you ever even spent twenty-four hours of your life in solitude and silence without another person defining you, needing you, talking to you?

What happens is like losing shells or encasements. As the days go by, these masks fall away: No one needs me now. I'm not important to anybody. I could die here and no one would know for at least two more weeks. I'm not a public speaker, I'm not a priest, I'm not a Franciscan, I'm not this, I don't have that kind of education or those kind of friends or that kind of family, or I'm not the pastor of New Jerusalem. I got more and more naked. I had to keep going back to the Lord for my identity: Who am I now, Lord?

In solitude, at last we're able to let the Lord define us the way we are always supposed to be defined: by relationship, the I-thou relationship, in relation to a Presence that demands nothing of us but presence. If we've never lived in the realm of pure presence without our world of achieving, we don't know how to breathe there at first. And that's precisely why the Lord has to breathe through us. The Lord has to be our life, the Lord has to be our identity. At last, we allow ourselves to be defined by relationship instead of by the good—even the holy—things we've done.

from *Letting Go: A Spirituality of Subtraction*

Jesus' Commandment Is, Love

We must learn to move beyond ourselves, to say no to instant gratification, to set limits on our own needs and somehow to meet somebody else's needs. That's why Jesus *commanded* us to love. He didn't suggest it. He didn't say when you get healed, love; when you grow up, love; when you get it together and have dealt with all your mother/father/husband/children wounds, then start loving. No, the commandment for all of us is, Love.

Until we love, we really do not even know who we are. In fact, we can buy into all the self-discovery the world has to offer and *still* not know ourselves.

That's countercultural. We are supposed to keep telling people they're good and beautiful; they're great and fantastic, Jesus loves them—and eventually they'll believe it. But I haven't seen that work. I think we know the love of God is within us when we ourselves can "do love" much more than when people tell us we are lovable. We can always disbelieve the second, but the first is an unexplainable power.

from *Letting Go: A Spirituality of Subtraction*

Praying in Your Rhythm

People have different temperaments, rhythms and seasons. There isn't just one way to be in prayer, communion or relationship. There isn't just one way to be in dialogue.

Laity and clergy used to think we had to adjust to a monastic prayer style. We still have not recognized the rhythm of American society, or the rhythm we live as parents, workers and families.

My rhythm has changed at different periods in my life. I often feel that I prayed much better when I was in the seminary than I pray now. The rhythm of my life now is so unpredictable and so dependent upon others' needs and expectations. There have been periods in the last few years where I discovered I was much more in a weekly rhythm than a daily rhythm. I would take Friday afternoons, listening and waiting upon the Lord. Now I take Wednesdays, where I really spend a longer period sinking into that presence and resting in that presence. There have been times where we were encouraged to take a monthly day of recollection. And there are days when I can't survive without a twenty-minute rosary or a contemplative sit in the middle of a busy day.

Respect your own temperament. Respect the rhythm of your life and know that it will change at different periods of your life.

from *The Price of Peoplehood*

Longing for Union

We long to expose ourselves, even though it's the most threatening thing in the world. We long for the self-disclosure of another person. That's the power of sexual interaction, the intimate exchange between people.

We Western men have been trained not to share ourselves, because we've been trained, especially as priests, never to look weak but always to be in control. We find it hard to be weak before God, to speak simply to God from our hearts. We find it easier to talk *about* God than to talk *to* God. Most spontaneous prayer I hear is in the form of an announcement to the groups instead of a personal address in the second person.

Many of us think prayer is meditating on good, holy, churchy thoughts, or preparing sermons, all up in the head. Why don't we, as sons and daughters, talk directly to our Father as if we know and believe he's there? To talk to God takes a childlike attitude. If we need always to be in control, we can't talk like a child to our Mother.

from *The Price of Peoplehood*

The Self-revelation of God

The dialogue between God and humanity is the give-and-take of self-revelation and response. That's what's happening in every relationship. If you don't understand self-disclosure or the rules of relationship, you can't understand the rules of prayer.

In prayer God is gradually disclosing himself, revealing herself. So revelation and faith are correlative: There cannot be faith without revelation. We cannot believe in a person who has not shared himself or herself with us. To the degree that person has shared with us, we can believe in that person.

It's the same way with God. When we waste time with the Lord and listen, we're allowing God to reveal not information but self. This is what's symbolized on the cross: God is totally disclosed, God is the totally given God. But it takes us a lot of scraping and converting to open ourselves up to that disclosure. If we are filled with ourselves, there is, quite simply, no room for the other, and surely not *The Other*.

from *The Price of Peoplehood*

Real Prayer

The most simple rule for good prayer is honesty and humility. One can never go wrong with those two. Talk honestly to God. Don't give God the self you think you're supposed to be. Give God yourself in your nakedness, who you really are, even if that means giving God your anger or distractions.

We used to try to avoid distractions. But it's much better to use our distractions. If you're obsessed with a thought all afternoon, that's what you give to God. Lord, why am I so caught up in this fantasy? Why am I so caught up in this preoccupation? Why am I so worried about this bill or this mortgage or whatever it might be? Make that the subject of your prayer instead of trying to avoid it and getting into some spiritual or theological world. That's the meaning of integrated, incarnational prayer.

St. Paul speaks of unceasing prayer. He's not talking about us spending time thinking spiritual thoughts or even spending time thinking about God. Prayer is seeing what is in front of us in all its fullness. This is a truly secular, biblical, Hebrew form of prayer. It's responding to life in a holistic way in the ways it comes to us.

Instead of our life being a self-centered monologue, our life becomes a God-centered dialogue. Are your control needs, your fears, your guilt, your worries, your success needs in charge? Is Jesus your natural reference point, so that he reigns over your life? Then you've accepted the lordship of Jesus. It's not a matter of having words, but of having a Center beyond yourself.

from *The Price of Peoplehood*

God Is Seducing Us

We've been afraid to say it, but there is a genuine sexual element in God's love for man and woman, and our love for God. The sexual element in God is passion for the other. That's why God put passion within us, so we could understand some of what God is about.

The truth beyond logic is that God is both seducer and continually on the make. God is after our body, our spirit. That's what the Scriptures are trying to say in many places. That's how much God wants us. And unless we've been wanted, unless we've been sought after, unless we've been desired, unless someone has called us beloved, we probably don't know how much God wants us.

We don't begin to know how much God wants us. Will we ever trust that desirous and desiring place within our own hearts, where God is a passionate God? In many ways the Western Church has been negative about our bodies, feelings, emotions. We've been afraid to discover, to trust that passionate part of God.

God is continually finding ways to draw close and to get inside, to become one in intimate ways that always threaten us and in the very same moment delight us. We know that's what we were made for. Until we experience and trust that, we are not made. Or even more sadly, we could say we've been made in vain. God is on the make.

from *The Passion of God and the Passion Within*

Love Your Enemies

Fear is the major barrier to the emergence of great faith and great-souled people. To enter into the mystery of forgiveness, we must first recognize our fears. Most of what we hold in unforgiveness we fear.

I was given the impression, when I grew up in the Church, that the problem was doubt. And so all our teaching was head education. Teach people up here how to get the right answers about God and then they will have great faith. Show me where head information alone has created great-souled people, prophets of great desire, freedom and courage for the Church!

God speaks to us, heals us and frees us at another level, at the level of our fears. Until you allow God to address your fears, you'll never recognize them yourself and you'll undoubtedly be trapped in them.

As we grow in faith, we move beyond the need to exclude (He, she, they are the enemy). We gradually move into that place where we can risk letting the would-be enemy in. And then begins the way of wisdom. We find ourselves capable, at last, of obeying what is the greatest of Jesus' commandments, the most radical of all of his teaching: Love your enemies.

How many of us love other people who kick us around, who make it hard for us? We haven't internalized the commandments of Jesus. Scriptural language, though, is both introverted and extroverted. If we haven't been able to love our enemies out there, if we still think the Russians or Iraqis are the problem, it's probably because we haven't first loved the enemy within. And if we haven't forgiven the enemy within, we will never know how to love and forgive the "enemies" without.

from *The Passion of God and the Passion Within*

I Will Be With You

Moses said to God, "Who am I to go to Pharaoh and bring the people of Israel out of Egypt?" (Exodus 3:11). The Lord answers, "I shall be with you." That's all. Simply, I'll be with you! He wouldn't tell Moses how to do it. He doesn't give him a timetable, any directions, simply—"I'll be with you" (3:12).

Moses's power is the presence of the Lord. That's all! In every religious experience in the Bible, a person comes to an experience of God and God says, simply, I shall be with you. I will do it. Trust me. The directions come as you walk the journey. The word is not fully given until the first steps are taken.

This is perfectly borne out as the Hebrews journey through the desert. Moses said to Yahweh's face, in his fourth attempt to get out of the job, "I am slow of speech. Why should Pharaoh listen to me?" (Exodus 4:10). Yahweh again comes back to him and says, I've given you the command. Go ahead. I will be with you. *Do it!* (4:12).

from *The Great Themes of Scripture*

Keep a Blank Sheet Ready

In Christianity, seeking emptiness is for the sake of an in-filling, for the sake of a readiness or an openness. It is creating the empty womb of Mary so that Christ can be conceived within it.

Seeking some sort of transcendental empty consciousness state, I agree, is not the goal of Christian prayer. But our goal is detaching from the private ego, the private self, so that Christ can do what he wants with us. Whatever word God wants to speak to me, I'm out of the way. Emptying, for us, is for the sake of fullness. But that fullness is something we don't even know we are waiting for; we don't know how to define it or to say when we've got it. And when we've got it, we can't hold onto it, or it will become an idol.

I do most of my writing right in front of my typewriter. I just sit there. And sometimes I sit for I don't know how long so that when the words come I'm ready to type. When it comes, I've got the paper in front of me. I try to keep that blank sheet as much as possible in my life, and it's a blank sheet you've got to seek again every day. Get your own agenda, hurts, neediness and fears out of the way, so that you've offered God a blank sheet to write on when it's time to write some words on your soul.

from *Catholic Agitator*, "Finding a Place for Prayer"

Our Daily Bread

When Moses prays to God, "Yahweh, feed these people," Yahweh replies, "I will feed them. I will let manna drop from heaven but they are to pick up only enough to feed themselves for one day" (Exodus 16:4).

The whole message of the desert is a message of continual dependence on God, minute-by-minute learning to trust in Providence. Some of them want to store up the manna in order to have some for tomorrow. They want to plan for the future, and allay their fears. Moses says, "No! Only enough for today. Yahweh will give you your daily bread. But some kept an excess for the following day, and it bred maggots and smelt foul" (Exodus 16:20). Instead we say, "Give us this day our *daily* bread." How strange these words sound to a people with savings accounts, insurance policies and three-year warranties, even on their toasters!

from The Great Themes of Scripture

The Security to Be Insecure

Imagine walking in a darkened room. We put our hands in front of us, afraid we are going to bump into a piece of furniture or slip on a rug. We walk very slowly. This is very much what God calls us to on the journey of faith.

It's not easy, because we want to have our pathway illuminated in front of us. We want to know where, how, why we're going. Faith, though, is the security to be insecure. Our trust is in God and not in our own cleverness. It's not in our ingenuity, our planning, our personality, status, money.

The desert is the place where all of the false names for God are taken away from us. The storehouses are always empty. It is the time for learning total dependence on God, minute by minute. What happens in the desert? We will constantly experience a new name for God, like the Hebrews did. God always has a new face.

from *The Great Themes of Scripture*

Thursday of the Fourth Week of Lent   Day 140

Stripped in the Desert

The Hebrew people entered the desert feeling themselves a united people, a strong people, and you'd think that perhaps they would have experienced greater strength as they walked through. But no! They experienced fragmentation and weariness; they experienced divisions among their people. They were not the people they thought they were.

When all of our idols are taken away, all our securities and defense mechanisms, we find out who we really are. We're so little, so poor, so empty—sometimes, even so ugly. But God takes away our shame, and we are able to present ourselves to God poor and humble. Then we find out who we are and who God is for us.

The desert is where Israel experienced its sinfulness, that it was weak and unable to do any good. Our temptation is always to shorten the time, make our timetable God's timetable. We want to get out and get it over with. But we cannot rush the journey of faith. We have to attune ourselves to its times and seasons. You can't bake a cake quicker by turning up the heat to 450 degrees, nor can you slow it down by lowering it to 200. It will flop either way.

from The Great Themes of Scripture

Love Challenges the Beloved

Humans do not want a God of love, because a lover always makes demands. That is the very nature of love and humanity doesn't want it. We seek to hide from it and destroy it. So people sought to destroy Jesus, brother to creation. Jesus did not have to be a great prophet to see the handwriting on the wall, to see that his word was not being received. The people did not want relationship; they wanted religion.

Should that seem so unreal to us? It is the same for us today. It is the same for the Church for the last two thousand years. Humans do not want love relationships; we want religion and all its trappings because that is much more comfortable. A love relationship continues to challenge and make demands. It also offers a joy that we cannot tolerate: too near, too lavish, too spacious. What might we do with such freedom? It's easier just to go to church.

from The Great Themes of Scripture

Jesus Saves

Once, when Peter and John were going up to the Temple for the
prayers at the ninth hour, it happened that there was a man
being carried past. He was a cripple from birth; and they used
to put him down every day near the Temple entrance called the
Beautiful Gate so that he could beg from the people going in.
When this man saw Peter and John on their way into the
Temple he begged from them. Both Peter and John looked
straight at him and said, "Look at us." He turned to them
expectantly, hoping to get something from them, but Peter
said, "I have neither silver nor gold, but I will give you what
I have: in the name of Jesus Christ the Nazarene, walk!"
(Acts 3:1-6, JB)

The lame of the world still come to the Body of Christ and
look at us expectantly, as they looked at Peter and John, hoping
to get something from us. What does the Church say to them in
many and varied forms? "Silver and gold we have plenty of.
Come, join our parish. We have a credit union, very democratic.
We have a pastoral council. We have a guitar Mass. We're very
avant-garde, hanging banners in our church. We're up to date
and will meet your every need. We have a St. Vincent de Paul
society."

But no one has the courage to say: "May I talk to you about
Jesus? Let me pray with you. The Lord will teach you the meaning
of forgiveness. The Lord will teach you the meaning of Church, of
the Scriptures. Come, follow Jesus!"

Are we ashamed of Jesus? Do we share him? It feels naive,
old-fashioned, pious, and a bit Protestant, to talk about Jesus. We
have Church. We have sacraments, we have priests and bishops!

Yet Jesus alone saves. The apostles speak with boldness and
with fire. Jesus did it! In the name of Jesus all power is given to
me! Every time they return they proclaim the name of Jesus

Christ. What has happened to the Church that so many are no longer proud of Jesus?

from *The Great Themes of Scripture*

Fifth Sunday of Lent   Day 143

The Attitude of Faith

Unless we can presume that the Lord is speaking right now, how can we believe that he ever spoke? This is the premise on which we're proceeding: that the Lord is acting and speaking in our lives right now.

To have an attitude of faith is to hear the Lord speaking everywhere and all the time, in the concrete and ordinary circumstances of our lives. Then religion and life have become *one*, and we are never far from God. That's why people of faith never grow old and never grow tired. They don't need signs and wonders, apparitions and visions. God has quietly broken through and stands perfectly revealed in the *now* of things.

from *The Great Themes of Scripture*

Fought-for Faith

God gives us meaning, not answers. The suffering of life is the
suffering of every marriage union, every love relationship, like the
suffering of Job in his relationship with God.

The Book of Job is a dialogue between institutional,
respectable and unpersonalized faith (Job's friends who come and
give him reasonable intellectual answers) and the charismatic,
gut-level, fought-for faith of Job. Job searches and struggles and
receives his answer only in the tempest. And the answer always
has the character of paradox: inconsistent, contradictory, but
utterly true.

So the answer will be the same for us. The answer will come,
out of the tempest, an answer that cannot always be verbalized to
your children and husband or wife. But it will be an answer that
you know. It is a conviction that is deep and all-pervasive. No one
can give it to you, no one can take it away: It is a gift from God.
You cannot prove it to anybody, but you no longer need to.
Believe me when I say it: The deepest levels of faith will still feel
like confusion—but you are no longer confused by your
confusion!

from *The Great Themes of Scripture*

Becoming Who We Really Are

God takes human life seriously. To come into this world we will discover ourselves as beloved son, daughter, brother, sister, mother and father. This is not just a time-consuming preliminary; it is the entire process. The end is summed up in the beginning.

Baptism, our initiation into the new family of God, is everything all at once, symbolized and celebrated. It takes the rest of our life to understand it, to suffer it and live it. The reality precedes the word and gives authority to the word. The reality must be lived first and only then spoken about. Christian life, then, is a matter of becoming who we already are.

from *Sojourners*, "My People, I Am Your Security"

Earning God's Love

The greatest act of faith is to believe God loves you, even in your nakedness, poverty and sinfulness. But human beings always think we have to earn God's love. We work for it and, by doing good things for God, think we are going to get God's blessing and love in return. This is Jesus-and-me religion. It ends up being a self-centered morality of self-perfection and discipline.

Christians have so commonly used the phrase, "I must save my soul," or, "Priests are here to save souls." That is not New

Testament. It is pure heresy to think you can save your soul. *Jesus* means "Yahweh saves." As long as *you're* busy saving your soul, you're preventing *God* from saving your soul.

from *The Great Themes of Scripture*

Thursday of the Fifth Week of Lent   Day 147

I Thought I Was Perfect

During my novitiate, we did all sorts of good things for God. We were achieving salvation, obeying all the laws. I was the perfect novice. (You can ask my novice master.) I bowed when we were supposed to bow. I was never late for Office. I was never late for meals. If I was late, I quickly fell to my knees as we were supposed to do.

One day while kneeling in the choir I realized I was not coming to know or love the Lord; I was coming to love myself. I was becoming quite satisfied with this perfect novice who could sneer at his classmates when they came in late. I knew I was going to be a good Franciscan and a good novice. I could get along quite well, being a good friar, without knowing the Lord. I could gain a feeling of togetherness, of wholeness, of maturity, of righteousness.

That day, that moment, more than any other, explains why I am here today: God revealed to me that I was loved exactly as I was. There was nothing to attain. That day I was set free. And chains flew from my body in every direction, from the top of my head to my toes. And I knew that I didn't have to apologize for my humanity, I didn't have to apologize for who I was, I didn't have to prove myself to my novice master or my classmates. I was a child of God. And I could go on my way rejoicing. I could go on my way lifting up my heart to the Lord knowing that I was going to fail. But somehow it didn't matter anymore. I was loved and that alone mattered. It was my baptism in the Spirit.

from *The Great Themes of Scripture*

The 'This-ness' of Things

I believe with all my heart that creation is already redemption. That's good Genesis theology, that's good Franciscan theology. Already in the act of creation, God has named you. Your "you-ness" is written in the core of your being. The Franciscan philosopher Duns Scotus called it the "this-ness" (*haecceity*, in Latin) of things. He said that God only created individuals, not genus and species. God created you as *you*, in your unique "this-ness."

Spiritual life is a matter of becoming who you *truly* are. It's not becoming Catherine of Siena, or some other saint, but who *you* are. It sounds easy enough, but being who you truly are is work, courage and faith.

In some ways religious people are the hardest people to work with—they're so addicted to judgments that they can't let reality be. Maybe that's why Jesus said not to judge. We've got a lot to learn from creation spirituality, Native American spirituality and Franciscan spirituality, in terms of letting creation, nature, earth—what *is*—speak to us. We religious people come on with our predetermined conclusions, Bible quotes and dogmas—all so that we don't have to *receive* reality, *receive* the moment as it is. For some reason it is easier to hold opinions than to just be *aware* and *awakened*.

from *The Enneagram: Naming Our Illusions* and *Enneagram II: Tool for Conversion*

Saturday of the Fifth Week of Lent   Day 149

Foundation of Life

We became convinced in nine years of community building at New Jerusalem that you can only build on life. All else is sand. You cannot build on fear, guilt, coercion or even idealism. You cannot build on gospel passages, Church commandments or papal mandates unless they are ultimately putting you in touch with life.

You cannot build on death. Unforgiveness, repressed hurts, denied feelings, unconscious anger will eventually show themselves as unfit foundations for community. They might appear to be energy in the short run, but they will in time show themselves to be negative energy, incapable of real life. "Wisdom has built herself a house" (Proverbs 9:1, *JB*). And wisdom knows that you can only build on the foundation of life.

This journey into ever deeper life is the essence of faith community.

from *Sojourners*, "All of Life Together Is a Stage"

Passion Sunday: 'I Love You'

The supreme irony of the whole crucifixion scene is this: He who was everything had everything taken away from him. He who was King of Kings and Lord of Lords was crowned with thorns. All of the humanity to which he was brother was taken away from him and he walked the journey alone. Jesus, the brother to creation, was nailed to the wood of the cross, his arms nailed open. He is the eternal sign of God to humans, yet his arms were nailed open because he said in his life three most dangerous words: "I love you."

When you say, "I love you," you give the other power over you. You give the other power to destroy you and the power to create you. Jesus spoke those words to his creation and we took him at his word.

What happened in the body of Jesus is what humans do eternally: We hate what we should love. But God says, in effect, in the words of *Superstar*, "Hate me! Hit me! Hurt me! Nail me to the tree!" I love you anyway! That is God's great act of reconciliation, not just toward individuals but toward all institutions and creation. What hope!

from *The Great Themes of Scripture*

The Lord's Prayer

Jesus is set free in the relationship which he has learned from the Spirit—that he is a son of a loving father. Notice the absolute God-centeredness of his prayer:

> "Our Father in heaven, hallowed be your name, your kingdom come, your will be done on earth as in heaven."

These are all said as *imperatives*, not requests! With the authority of daughters and sons, we are saying to God, Do it!

> "Give us today our daily bread."

Give us each day the manna you gave our fathers in the desert, just enough for the day so that we will trust you tomorrow.

> "Forgive us the wrong we have done as we forgive those who have wronged us." (Matthew 6:9-13)

Why would God give us anything we ourselves were not willing to work for? We don't want it very bad if we are not cooperating in the effort. We pray, "Do it, God!", but also, "We will do it, too!" God creates and invites us to co-create. What trust and infinite patience!

from *The Great Themes of Scripture*

The Time Is Here!

Salvation is now. We have a tendency to point ourselves backward or forward in time, but the Gospels say either we are letting Jesus save us now or we aren't letting him save us at all. It's called the always-available grace of the present moment.

But it's the first word Jesus preaches: "The time is now! The Kingdom is present and here. Turn around. Believe the Good News" (Mark 1:15). In these four phrases we have the summation of all of Jesus' teaching. It's nothing esoteric or pseudo-mystical, just the infinite nature of now. Just let go and let yourself fall into it. It's a net you cannot fall out of. You are seeking what you already have. You have been knocking on the door from the inside.

from The Great Themes of Scripture

Father and Son

Who is the Christ? First, most obviously he was a man. He was a man who walked the journey of faith, who grew, as Luke says, in wisdom and grace. It was he who returned to the desert to seek the will of his Father, to seek to hear what the Father was telling him, to seek to be true to himself and the word of the Father.

Why did Jesus call God *Father*? My own opinion as to why

he chose the masculine word (although he often uses feminine images) is that it is the harder and more necessary word to speak. Perhaps many more people have been wounded by the masculine.

In Luke's Gospel every time Jesus prays (five times explicitly), his words are always preceded by "*Abba*," "Daddy." This brings out the beautiful relationship in which Jesus grows with his Father, of being the loving, trusting son. Three times at the end of the Gospel, in Gethsemane, and two times on the cross he calls out "Daddy!" Jesus seeks at all cost to be true to his Father, true to this relationship.

Whenever he goes to the desert he returns to the city to preach the word with new power. What is this word? That the Father has absolute claim to our fidelity, our love and our life, that God's love is unconditional and forever.

from The Great Themes of Scripture

SACRED TRIDUUM

The Breaking of the Bread

There's no real story of the Last Supper in the Gospel of John as
we find it in the other Gospels. There is no passing of the bread
or passing of the cup. Instead we come upon the story of Jesus on
his knees washing the Apostles' feet. Perhaps John realized that
after seventy years the other Gospels had been read. He wanted to
give a theology of the Eucharist that revealed the meaning behind
the breaking of the bread.

Peter symbolizes all of us as he protests, "You will never
wash my feet!" (John 13:8). But Jesus answers, "If I do not wash
you, you can have nothing in common with me."

Sometimes we think we are being heroic in not letting God
love us. We want to do the loving thing ourselves. Yet only when
Peter capitulates and allows Jesus to minister to him does he
experience the meaning of Jesus. He has to let Jesus get down
before him as a servant. John is saying Jesus wants to do that for
all of us. Eucharist in John's Gospel is not ritual or liturgy but
suffering service.

from *The Great Themes of Scripture*

The Price of Truth

When one attempts to live the reign of God in this world, one comes to know the cross through misunderstanding, difficulty, privation, persecution. To take the cross means turning your face against the darkness and arrogance of Jerusalem when it tries to supplant the city of God.

The cross is our obedience to the price of truth and love—with no assurance that it is going to "work." As in the life of Jesus, the cross leads us to perfect faith. Love led to its logical conclusion demands that we trust in a goodness and a life beyond our own. The doctrine of the cross says that no life can last forever, but there is a price to the breaking down of the lie. It is love become alive and personally engaged. Finally, there is no other word for love—except sacrifice, the cross, "laying down one's life for one's friends" (John 15:13). The cross is *doing the truth.*

While the affluent and unpersecuted Churches of the North have abandoned the life of the cross and pursued happiness and survival in this world, the Christians of the South have been led to a different kind of joy and survival based on the cross of Jesus. Thus their lives have the power to shake, subvert, save and sanctify our Churches—precisely through and because of the cross! We are forced to recognize that we are "only strangers and nomads on earth" (Hebrews 11:13) when some like ourselves are free to scorn the rewards and comforts of this world in favor of a greater vision—the coming of the Kingdom of God.

Yes, the cross is our salvation. It makes us holy. It frees us and liberates us for God and the great picture. It "opens the gates of heaven" by closing off our loyalties to hell. It "buys" us the truth, which is always expensive in this world. Through the cross Jesus paid the price, not so we would not have to, but so that we would in fact know that there *is* a price for truth and love: everything.

from a Coalition for Public Sanctuary pamphlet,
"The Cross of Jesus and Human Suffering"

Holy Saturday   Day 156

Love It to Death

Jesus is our guarantee of God's promise. What happened in his body is the pattern of what must happen in all of the cosmos. We are making up in time, in our body, what happened in thirty-three years in the body of Jesus. We are optimistic because we look at him and see the final pattern.

To be a Christian means to be an optimist because we know what happened on the third day. We know that it worked, that Jesus' leap of faith was not in vain. His trust was not in vain, and the Father raised him up. He trusted enough to outstare the darkness, to outstare the void, to wait upon the resurrection of the third day, not to try to create his own but to wait upon the resurrection of God. The Scriptures and early Church seldom said Jesus "rose" from the dead. They always said, "God raised him up!"

Good Friday inevitably comes into every life. So does Holy Saturday. In those moments of absurdity and darkness we want to say it's unreal, but Easter Sunday will come. It is as certain as the dawn. No longer is it an act of faith to believe in immortality, no longer is it an act of faith that some theologian must prove to me, because I have seen the pattern worked out again and again. The

Paschal Mystery, the death that is embraced with love, does not lead to death but to life. Absurdity which is embraced and forgiven will not lead to meaninglessness but to freedom.

So what was Jesus' plan to overcome evil? Attack it? No! Love it to death. What is given to God is always returned transformed. That is the eternal third day that we forever await.

from *The Great Themes of Scripture*

Easter Vigil/Easter Sunday   Day 157

The Subversive, Risen Christ

Jesus is among us now in a new way as the Risen Christ, the Christ who is everywhere, beyond all limits of space and time. On Good Friday we saw the relationship of all humanity to God: We kill what we should love. We're afraid of the gift that would free us. On Easter Sunday we celebrate Jesus coming back into a world that rejected him.

If you have ever been rejected, you know how unlikely it is to come back into the midst of those who have said, We do not want you. Yet that's the eternal mystery we celebrate: God is always coming back into a world that for some unbelievable reason does not want God. It's almost impossible to believe that could be true. And yet Jesus, in his humility, finds ways to come back.

Jesus knows we didn't like the first time what he had to say. We weren't ready for that much freedom or that much truth. Humankind can't bear that much reality or that much love in one moment of history.

So God had to come back in a disguised form. God had to come back, as it were, secretly, as a subversive, hidden—the Risen Christ. Now he can be everywhere, but we can't capture him. We can't name him too precisely. He can always break through in new and unexpected ways. That's the Risen Christ the world is never ready for and never expects, and sadly, does not even want. That's the Christ who energizes his Church, the Christ forever beyond our control.

from *For Teens on the Risen Christ*

Easter Monday   Day 158

The Meaning of Resurrection

Jesus taught us something about resurrection not long before his own Resurrection, when he called his friend Lazarus back from death. In John's telling of the story, Jesus comes before the tomb, the tomb symbolizing the deadness, the coldness, the hard-heartedness in all of us. He stands as the powerful warrior, the victor, the conqueror before that deadness. Jesus tells them to take away the stone, then he asks of them a further sign of faith. Do you believe that I can do it? Can you be with me as I do it? Step out. Make a bit of a fool of yourself, move away the stone. "Untie him," Jesus told them, "and let him go free" (John 11:44).

Notice what John may well be saying to the community. Though Jesus brings us to life, he needs us, the Body of Christ. He needs the community to unbind Lazarus. We now share in the power of resurrection. The eternal Christ says to the eternal Church: Unbind the suffering world and let it go free! That is the meaning of Church. It is our call, our burden, our task in human history. The risen Christ invites us on his path of liberation.

from *The Great Themes of Scripture*

The Risen Jesus:
The Future Shock of God

Except for the raising of Jesus, "there is nothing new under the
sun." All is the eternal return, cyclic history; everything bears the
seeds of its own destruction. All the great moments of history are
as nothing before the moment of Christ's resurrection: All else is
hopeless, absurd and driving toward death. As St. Paul wrote,
"And if he is still dead, then all our preaching is useless and
your trust in God is empty, worthless, and without hope"
(1 Corinthians 15:14).

In the risen Jesus, God reveals the final state of reality. God
forbids us to accept it "as-it-is" in favor of "what-God's-love-can-
make-it": To believe means to cross and transcend boundaries.
Because of Jesus we realistically can have a passion for the
possible.

The risen Jesus reveals the true meaning of this world:
paradise regained. The Resurrection is heaven—here, now—
created by the risen Christ. He is not rising up to some preexistent
place, but he is defining in himself the longings of every human
heart—a real sharing of life between the human and the Divine
(see Revelation 21:1-7).

We should not speak of survival or immortality but
Resurrection, a new creation!

from unpublished sermon notes

The Risen Jesus: God's Hidden Plan

You cannot see Jesus until you have believed in him (see John 20:16, 28). If you accept that there was a Resurrection, that will not necessarily lead to faith. But if you receive the gift of faith, you will necessarily experience the Resurrection. "And that joy no one shall take from you" (John 16:22).

We cannot see love itself, but we can see what happens to those who have been loved. We can see the power and gentleness of those who let themselves be loved by Jesus. We know that there is endless life welling up within us. We know that when we dare to look at others with "unveiled" faces, they begin "reflecting like mirrors the brightness of the Lord and all grow brighter and brighter as we are turned into the image that we reflect; this is the work of the Lord who is Spirit.... And where the Spirit of the Lord is, there is freedom" (2 Corinthians 3:18, 17, JB).

from unpublished sermon notes

The Victory of Resurrection

The voluntary self-gift of Jesus was his free acceptance of all creation—even in its weakness and imperfection. He chose to become brother to humanity, and by giving himself to God totally, he invites all of his brothers and sisters with him in that same relationship. Jesus thus proclaims and celebrates the universal Motherhood and Fatherhood of God. The raising up of Jesus is God's confirmation of this relationship. Jesus becomes our Promise, our Guarantee, our Victory!

In the Resurrection Jesus passes from individual bodiliness to total presence. Matter has thus become spirit—which is boundless, limitless, shareable and communicable. " ' As the Father sent me, so am I sending you.' After saying this he breathed on them and said: 'Receive the Holy Spirit'" (John 20:21-22).

Thus the victory worked out in Jesus becomes power (the Spirit) whereby Jesus is universally available. Our opening to this love-power is faith. *He* died, and *we* arose!

We cannot free ourselves. We can only be set free by the love of another. Jesus is totally set free only by the love of *the* Other! Amazingly, this faith-surrender does not destroy the self or individuality, but it actually creates it and recreates it. For the highest form of self-possession is the capacity to give oneself.

from unpublished sermon notes

Easter Friday   Day 162

The Promise of Jesus

Jesus promised that when we celebrate the Eucharist, he will be present to us. That has been the unwavering faith of the Church catholic since the New Testament. The Eucharist has been at the center of our Church from the beginning, and rightly so. It has given us the power of community, the power to understand ourselves as one universal people, beyond nations and races. It's given us the power of healing and reconciliation. Every time we celebrate the Eucharist, the Church is redefined as people, as a big family, around our family table, the altar.

Jesus gives us himself at Eucharist to remind us: We are becoming what we eat. We are his body, we are his flesh for the life of the world. When we eat this meal we are united to Christians all over the world, who this very hour are celebrating this same Eucharist in many different languages and countries. Someone said, If we really understood Eucharist, how could there ever again be war? How could we go out in that world and kill people who have eaten this same bread and have drank from this same cup?

The Eucharist defines humanity as one flesh, one people, and if you hate this flesh, you hate the flesh of Christ himself. Eucharist is the gift that makes us a sacred and universal people.

from *The Symbolism and Meaning of the Mass*

Easter Saturday   Day 163

The Life on the Other Side of Death

Eternal life, the life that the Virgin Mother bears into the world, is the life that's on the other side of death. It's for those who can face the death, demons, darkness, and still live. One cannot take that journey without a mother.

Whatever we find in the eyes of Jesus must first have been in the eyes of Mary. The mother's vision of life is powerfully communicated to her children. Mary had to be the spiritual director, the one who gave the vision to Jesus, who taught Jesus how to believe. What was in his eyes was somehow first in hers. And in both of their eyes is what they both believe about God.

Mary holds us naked at each end of life: the Madonna bringing us into life; the grief-stricken mother of the Pieta handing us over to death. She expands our capacity to feel, to enter the compassion and the pain of being human. She holds joy deeply, where death cannot get at it. He learns by watching her.

The mother of the suffering servant is the one who teaches us to trust life, to trust the space in between, to say yes to it, and on the other end, to trust death. But the life she calls us to trust is not an easily created life. It's not just a life that happens in a moment. It's the life on the other side of death, and therefore indestructible.

The mother teaches us by the way she stands at the foot of the cross. Not a word is spoken; she simply trusts and gives space and silence. She is present. The Church without Mary is a Church of technique, product and function. It is a Church that is driven to win and to control. It is overly rational, ideological; it is obsessed with trying instead of trusting. Faith is not for overcoming obstacles; it is for *experiencing* them. The Church without Mary does not understand faith; it does not understand love. Therefore, it does not understand resurrection.

from *How Mary Faced Life*

Walking in the Spirit

When you no longer expect something more from life, you are for all practical purposes an atheist. When you are no longer open to do something new, to see and feel in new ways about old things, you might as well hang it up. There always is more of the Spirit for you to receive, or you would not be sustained another moment.

The experience of the Spirit is an undeserved, unmerited becoming, a new whole greater than the sum of all the parts. It draws us out and beyond ourselves in spite of ourselves. It is radical grace. To walk in the Spirit is to allow yourself to be grabbed by God and taken into a much larger world of meaning.

from *The Great Themes of Scripture*

A Week of Easter Prayers: Help Us to Love

Loving God, we love how you love. We love how you have freed us. We love what you have given. Help us to recognize, Holy One, and to rejoice in what is given, even in the midst of what is not given. Help us not to doubt, Lord, what you have given us, even when we feel our shortcomings. We praise you, and we thank you for the promise and sign of your love in Jesus. We thank you, and we praise you for sharing your. life, your Spirit with us.

We offer you our lives. We offer you our bodies, our hearts. Bless this people, heal us, make us signs of Jesus. Do in us what you did in him, Father. Make us your sons, name us your daughters. Renew our Church in love and in forgiveness. We ask, Lord, for all of this. We trust in your love as Jesus trusted. And we pray as Jesus prayed. Amen.

from *Days of Renewal*

A Week of Easter Prayers: Help Us to Love our Manhood and Womanhood

Mother/Father God, we thank you for life. We pray that our lives can be a real adventure, that you can open up some new parts of ourselves, that we can recognize and love some new parts of our own manhood and womanhood.

Guide us, teach us what it means to be father, brother, son; to be mother, daughter, sister. Teach us what it means to be man and woman. We are all still learning, Mother, but we trust that you are with us, we trust that it matters. We know, Father, that you have made us male and female, and that there is great power in those two energies. Help us to discover ours and to trust it.

from *A Man's Approach to God*

A Week of Easter Prayers: Make Us Truly Catholic

God, make us truly catholic people. Make us bearers of the Incarnation. Make us not afraid of life and not afraid of this earth. Make us strive for justice and believe in peace. Make us not afraid of the cross and neither afraid of the Resurrection. Make us, Creator, not afraid of enjoying this world, of celebrating and protecting this world.

Teach us, Jesus, how to do liturgy, how to do life. Teach us, God, how to continue to make things beautiful, because you have made us beautiful by your choice of flesh.

We thank you for this world. And we thank you for our Holy Catholic Church.

Eternal God, make the Catholic people truly catholic. Make us whole. Renew our Church, Lord, in our time. And make us a whole and holy people. Heal us, Lord, from our hurts from Holy Mother Church. Show us how to forgive our Mother. Reconcile us to our tradition, to our past, so we can move into our future, so we can walk with you, loving God.

We ask for all of these blessings. We invite you into our world. We invite you into our lives in Jesus' holy name. Amen.

from *The Price of Peoplehood*

A Week of Easter Prayers:
Help Us to Forgive Ourselves

Lamb of God, we ask that we might be defense-free people, that we might be able to live a truly disarmed life, that we might be able to be secure enough in your love, Jesus, to be insecure in this world, to let go, Lord.

Heal us from the lie. Heal us from the doubt. Heal us from the darkness. Heal us from the untruth that controls us. Take us close to you today and teach us the truth. Accept our flaw, Lord, that we cannot accept. Heal our wound. Forgive that fatal flaw, Lord, that we cannot forgive. Help us to forgive ourselves. None of us has become who we thought we wanted to be. We thought our life was going to be so different. Our judgment is not greater than yours. Free us to forgive what you so readily forgive. What you have let go of, help us not to hold on to.

from *The Price of Peoplehood*

A Week of Easter Prayers:
We Want to Be Family

Mother/Father God, teach us how to create family on earth. Teach us how to love one another as you have loved us, to lay down our lives so that the Church might be renewed. Lord, we want to love you and we want to love one another. We want to receive your life from one another. We want to enter into the great adventure that is before us. We want to be a part of what you are doing.

But Lord, there's so little we understand. We know that all we can do, God, is try to love and try to live in faith. We ask for that grace and that gift for all those who hear these words. And we put our lives, our families and our Church in your hands. We give history back to you. May you be praised, Lord, God of the Ages, tonight and forever. Amen.

from The Spiritual Family and the Natural Family

A Week of Easter Prayers:
Francis, Teach Us How to Be Poor

Creator God, give us ears, make us rich soil like the rich soil in the Gospel parable of the seeds. Fill us with life so that we can receive the words of life that you offer. We thank you for loving us and for leading us to this moment of life.

This day, allow us to hear anew. Allow us to receive afresh. Allow us to become all that you want us to become, for your sake, for the coming of the Kingdom.

St. Francis, teach us how to be poor. We don't know how—we're rich Americans. We've had everything. We don't know how to live without. We don't know how to trust God the way you did. We don't know how to let people call us names. We want to be loved and be popular.

Little Francis, teach us how to be little. Renew our Church. Renew the Franciscans. Renew our world in the love of Jesus. Give us hearts on fire for Jesus so we can look and see nothing else but only the Lord. We ask for all of these good things, together with Francis, and in Jesus' name.

from *Letting Go: A Spirituality of Subtraction* and
On Pilgrimage With Father Richard Rohr

Third Sunday of Easter   Day 171

Why Be Catholic?

Grace operates best in the realm of freedom. As free people, we listen to the Lord and say, "What are you asking of me, Lord?" and, "Where are you leading me?" That is the nature of a dialogue, of a relationship, in which we are listening and being called.

We shouldn't ask, "Why do I have to be Catholic?", but rather, "What's good about Catholicism? How can we make it good in our specific moment of time?"

Being a Catholic is not the same as being saved. Love saves us. Education gives us the right questions, if we get a good education, that is. Society makes us practical and effective. Christ, though, makes us free for love, for life and human history. The Church is a means, not an end.

The Church is not a necessity any more than Christ is. As the Franciscans once believed, even Christ is a gift, not a necessity. Yet for some reason gifts are considered less important than necessities! How strange!

Catholicism offers the gifts of wisdom, time and universal connection. That's all—but that's a lot.

from *Why Be Catholic?*

Monday of the Third Week of Easter   Day 172

The Catholic Worldview: Sacramental

Catholics have a sacramental worldview: For us, material reality mediates spiritual reality. All spiritual reality, all grace is mediated to us through this world, through history, through concrete objects, things, moments, events, persons.

It is deep within the Catholic consciousness that grace is always mediated. It always comes through our human, sensate experience. Even sinfulness itself became something that mediated God's grace. That's why so many Catholics, and even ex-Catholics, become artists, novelists, movie directors and poets. Both Carl Jung and Andrew Greeley say they can prove that Catholics *imagine* differently.

Ours is very different from the Protestant worldview. If

you've been raised Catholic, maybe you don't even realize how different that is because you've always taken it for granted. My great disappointment is that we might not be passing on the Catholic imagination to the younger generation.

from *Why Be Catholic?*

Tuesday of the Third Week of Easter   Day 173

The Catholic Worldview: Whole People

In Catholicism there is a kind of holism, a kind of mystical desire to connect all things and a realization that all things are already connected. It's no surprise, therefore, that Catholicism throughout its history moves toward mysticism. Mystics have a profound sense that all is united. They don't departmentalize life because they know deeply that God is the center, and all things are connected to the center. Their circle is very wide and broad, and there is room for everything inside of it.

Mystics are the best of the Catholic tradition. They're wide-open people, with room to integrate everything: faith, intelligence, politics, science and the humanities. I hope in your lifetime you have at least one great Catholic teacher. They fascinate you, pulling everything together and making it all subservient to the gospel and to Christ.

Look at Thomas Merton, Dorothy Day, Graham Greene, Teilhard de Chardin, Flannery O'Connor, Cardinal Newman, Thomas More. Our Church creates this kind of people. They emerge out of the holism of the Catholic tradition. If Catholic schools are no longer creating such people, we must ask why we

prefer propaganda, law and order, and job preparation to
education in wisdom.

from *Why Be Catholic?*

Wednesday of the Third Week of Easter   Day 174

The Catholic Worldview: Process

On the walls of our Catholic churches we have fourteen stations.
That's good process theology. It's movement, stages and phases:
First *this* has to happen, then you have to go through *that*; you
have to remain on the path in all its stages and relationships. The
path itself will be your teacher.

Elizabeth Kübler-Ross wasn't the first to discover the stages
of grief and dying. The way of the cross did, and it was inside of
every Catholic church. The Franciscans started it, in fact. We said,
there is going to be an experience of condemnation in your life, an
experience of judgment, an experience of betrayal. There's going
to be a time where you'll finally have to do his will, not your own.
When you try to do it, you're going to fall at least three times.
Probably a lot more than that. But God is going to give you people
like Simon of Cyrene, Veronica, Mary and the weeping daughters
of Jerusalem. God is going to give you friends who will support
you.

That's process theology. It's not the static theology some of
us unfortunately grew up with, the game of: mortal sin, I'm out;
go to confession, I'm in. Push-button theology is very different
from healthy, rich Catholicism.

from *Why Be Catholic?*

The Catholic Worldview: Community

Jesus used the image of the Kingdom; Paul, the image of the body of Christ; John, the vine and the branches. But it's all the same sense of mystical union: that, first, we are one; secondly, we became separate.

I don't suppose that most of us can think that way. I want to think that way, and I try to let the Lord convert me, but I'm still an American individualist. I wish I were not. Such an exaggerated sense of the private self breeds competition: Your good becomes a threat to my good.

Do you know what the Greeks called a private person? They called someone who had no sense of the common good an idiot. The original meaning of *idiot* is one who simply thinks of himself and has no sense of the city-state.

Paul said the Spirit is given "for the sake of the common good" (1 Corinthians 12:7). We cannot make any claim to being Catholics or even people of the Spirit if we do not have that profound commitment to the common good *first*.

from *Why Be Catholic?*

The Catholic Worldview: Tradition

It is said the Roman Church looks at history in terms of centuries. For example, we should be ready to deal with the problem of infant Baptism by about 2020, one cardinal was to have said. By that time people will have matured and understand that the ideal is adult Baptism. But right now they're not ready for that. That's thinking in the big picture. The Catholic Church, for good and for ill, thinks that way. We've been around for a long time. It does keep us from momentary cultural fads, but it makes it hard for us to live in the moment.

I hope you've met a sister who taught you at college, or a good priest or wise Catholic layperson who had that profound sense of time, history, tradition and the future. That's Tradition with the big *T*. That's great Catholicism. The unfortunate thing is that so many people who think they are traditionalists have only a sense of tradition with a little *t*. Most conservatives and restorationists are more committed to their childhood myths than to the Great Tradition. The Great Tradition forces all of us to move beyond our private comfort zone, both liberals and conservatives.

from *Why Be Catholic?*

The Catholic Worldview: Optimism

Catholicism has a rather optimistic view of human nature (contrary to popular opinion!). I was with some members of another tradition recently, folks who came from a Calvinist, or Reformed, tradition. One man said to me, "The human heart is endlessly depraved." There's a small amount of truth to that, but we Catholics would never start there.

The Catholic worldview starts with, "And it was good" (Genesis 1:10). We get to original sin afterward. It's original blessing first, then realism. Many of our Protestant brothers and sisters will start with the hard realism. The tendency, then, is to protect us against that dark, realistic side by law and salvation theories.

Catholics don't begin there. We legitimate Mardi Gras, the wine and the dancing, the singing: It's all OK, we say. God loves us. Enjoy life, but be willing to repent. Witness the Mediterranean cultures, as opposed to the Anglo-Saxon culture. The first are more formed by the Catholic ethos—for good and for ill. I'm not idealizing all of that, but Catholics really do have a different starting point.

To look at the dark side, Catholic regions often suffer a huge amount of social injustice, in the form of materialism, racism, sexism and militarism. The powerful enjoy and the poor suffer because we refuse to be *realistic* about the also "depraved" human heart.

Optimism is both our gift and our greatest sin.

from *Why Be Catholic?*

Despair and Hope

Rising and dying are closely related. Despair, I suspect, is another kind of dying and another kind of pain. It is not so much the loss of persons as the loss of ideals, visions and plans. For people who hitched their future or their hopes to certain stars, the loss of those stars is bitter and disabling.

It usually happens slowly as we recognize unfulfilled dreams and as we gradually face our own impotence and the "sin of the world" (John 1:29). We are forced to let go of images: images that we built in our youth, images that solidified and energized our own self-image. The crash of images is experienced as a death of the spirit, as a loss of hope, as a darkness almost too much to bear. Many, if not most, become tired and cynical while maintaining the old words that have become cliches even to themselves.

Spiritual growth is the willing surrender of images in favor of the True Images. It is a conversion that never stops, a surrender that never ceases. It is a surrender of self-serving and self-created images of self, of others, of God. Those who worship the images instead of living the reality simply stop growing spiritually. In this light, the First Commandment takes on a whole new power and poignancy:

> "You shall not make yourself a carved image or any likeness of anything in heaven or on earth or beneath the earth. You shall not bow down before them." (Exodus 20:4-5)

It seems that many people, religious people in particular, would sooner relate to images than to the reality where both despair and God lie hidden.

Until we walk with this despair, we will not know that our hope was hope in ourselves, in our successes, in our power to make a difference, in our image of what perfection and wholeness should be. Until we walk with this despair, we will never uncover the real hope on the other side of human achievement. Until we allow the crash and crush of our images, we will never discover the real life beyond what only seems like death.

from *Radical Grace*, "The Other Side of Sadness: Naming Despair"

Monday of the Fourth Week of Easter   Day 179

Against Deterrence

We Catholics have had no training or encouragement in the prophetic charism. It is a lost gift except in the area of private morality. We are accustomed to forming teachers, pastors, administrators and even apostles and healers, but the highly listed charism of prophecy (Ephesians 4:11) is still scary, foreign, thought to be unnecessary by Churches that have bought into the system.

Fortunately, we are again discovering the older and biblical notion of social and structural sin ("the sin of the world") that John the Baptist points out (John 1:29). Pope John Paul II speaks of it in his hard-hitting encyclical *Solicitudo Rei Socialis*. His critical analysis of both Western capitalism and totalitarian communism shows the type of courage and prophetic leadership that we need from our American bishops in confronting the myth of deterrence and nuclear superiority.

People and nation-states do have a right to safety and security. A certain degree of it is necessary for psychological, economic and human growth. But that is quite different from the overarching and overbearing need that now seems to dominate all other human concerns. What allows us to think that food, housing, education, welfare, ecology, medicine, aesthetics, the animal and plant world, wisdom, family and holiness are all supposed to be put on hold until American people can feel absolutely secure and victorious?

It is spiritually destructive for the individual, and it is equally destructive for the collective. Until Catholicism recovers its great medieval synthesis, until it again sees itself as preaching the gospel to the *nations* (Matthew 28:19), until it again acts as the corporate conscience and not just the comforter of private lives, we will surely continue to lose our moral credibility and moral leadership.

American bishops, our teachers and overseers, we ask you to pray, to reread the sermons of Jesus, to follow the prophetic leadership of the bishop of Rome in regard to social justice. As many have said, the social encyclicals are still the best-kept secret in the Church! We ask you to firmly and courageously condemn the American myth of nuclear deterrence before we have lost both our planet and our spiritual soul.

from Radical Grace, "Why Deterrence Is Death"

Jesus' Attack on the Temple

Pyramids are always pyramids of sacrifice. Whether it is the hundreds of thousands of slaves creating monuments to Egyptian kings, the sacrificial victims offering their hearts to Aztec gods, or the underpaid maids and janitors in the tourist hotels of the world, someone always has to give his life or her life so that someone else can be "special." When that elitism is idealized and protected, instead of avoided and made unnecessary as Jesus taught, we have the destructive and dark side of power.

Jesus struck at the nerve center of all of these when he empowered honest human relationships instead of degrees of religious worthiness. Jesus built circles of disciples instead of pyramids. What they could not forgive him for, even on the cross, was that he announced the necessary destruction of the holy temple. "Not a stone will stand on a stone. Everything will be destroyed" (Mark 13:2).

He knew that the temple, now divided into courts of worthiness, was not a place where God was first, as much as a place that kept the central storehouse economy in control and the widow with her mite outside. Thus he revealingly called it "the treasury" (Mark 12:41) and committed the unforgivable sin of overturning the tables of "those who were selling and buying there" (Matthew 21:12). In attacking the temple, Jesus attacked Judaism's final tower, and he democratized religion once and for all. But like Aaron, the first priest, we priests have been building golden calves and golden temples ever since. With priests and ministers, the assumption is that if it is good for religion, it is good for God. "False!" said Jesus.

from *Radical Grace*, "Is This 'Women-Stuff' Important?"

God's Building Block

God's basic building block for his self-communication is not the "saved" individual or the richly informed believer—or even personal careers in ministry. It is the journey and bonding process that God initiates in marriages, families, tribes, nations, peoples and Churches who are seeking to involve themselves in his love.

The body of Christ, the spiritual family, is God's strategy. It is both medium and message. It is both beginning and end: "May they all be one...so that the world may believe it was you who sent me...that they may be one as we are one, with me in them and you in me" (John 17:21-22, JB).

Until Christ is someone happening between people, the gospel remains largely an abstraction. Until he is passed on personally through faithfulness and forgiveness, through bonds of union, I doubt whether he is passed on at all.

from *Sojourners*, "Building Family: God's Strategy for the Reluctant Church"

Wisdom From St. Bonaventure

Self-conscious prayer is not necessarily the best or the only form of prayer. To be praying, you don't need to know you are praying! How else could the Apostle Paul tell us to pray without ceasing? Paul was not naive or unaware of practical demands. He was, quite simply, mature in his spirituality. He was a "contemplative charismatic": Life and religion were synthesized; he had the vision of the whole.

St. Bonaventure, building on the Franciscan experience of the Incarnation, saw the "traces" or "footprints" of God everywhere. The "journey of the mind to God" was to learn how to see the unity of all being, how to listen to the hidden God and how to read the footprints that were everywhere evident. The result was a life of gratitude and reverence and simple joy—a Franciscan spirituality. Thus Bonaventure, like most great saints, combined a highly contemplative personality with a very active and effective ministry in secular and practical affairs.

from *Catholic Charismatic*, "To Be and to Let Be: The Life of Reverence"

Friday of the Fourth Week of Easter   Day 183

Learning How to Pray

Prayer isn't bending God's arms in order to get things, or talking God into things. God is already totally given. Prayer is us learning how to receive, learning how to wait, listen, possess something. It's not that we pray and God answers; our praying is already God answering. Your desire to pray is God in your heart. Your reaching out to enter into dialogue with the Lord is already the answer of God. It is grace that makes us desire grace.

When you don't even have that desire to pray, to want to listen to God, then perhaps your openness to the Spirit has come to a halt. If you're not really wanting or choosing God anymore, what can you do? All you can do is ask for it again: "Lord, give me

the desire to pray. Give me the desire to be in union with you."
Pray for the desire to desire. Prayer is unmarketable. Prayer gives
you no immediate payoff. You get no immediate feedback or
sense of success. True prayer, in that sense, probably is the most
courageous and countercultural thing an American will ever do.

from *The Price of Peoplehood*

Patriarchy and Power

Christian men of power apparently have decided that happiness
is optional. What is mandatory and necessary is that the world be
divided into those who have power and those who don't. It makes
for good order, at least for those on top, and order is more
important than happiness. Our word for this addictive view of
reality is "patriarchy," which means the "rule of the fathers." It is
the basis of *all* major relational systems in the Western world.

    In the patriarchal view (1) all relationships are eventually
defined in terms of superiority and inferiority and (2) the
all-important need for order and control is assured by the exercise
of dominative power. Now that does not sound so bad if the status
quo happens to be working in your favor. But it has served to
dehumanize and therefore de-spiritualize generations of races,
nations, professions, women, sexual minorities, handicapped
people, the weak and the elderly whom the powerful are able to
culturally disparage and dismiss as "of no account."

    Not only are the rich and powerful able to project their own
darkness onto such groups, but the groups normally accept that

darkness as their true value. The utter evil of such patriarchy is that both the oppressor and the oppressed are incapable of real spiritual growth. The powerful, by rejecting their shadow, are hopelessly inflated. The powerless, by receiving others' shadows, are endlessly deflated. Both lose. That is why patriarchy is evil.

from *Radical Grace*, "Is This 'Women-Stuff' Important?"

Fifth Sunday of Easter   Day 185

The Church Tells Us Who We Are

It has been said over the years, with some degree of truth and some degree of heresy, "Outside the Church there is no salvation." I interpret it like this: Outside of those redeeming relationships that speak truth to us, that challenge us, that father us, that mother, brother and sister us, we do not know who we are. How many people are living in that kind of enslavement! They don't know who they are or what they want.

When individualists come with their problems, one has no power to help. You pray with them, assure them that God loves them, that God forgives them, then they go right back to sick relationships—and a sick world system to which most people are addicted. They're all tied up by put-downs that have gone on for so many years they've become natural and accepted.

Often the only way we can free these brothers and sisters from the lie about themselves is by inserting them in a new set of relationships that finally tell them the truth. That truth-telling of God's grace is what the Church is all about. It might be as simple as "two or three gathered" in the name of truth, it might be a vulnerable Twelve-Step group, but still it is the eternal mystery of Church and Christ at work.

from *The Spiritual Family and the Natural Family*

Monday of the Fifth Week of Easter   Day 186

The Prodigal Son's Father

The Father who Jesus knew looks amazingly like what most cultures would call mother. In Luke 15, the story of the prodigal son, Jesus makes his most complete presentation of the character of this Father, whom he called God. The father is in every way the total opposite of the male patriarch and even rejects his older son's appeal to a world of worthiness and merit. He not only allows the younger son to make choices against him, but even empowers him to do so by giving him money!

After the son's bad mistakes, the father still refuses his own right to restore order or impose a penance, even though the prodigal son offers to serve as a hired servant. Both his leaving and his returning are treated as necessary but painful acts of adult freedom. In every way he can, the father makes mutuality and vulnerability possible.

from *Radical Grace*, "Is This 'Women-Stuff' Important?"

Patriarchy and Masculinity

Patriarchy and masculinity are not the same thing. Patriarchy is wounded and un-whole masculinity. If we believe that we are created in the image of God—"Male and female, God created them"—then half of God is what it means to be masculine. Half of God is what it means to be feminine. Anybody who only gives you half of that truth is only giving you half of the mystery of God. The journey for all of us is to find the opposite, the contrasexual. For men, this is called the *anima*, or feminine soul.

Patriarchy is immature masculinity. It's males who don't know their souls, who don't know who they are. So they overdo it. Whenever you see people dominating others, you know they haven't found their soul.

from *Is There a Masculine Spirituality?*

The Gift of Life

On this earth nothing lives unless something else dies. It's true in the animal world, it's true in the chemistry world, it's true in the whole physical world. Jesus comes into this world and says, I, your God in your midst, will die so that you can live. Our vocation is to be like him, to die and be bread that is broken to feed the hungry world so that the world can live.

When we can acknowledge that no one owes us anything, that all of life is a gift, we move toward freedom. And in that freedom, the amazing thing is, we're able to enjoy our life, because we don't have to grasp it anymore. We don't have to prove or assert it anymore. We're finally allowed to sit back and to enjoy God's presence, and to enjoy our own, too. Now we can enjoy other people because we don't need them to meet our so-called needs.

We are called to live in that beautiful place of dying and living. It's *the* mystery of faith that we shout at the center of the Eucharistic Prayer. As I give him my dying, as I say, "Welcome, sister death," as I hand myself over, God gives back life in new form. Now I've lived long enough to see the pattern played out for myself. To me the pattern is evident. I can believe the dying and the rising of Jesus is the pattern that connects all things. I believe that it *is* the mystery of this world, in all of the cosmos, in all of the stars, in all of nature, in water, in plants, in animals and in my human flesh. Christ is dying, Christ is risen, this Christ will show himself in all ages and all things.

from *The Price of Peoplehood*

A Little Bit of Unity Is Worth Your Life

As long as we think that we alone have to save the world, we become arrogant in our methods, impatient in our attitudes and quick in our solutions. We instead must seek the patience and peace of God. The man and woman of God are content simply to lay down their lives for some little bit of unity. Wherever you are, let God create unity. I believe that's what God's doing on earth. I know one sister who sees her primary call as bestowing "benevolent smiles" on everybody she meets. What a threat she must be to disunity!

If Jesus is to be risen among us, we must each individually and in groups together surrender to a love and mystery that is greater than our hearts. We must humbly admit that we really don't know much at all. We have few right answers, it seems to me, and even fewer conclusions. All we can be is what Jesus was: *present* and *enfleshed*. In the end it seems to me there's only one gospel: Jesus incarnate, Jesus crucified, Jesus resurrected. Solidarity in suffering and in ecstasy is God's gift to the world.

To be in the Church is to be willing to be part of the rhythm and create little bits of unity wherever we can.

from *The Spiritual Family and the Natural Family*

Friday of the Fifth Week of Easter   Day 190

Solidarity Is Our Calling

The term *Third World* was coined at the United Nations back in the 1950's. I remember thinking, Well, that's about as low as you can go. Third World countries are those with low potential and low development. But there are Fourth World countries with some potential and no development. And there are Fifth World countries with no potential and no development, like Nepal. I was in Nepal, in fact, giving a retreat to the Jesuits. They said,

Welcome to a Fifth World country. And I said, What? There is such a thing?

It's hard for us even to comprehend that two people living on the same planet could live in such utterly different worlds. The gospel isn't asking us to be do-gooders or altruistic, the big white fathers and big white mothers. I think it's calling for something that's really much harder than altruism and generosity (although that certainly is asked for in cases). The gospel is calling us into solidarity.

The First World Churches will never be converted until they receive the Second, Third, Fourth and Fifth parts of Christ's Body.

from *Letting Go: A Spirituality of Subtraction*

Prayer Is a Place

Prayer is a psychological place, a spiritual place, a place where we go to get out of ourselves, a place created and inhabited by God. Whatever disciplines can help us to get to where reality can get at us (the Real in its ultimate sense being God) I would call prayer. That opens up many possibilities and styles.

Prayer is whatever calls us to detach from our own self, from our own compulsions and addictions, from our own ego, from our own "place." We are all too trapped in our own places by virtue of the egocentricity of the human person. In prayer the Spirit entices us outside of our narrow comfort zone. No wonder we avoid prayer: We have to change places.

from *Catholic Agitator*, "Finding a Place for Prayer"

Self-image

If there's one thing that human beings are attached to, it's their self-image, whether it's positive or negative. We need a self-image; there's nothing wrong with that. The spiritual problem is our *attachment* to it! It determines most of what we feel free to do, to say, whom we link with or don't link with. "I am a well-educated, middle class, intelligent woman." "I am a fun-loving, only partially responsible, casually dressed man." Those are the things that determine most people's lives. And most of us have to say, Am I free to be something other than that? Much of spiritual direction is aimed at helping people detach from false self-images. Amazingly, we are just as attached to negative and destructive self-images as we are to positive, flattering ones.

In order for the Great Lover to be able to get at us, we must let go of our secret attachment to our self-image. It limits what we pay attention to, what we ignore, what kind of God-lover we will accept or avoid. We probably have to have a self-image, but just don't take it too seriously.

from *The Enneagram: Naming Our Illusions*

Why the Enneagram?

"You must give up your old way of life; you must put aside your old self, which gets corrupted by following illusory desires. Your mind must be renewed by a spiritual revolution so that you can put on a new self that has been created in God's way, in the goodness and holiness of the truth." (Ephesians 4:22-24)

The earliest roots of the Enneagram, perhaps, are among the Sufis, who were the charismatic Muslims. They had a tradition of direction, and their goal was to help people meet the Holy One. In years of refining this, they came to see patterns of why certain people didn't meet God but just continually met themselves. Human nature hasn't changed much, and that's why we still need the Enneagram: We keep meeting ourselves instead of the Other.

That's especially true for our very egocentric culture. It's very easy for us to just rattle around inside our own heads and emotions. God for many Western people today becomes a projected image of the self: what we need, like or want God to be. There's not really meeting the Other, the not me, the non-self. The Enneagram helps us get our false self out of the way by naming nine capital sins.

The Sufi spiritual directors wanted to help people see the inner obstacles they had. They identified nine "styles of attention," nine compulsive ways of looking at life. In the same spirit, the medieval Christians talked of "getting beyond the passions" so they could read and receive reality as it is instead of what we need it to be.

from *The Enneagram: Naming Our Illusions*

Your Enemies Are Your Best Friends

In the spiritual life your enemies are your best friends. That's why Jesus makes his most daring commandment, that you must love your enemies. Until you allow the enemy at the gate to come in, allowing the "not-me" to enter your world, you'll never be able to face your sin, your dark side.

People who turn you off, people you're afraid of, have a message for you. We reject and hate our own faults in others. I'm not saying you have to go out and become best friends with them, but you should put up your antennae: They're triggering something within *you*. You need them.

from *The Enneagram: Naming Our Illusions*

God Uses Our Sin

It's so humiliating to know that God uses your sin for God's purposes. We are imperfect, we are full of compulsions, yet this is how we've been created by God! It's humiliating, but it's so freeing! Your sins and your gifts are two sides of the same coin. It seems you can't have one without the other.

For your gift to unfold, you must face its dark side, which is your addictive sin. To understand your sin, you just see that it is partly a gift, but on a destructive course. God is humble and able to use both of them for our liberation. It's *we* who have a problem living with both sides.

from *The Enneagram: Naming Our Illusions*

Ascension Thursday (Solemnity)   Day 196

Jesus Is Lord

"Then he took them out as far as the outskirts of Bethany, and lifting up his hands he blessed them. Now as he blessed them, he withdrew from them and was carried up to heaven. They worshipped him and then went back to Jerusalem full of joy; and they were continually in the Temple praising God." (Luke 24:50-53, JB)

Some of us have gone through twelve years of religious education and have never heard the lordship of Jesus Christ proclaimed. We don't even know what it means when we say, "Jesus is Lord." Yet the lordship of Jesus Christ was the first creed of the Church. It is mythically symbolized by Jesus "standing on the clouds of heaven." The Ascension might be called the feast of the lordship of Christ.

We don't experience God's power, God's lordship, unless we allow God to be first. I call it the radical first-ness of God. God is by definition not *your* God unless that God has primacy of place. No one else may be first in your life. Your husband, your wife, your children, your job have no right to be first. Fortunately, God is willing to wait!

Where does your heart usually go when it is free? Wherever it goes, that is your momentary God. How you use your time and

– 183 –

your money are probably the most honest revelations of your real gods. The God who is in fact God waits like a patient but jealous lover. God's lordship is not dominating but enticing and seductive, and ever so patient.

from *The Great Themes of Scripture*

St. Catherine's Tree

St. Catherine of Siena in her *Dialogues* pictures the spiritual life as a large tree. The trunk of the tree is *love*. There's no other goal on this earth for the Christian but to grow in love—spirituality is always about love. She says the core of the tree, that middle part that must be alive for the rest of the tree to be alive, is *patience*. No virtue happens until you are patient with yourself. The roots of the tree are *self-knowledge*. You will not grow in love without self-knowledge. The branches, reaching out into the air, are *discernment*, to know how to listen, to know how to weigh the voices, to know how to hear deeply what's happening.

In other words, says Catherine, love does not happen without self-knowledge, patience and discernment.

The discovery of the past decade has been that an awful lot of what we call love has merely been codependency. And if you have any doubt of whether we are a discerning people, just look at the public opinion polls surrounding the Persian Gulf War. One day before the war began, eighty percent of the American people were against it. One day after it, when apparently they think they're winning, eighty percent are for it. When the real issues arise, there is no spiritual discernment, little self-knowledge and almost no patience. Whatever the mass consciousness is, our people just kind of slip into it. And we lose another chance to love. We need St. Catherine's tree.

from *Enneagram II: Tool for Conversion*

Leaven and Salt

I hope that we will have the courage to stop rewarding and confirming people's egos and calling it morality, ministry and Church. I hope that we will have lower expectations of leadership and the institution and therefore less need to rebel against it or unnecessarily depend upon it. After all, as the poet Rilke put it, "There is no place on earth that isn't looking for you. You must change your life." The Church cannot make that happen. It can only announce its possibility and offer its Risen Life as leaven and salt. I always wonder why such a glorious power and privilege is not enough! It is more than I ever hoped for or will ever do! Many people are upset with the Church because they expected too much from it.

    More than anything else I hope that we will be a people who have entered into mercy and allow others to enter. I once saw God's mercy as patient, benevolent tolerance, a form of forgiveness. Now it has become an understanding, a loving allowing, a willing "breaking of the rules" by the One who made the rules, a wink and a smile, a firm and joyful taking of the hand—while we clutch at our sins and gaze at God in desire and disbelief.

from "A Church Unashamed to Be Leaven and Salt"

Fingerprints of God

If creation history were a calendar year, humans would first show up in the last three minutes of December 31. That means the entire Judeo-Christian tradition appears in the last millisecond of December 31. Do you think God waited until the last millisecond to start telling us who God is? How absurd! The Bible didn't start revelation! I think that's the Achilles heel of some narrow forms of Protestantism.

We listen to human experience, to history, to the natural creation! We look at all of it, and say, this is already, as St. Bonaventure said, the footprints and the fingerprints of God. That's also in Romans 1:20: "God has been there ever since creation for the mind to see in the things God has made."

Our task is to look at things as they are, and in all their seasons: in their agony, in their ecstasy. That will be your best teacher. Creation itself is the primary revelation of God and truth.

I'm ashamed of Catholics who are fighting the Enneagram (although it's mostly Catholics who are teaching the Enneagram, too). They don't know their own tradition! Our tradition has always known how to integrate. For example, Aquinas integrated Aristotle and was called a heretic. That's always been our tradition, though: Pull it in! If it can't be integrated, it isn't Christ for us. Because Christ is the whole one who includes all things. And if God is truth, then we have no truth to be afraid of: psychological truth, political truth, metaphysical truth, scientific truth, evolutionary truth—if it's truth, it's of God.

That's Catholicism at its best. But I find so few Catholics today. *Catholic* (*kata holos*, in Greek), means "according to the whole." I'm afraid, though, that we've had a lot more provincialism than Catholicism. We've had a lot more ethnicity than catholicity. And catholicity makes no sense unless it includes Judaism and the Islamic tradition which also comes forth from Abraham. The Enneagram, some say, comes out of Islam. There's room for everyone underneath the Cosmic Christ.

from *Enneagram II: Tool for Conversion*

Monday of the Seventh Week of Easter   Day 200

The Providence of God

God cooperates with those who love by turning everything to their own good. (Romans 8:28)

St. Paul says that God both initiates and cooperates in all human growth. God "works together with" us, which means both our workings are crucial. Every moment, God is trying to expand your freedom. Can you imagine that? God is trying to make this choice more alive, more vital, more clear, more true. God even uses your mistakes and your sin in that regard. Nothing at all is wasted. I believe that's profoundly true. If that's not the providence of God, what else would be "providential"?

The provident care of God is that God is working for our

wholeness, for our liberation, probably more than we are. We can only keep our desire awakened, and keep ourselves out of the way so we can work together. It's co-creation spirituality. "With such a God on our side, who can be against us?" (Romans 8:31).

from *Enneagram II: Tool for Conversion*

Tuesday of the Seventh Week of Easter   Day 201

Most Are Called to Marriage

Most people are rightly called to marriage. Most are called to stay with one relationship long-term, to go through the agony and the ecstasy of one other person. If we Christians believe that God is relationship, the Trinity, then the foundation of reality is also relational: giving and receiving.

To live in the Spirit is to live in the flow of relationship, with all that it offers you. It offers you the paschal mystery, the mystery of agony and ecstasy, light and darkness. A companion is a mirror who will show you your greatest and deepest beauty, and who will show you your greatest and deepest sin.

from *Enneagram II: Tool for Conversion*

Love Is the Foundation

The saints are so aware that love is not something to be worked for—to be worked up to or learned in workshops. It breaks through now and then, in ways suddenly obvious. Maybe it's looking at a sunset or a beloved one; maybe it's a moment of insight or a gut intuition of the foundational justice and truth of all things. But when you discover love, you want to thank somebody for it. Because you know you didn't create it. You know you didn't practice it, you are just participating in it. Love is that which underlies and grounds all things. As Dante said, love is the energy "that moves the sun, the moon and the other stars."

St. Vincent de Paul would thank the poor for letting him help them. It's as if he said, "Thank you for letting me see this. You are the window that lets me see the real."

I didn't love, you didn't love. Love just *is*, and suddenly we see it standing between us.

from *Enneagram II. Tool for Conversion*

Living Between First Base and Second Base

Carl Jung said, "If you get rid of the pain before you have answered its questions, you get rid of the self along with it." Our Christian way of talking about this is the cross. The pain is the way through. We must face our compulsions, our lie. Each of us has a false image of God, one of the nine false images of the Enneagram.

Faith, for me, is letting go of the images. Then you'll feel like nothing. Faith is so rare—and religion so common—because no one wants to live between first base and second base. Faith is the in-between space where you're not sure you'll make it to second base. You've let go of one thing and haven't yet latched onto another. Most of us choose the security of first base.

Yet faith happens in the in-betweens, the interruptions, the thresholds. It happens when I've left this room where I was in control, where I had my self-explanation, where I had my ego boundaries, where I had my moral sense of my own rightness and superiority.

We all fall into the trap of trying to justify ourselves. But justification by faith is the decision to stop pulling yourself up by your bootstraps, to stop any process of self-justification. Do you realize what a surrender that is? Only God can lead you on that path. Often that happens in times of personal loss or humiliation. We must listen to the questions that pain offers us. Then we can move through the pain to truth.

from *Enneagram II: Tool for Conversion*

Find the Great Love

When you can trust, as Gerald May says, that "there is a part of you that has always said yes to God," then you can trust your soul, even if you've gone down a lot of dead ends. Even those dead ends will be turned around. That's the providence of God. Trust that even your dead ends, your mistakes, your sins were still misguided attempts to find love. Don't hate yourself, just be honest with yourself! Even your sexual forays, your drug problems, your alcoholism—they were all misguided attempts to find the Great Love. Your heart of hearts says, I know the foundation of reality is love.

You already know that! It's written in your soul! You came forth from it! It's what you can't forget! Religion reminds us what we've all forgotten and what our soul already knows.

When we see God, it will not be a new discovery. It will be a profound recognition of that heart and soul of yourself that is already in union with God. All contemplation, all true prayer, is an attempt to go back to that place. My hope in giving the Enneagram is that it will be an aid on that journey toward the great compassion: toward yourself and toward all the other eight—and eight hundred—types of sisters and brothers the Enneagram describes.

from *Enneagram II: Tool for Conversion*

Spirit, Come

We have been waiting for what will come tomorrow. Nine days, fifty days, fifty years, five hundred years we have been waiting. It is the day we are always waiting for, but never prepared for, the day of the great outpouring, the day that ties all other days together. It is the day when we can speak and be understood at last, the day when we can babble incoherently and people do not laugh, when it is OK to love God without apology or fear, when we know that all of the parts are different and yet all of the parts are enjoying one another. It is Pentecost, the day of the great gathering in and the great sending out.

We have been waiting for this Spirit—somehow forgetting that the Spirit was given us a long time ago—in fact it was hovering over chaos in the first lines of the Bible. We are waiting for one who has already come. We are waiting for water that has already been poured fresh and sparkling into our cup. We are waiting for a cool breeze in a desert of our own making. We are waiting for a fire that has been burning incessantly within. We are waiting for the life that we already have.

We are waiting, we say, and yet we have padlocked the door—out of fear. We are afraid of this part of God that we cannot control or explain or merit, which is seductive and cannot be legislated, measured or mandated. Let's be honest. We do not like this part of God which is dove, water and invisible wind. We are threatened by this part of God "which blows where it will" and which our theologies cannot predict or inhibit. We, like the disciples in the Upper Room, sit behind locked doors of fear, and still say that we are waiting and preparing for his Holy Spirit.

Fortunately, God has grown used to our small and cowardly ways. God knows that we settle for easy certitudes instead of gospel freedom. And God is determined to break through. The

Spirit eventually overcomes the obstacles that we present and surrounds us with enough peace so that we can face the "wounds in his hands and his side." We meet the true Jesus, wounds and all, and we greet our true selves for perhaps the first time. The two are almost the same. "Peace be with you," he says again.

from unpublished sermon notes

Pentecost

After the Ascension in Luke's Gospel, the apostles experience the absence of Jesus' presence and power. They recede to the Upper Room where they had known his love before and perhaps he seemed close and real there.

Mary is in their midst. They pray. They're scared, and the doors are locked. They don't know at this point if they have been fooled. *Maybe we wanted it so much we created it,* they must have thought. *Maybe we did it ourselves. Are you sure that was really Jesus who you saw on the road, Peter? You can't believe those women; they get emotional. How do we know that they really experienced Jesus?*

Perhaps it was then that Mary communicated to them her own experience of Jesus. Again and again she had pondered in her heart what he was to be, what his life was to mean. No doubt they shared again and again during those forty days. Yet it was jumbled and confused. There is no talk yet of conviction or power.

But they are praying together and sharing as a community. They're gathered together in faith, waiting upon the Lord. They're listening to the Lord, suffering with the Lord, knowing that no person who has put trust in God has done so in vain.

And they are not disappointed. The power comes. By no effort of their own they are made into persons of faith, of conviction, into those who can say, "Jesus is Lord!" That is the dividing line, the day of Pentecost. Finally they are purified. They are free to believe in the power of the Lord. They receive the gift of the Spirit. God had not changed; they had, by the Spirit's gift.

The Spirit is always unmerited favor. She always does it first. God is experienced as intimacy and warmth and fire, as love-power. She is surprising, elusive and free.

So the Church has always been afraid of the charismatic, has always feared those who speak of the Spirit because they cannot be easily organized. The Spirit blows where the Spirit will, like the wind: It comes from and goes where you know not.

from *The Great Themes of Scripture*

Part II:

ORDINARY TIME

Ordinary Time After Pentecost

Monday of the First Week After Pentecost   Day 207

Breakthrough

As Catholic Christians in America, we've got to make connections with all cultures, with all our brothers and sisters who share the bread and the cup with us. We must ask, How are they brothers and sisters? Are we really Kingdom people? Or, after all is said and done, are we only American people?

In this century, I think, Catholics have the greatest chance to make this breakthrough. The Catholic Church is an international institution. Our brothers and sisters from other countries keep telling us there's a bigger world. I think we're going to get converted. The U.S. bishops' pastorals on peace and on economic justice give us hope. The pope's social encyclicals are truly global in scope.

Yes, our eyes are opening. We're discovering that we North Americans just might be the most unliberated, and therefore the most ready for liberation. We who have the greatest blindness think we don't need liberation. We think *Time* and *Newsweek* tell us the whole truth, and we are content with that worldview. We must fight that blindness with *vision*. The global access of American Catholics is fated to become global responsibility.

from *Letting Go: A Spirituality of Subtraction*

We Still Need the Saints

The saints are our heroes and heroines: It's worth being Catholic to hope that we might be like them. It's good to stand on the shoulders of these giants, these free, poor and in-love people.

Catholicism at its best wants to give you the freedom of a saint. It can lead you on a wisdom journey, a universal tradition that includes Abraham, Sarah, Moses, the prophets, Jesus, Mary and two thousand years of saints.

Saints, like all of us, are forgiven sinners. But saints have rejoiced in forgiveness and not been overwhelmed by the sin. Many of them, frankly, were ignorant, biased, broken and neurotic. That gives me hope.

I've been inspired, motivated and energized much more in my Catholicism by reading biographies and lives of saints than any book of theology. They were the heroes and heroines who formed my ideals as a young man. We still need to read the lives of the saints, and I think our young people do, too. Every culture I am aware of forms its next generation by heroic epics and myths.

from *Why Be Catholic?*

Don't Save Your Soul

We prostituted Christianity when we told our people they had to "save their souls." That attitude often affirmed the ego "spiritually," which is very dangerous and deceptive. We called it the journey into holiness, but it was often disguised and denied self-interest.

Saving one's soul and falling in love with God are two very different journeys. Because we told our people to save their souls, they got into spiritual consumerism, gathering sacraments, holy works, ascetical practices—all affirming the false self. Now we've got these big Christian egos walking around, who are very self-protective, satisfied and conservative in the wrong way. Conversion is not on their agenda. Every preacher or teacher knows what I'm talking about.

An unhealthy conservatism is incapable of exodus, of risk, of passion, and, therefore, perhaps incapable of the living God.

from *Letting Go: A Spirituality of Subtraction*

Silence Is Golden

As a people, we are afraid of silence. That's our major barrier to prayer. I believe silence and words are related. Words that don't come out of silence probably don't say much. They probably are more an unloading than a communicating. Yet words feed silence, and that's why we have the word of God—the read word, the proclaimed word, the written word. But that written and proclaimed word, doesn't bear a great deal of fruit—it doesn't really break open the heart of the Spirit—unless it's tasted and chewed, unless it's felt and suffered and enjoyed at a level beyond words.

Blaise Pascal said all human evil comes into the world because people can't sit still in a chair for thirty minutes! I hope that's an exaggeration. Maybe he's saying that running from silence is undoubtedly running from our souls, ourselves, and therefore, from God.

If I had to advise one thing for spiritual growth, it would be silence.

from *Letting Go: A Spirituality of Subtraction*

Friday of the First Week After Pentecost   Day 211

A Humbling Experience

Americans come at life expecting everything to work. It always has. I was born with seven silver spoons in my mouth. I had a strong family and was loved from the beginning. My parents paved a path for me. Do you realize what a head start that is? It's wonderful.

But there's a dark side: People from privileged backgrounds expect that path always to be paved; they expect everything to work out. When it doesn't, they're not only disappointed, they feel wronged. They think, How dare reality not work out for me!

Why should I have to suffer? How dare the air conditioner not work!

That explains the morose, quasi-depressed state of so many affluent countries and peoples. When you go to poor countries, these people who don't have anything and for whom everything is going wrong from morning to night (and if you've been there you'll know that I'm not making this up) tend to be much happier than we are! And our tendency is to look and say they shouldn't be happy, they have no reason to be happy. They don't seem to have an agenda.

I remember visiting the Home for the Destitute and Dying in Jamaica. People lay in rags, with the smell and the lack of food and the sores. I thought, How could anybody live this way? From my world, it was like hell. And yet I came as a priest to talk and pray with people. I'd stop and say, "Well, how are you?" They'd say, "Oh, fine." And I'd want to say, "Fine? You're not doing fine. You're doing terribly! How can you say you're doing fine?"

"Can I do anything for you?" I'd ask. One woman replied, "Oh, just recite a psalm with me, Father, just recite a psalm." And here the big Scripture man couldn't think of a psalm (being a Catholic). This humble lady picked out my obvious embarrassment. Here I am, the great priest, coming to help her, and I can't even remember a psalm by heart. She sees it on my face and starts singing Psalm 23. "Just join in with me, Father. You just come along."

There is a profound message here for our affluent culture. I knew I had met "the first in the Kingdom of God."

from *Letting Go: A Spirituality of Subtraction*

Recognize Your Starting Point

There is a liberation theology for the First World. What is it that we need to be liberated from? How do we need to be freed so we can receive Christ? Inner biases must be faced, I'm convinced. Unless those inner liberations happen, we're not going to be that rich soil that can receive the more demanding word of God.

The beginning point of liberation theology is the experience of human beings. This theology isn't pulled out of philosophy or metaphysics, beginning with first principles and then deducing down to us. It starts at the other end, with the longings of the human heart, and moves back toward God.

Experience is the only honest place to begin. Because even when we don't admit that we're beginning out of human experience, we do anyway. We begin out of our so-called first principles, but even those are planted in the experience of Italian people, German people, American people or African people, who all read it through their own eyes but don't admit it. And that's why the gospel has been so culturally trapped.

We assume we've all been true to our totally objective first principles of philosophy and theology. But in fact it's all filtered through the cultural eyes, prejudices and assumptions of each country. In Germany you experience Catholicism, but you also experience Germany. In Italy it's Catholicism, but it's first of all Italy. Across the Atlantic it's Catholicism, but it's first of all America. We've got to be honest enough to admit that. Deductive theology never worked anyway except in the textbooks, and for those few who lived there. Every viewpoint is a view from a point.

from *Letting Go: A Spirituality of Subtraction*

An Image of God

When I was working with the peace movement in Germany, a Lutheran friend took me to a thirteenth-century Cistercian monastery. As we came into this old church, there on the wall was a picture that really expressed some truth about God and the Church.

First, it's a picture of the Father in the traditional style: the old, bearded man. But in this case he's holding the orb of power, that golden ball that kings held at one time. But it's sort of slipping out of his hand. And there was my first clue that this painter and I were on the same wavelength. How can anybody think that God is in charge? Much is happening to tell me that isn't true. Or, as Jesus much more wisely said, the prince of this world is in charge. So often the lie is in charge, the world, the flesh and the devil are in charge. God hardly ever gets his way. God is a wounded lover; *we* are running the show. That's the great risk God took in deciding to play for love instead of power.

In his other hand the Father has a sword. I suppose the imagery is dangerous—the God who demands and expects and desires reality to be what it is. It's the sword of great expectation. Right across from the Father is Jesus, naked and bleeding. He's got his hand in the wound in his side, and he's looking across at the Father, eyeball to eyeball. It's a gaze of great intensity; it's a gaze of understanding, of mutual giving and receiving. There's great power in it. And the very sword that the Father is holding, Jesus is restraining.

The Father symbolizes that part of God that demands and desires his sons and daughters to become all they can be, that demanding expectant part of God. Parents surely see that in relationship to their children: why it is sometimes hard to be soft or nice to them. If I don't teach them this, you say, then they will screw up or not live a good life; I've got to help them in this way, I've got to teach them. We call this the angry God in the Old Testament. That's not the right word. It's the expectant part of love, the part of love that pushes a bit. It's tough love. It is a necessary part of love. I call it the masculine side of love and the masculine side of God.

Jesus for me represents that part of God that is wounded, that part of God that is losing, that part of God that is failing, that part of God that doesn't get his way, that part of God that is broken and that we celebrate in every Eucharist. That part of God who has involved himself in love and therefore is involved in the suffering of the world: the Lamb of God.

So between the Father and the Son is the perfectly horizontal line of this sword, and yet there is a love gaze between the Father and Son; they're looking at one another intensely. It's a great image: They perfectly accept one another from their different positions—the Son, the weak part of God, if you'll allow me that word, and the Father, the powerful part of God. Maybe the Father is the powerlessness of power and the Son is the power of powerlessness, which is precisely the image of Jesus. They complement one another.

The picture doesn't stop there, because on that sword held between them is the dove symbolizing the Holy Spirit. In that relationship, *when each part accepts the other*, there is a huge explosion and release of power we call the Holy Spirit, the relationship between strength and vulnerability. There is the power. There is the passion. There is the water, there is the breath, there is the air, there is the wind. The Church is born in that creative love and tension between the Father and the Son.

But that's still not the whole picture: There's a big space, and on the other side of that space is the woman. It's obviously Mary, but it's also the Church, the Church that is feminine before God. The Church that is always receiving and believing and becoming pregnant; like Mary, saying, Let it be, let it happen. I trust it. Mary is standing there in a big and beautiful robe, looking across at this mystery of the Trinity. She's got a great Mona Lisa smile on her face, deep satisfaction and joy: She loves what she sees and she understands it. She lets it be; she doesn't try to explain it. She can live with the mystery and paradox. She's holding up, with her left hand, one of her big robes. Behind her robe are a bunch of abbots, cardinals and bishops. And they're all in their tiaras, croziers and miters, sort of peering over the top of Mary's arm. They've all got a quizzical look. What's going on over there? It's like they're not sure they understand.

Mary is holding up her robe, and with the other hand she seems to be gesturing to them: Boys, I don't think you're ready for this yet. Just stay back there. I don't think you're ready for what's happening. You're probably going to go on another thousand years trying to explain, "This means this" and, "That means that" instead of quite simply diving into the abyss, where it doesn't make a lot of sense, where there aren't a lot of answers, where there's only mystery, journey and an impassioned God. God oft-times doesn't give a lot of answers but just keeps telling us who we are. God just keeps inviting us into that place where love is alive and where God is in love.

from A Man's Approach to God and The Passion of God and the Passion Within

Monday of the Second Week After Pentecost   Day 214

Sacred Cows and Hot Potatoes

God comes to forgive our sin, yet we seem much more concerned about our guilt, which is a bit different. Sin is not just something we do. First, sin is a state of being. It's an incompleteness that we're born into and eventually choose.

Sadly, I don't think most people want to be freed from their sin. We've grown comfortable with it, almost become friends with it. It pads our insecurities. We don't know how to live without it. We've lived so long with our fears, we don't know how we would be without them. We've made friends with our sinfulness.

For example, we may have based our marriage on unforgiveness for twenty years. How could we change it? Or maybe we love to be angry. Our anger is what drives us day after day, our anger at our father or mother, our anger at the system, our anger at our work. We live on our anger; we feed on our anger. Most of us don't want to be freed from our sin. We've lived with our darkness so long we are comfortable with it. Our lives are full of sacred cows and hot potatoes, areas where we indulge our sin. No one can touch them.

That's why it's so hard to deal with sin: We've grown to like sin. And the greatest threat of all is someone who will come into the midst of our evil and rob it from us.

from *Days of Renewal*

The Thought God Is Lost In

We are God's prayer. We are, in fact, God's thought. And God is hopelessly lost in thinking us. All we can do is stay naked and self-forgetful, ready for lovemaking. The primary temptation is to cover ourselves with roles, controls, successes and satisfying explanations. The mind will discover a million ways to cover itself from its fears and its emptiness. But praying is living in a lover's world, with no need to affirm or deny, judge or justify. Praying is the unexpected uncovering of perfect goodness after we have done so many things wrong. There is no other place to begin listening or living. Prayer is the only foundation we can trust in ourselves.

Be quiet and self-forgetful, dear friends. Don't miss out. You must know for yourself that Someone is thinking *you* (as opposed to another) each creative moment. The only good choice is to love and trust yourself in God.

from *Radical Grace*, "The Thought God Is Lost In"

Wednesday of the Second Week After Pentecost   Day 216

Recognizing Grace

When Job's life is about to be taken away from him, he can say one of two things. He can curse God, as he does for a moment, and say, God, why not fifty-one years? Or he can surrender to love and grace and say, God, why fifty years? Why did I deserve anything? When we take on that attitude, we've made a decision for grace.

"Naked I came into the world, and naked I will leave" (Job 1:21). What do I have, brothers and sisters, that has not been given to me? All is grace. All is given. Who gave me this hand? Who wiggles these fingers? Who created this eye that I cannot explain or understand? I cannot even make this hair grow. It is all gift. From beginning to end, everything is grace, everything is given. There is nothing that we deserve.

We have no real rights. There is nothing we *have* to have. When you lose your friend, your lover, your life-giver, you can curse God and say, Why was he taken? Why was she taken? Or you can say, Why was she given at all? You can say, Why is that love gone? Or you can say, Why did I even deserve a moment of love? Why did I even deserve a second of this life? God is creator and I am creature. God created me out of nothing and some years back I did not exist at all. "Yahweh gives and Yahweh takes away. Blessed be the name of Yahweh" (Job 1:21).

from *Days of Renewal*

What a Friend We Have in Jesus

Relationship cannot be sought as an end in itself. If it is, it smothers us and destroys us. Relationship is a byproduct of a journey shared between those seeking the same goal, between those who eat the same bread and drink from the same cup.

A *companion*, literally, is "one who eats bread with us." Jesus calls us to be his companion on the journey to the Father. He says: Walk with me. Trust my faith. Trust my love. Trust my hope. And I will walk with you. He is a partner. He is a brother who is also lover. He eats bread with us.

Christians are afraid to believe how deep, real and powerful that relationship is between companions of Jesus, those who are on the same path together, who eat the same food.

from *Days of Renewal*

Freedom to Feel

Suffering is the necessary feeling of evil. If we don't feel evil we stand antiseptically apart from it, numb. We can't understand evil by thinking about it. The sin of much of our world is that we stand apart from pain; we buy our way out of the pain of being human.

Jesus did not numb himself or withhold from pain. Suffering is the necessary pain so that we *know* evil, so that we can name evil and confront it. Otherwise we somehow dance through this world and never really feel what is happening.

Brothers and sisters, the irony is not that God should feel so fiercely; it's that his creatures feel so feebly. If there is nothing in your life to cry about, if there is nothing in your life to complain about, if there is nothing in your life to yell about, you must be out of touch. We must all feel and know the pain of humanity. The free space that God leads us into is to feel the full spectrum, from great exaltation and joy, to the pain of mourning and dying and suffering. It's called the Paschal Mystery.

The totally free person is one who can feel *all* of it and not be afraid of any of it.

from *Days of Renewal*

Merton

Thomas Merton continues to fascinate much of the Catholic world. I think part of the reason for that is because he symbolizes a man of the world, well educated, who understood what he was leaving, who understood the costs. He was not running and yet he was willing to chuck it all for an ultimate truth.

If you've read his writings, you know he remains very current, very aware. In fact, many of his writings were twenty years ahead of his time. He was dealing with the nuclear arms questions in the early 60's with an understanding that many others only came to in the early 80's. He was saying things that our bishops said just recently in the pastoral *The Challenge of Peace*. Merton had enough freedom from the system to be able to understand the system and creatively critique it. He was enough apart from it to, in fact, enter back into it with insight, knowing what the questions are and often having the correct responses. That's the simple definition of a prophet.

from *Why Be Catholic?*

The Eucharist

The central symbol of Catholicism is the Eucharist. The Church
keeps giving the bread of Jesus and saying, "This is who you are,
you become what you eat. You are more one than many. You are
one, but you are also broken." That's the mystery Catholicism
constantly celebrates and tries to understand.

I don't think you become Catholic to get mystical, to get
metaphysical, to get transcendent, to achieve some kind of
nirvana. That might be Buddhist or Hindu holiness; it might be
some of the sects and groups today who remind me of
unidentified flying objects. That's not Catholic Christianity.

The Catholic understanding of Christianity, at its best, does
not emphasize how to get you in the skies, but how to get your
feet on the ground, how to get in touch with the real. Truly
Catholic Christianity tells us how to get into society, into history,
tied to the common good, how to be part of the muddiness and
fleshiness of it all. We *eat the body* of Christ; we don't just reflect
on his ideas. That's primal, archetypal, transformative energy.

from *Why Be Catholic?*

Reverse Mission

Folk Catholicism is no putdown. That's where most of the power is. Priests often discover that people put us to shame. We study faith or theology all these years and then meet people in a hospital and find we are not even close to their level of faith. Here we are giving them the sacraments and preaching the word, and we walk in and out dressed up as if we're the experts on religion. Then we meet saints who don't know they are saints. That's an example of "reverse mission."

All of us discover after a while in ministry that the people we think we are saving are really saving us. It's a wonderful discovery after coming out of the seminary thinking *we* are going to save souls. It's the way God set up the Church: We all save one another in spite of ourselves. Maybe that's what we mean when we say that Christ saves us. Surely, none of us save ourselves.

from *Why Be Catholic?*

Standing Together

If the gospel has taken on a kind of enigmatic quality in some places or cases, I think part of the problem is that we've tried to live the gospel alone. The gospel was meant to be lived by the Church, by the people of God, where there is a support system that says you can ask new questions. I think of the people in the New Jerusalem Community and at the Center in New Mexico who have, at great risks to themselves and their families, given up jobs building military hardware. They would never have been able to do it if there weren't a support system saying, That's an appropriate gospel question, and we support the risks you take in asking that question.

I don't think we can carry the cross alone. I'm not going to get to real questions of solidarity with the poor unless I know I'm not just standing out there naked and alone. I'm not just one silly, stupid person; there is a whole faith vision calling me to do it. That is the meaning of the Body of Christ and should be the meaning of the parish.

Our parishes have become so large and so anonymous, and we've been allowed to attend them instead of participate in them. Today people don't drop out of Church as much as drop in—occasionally! My hope is that little faith-sharing groups will continue to emerge, connected to parishes. The "base community" and the institutional parish need one another. The parish needs the small fervent group to keep it honest, to allow and encourage those who want to ask the deeper questions, those who want to go further, those who want to learn to pray, to minister, to study, advocate and lay down their lives for the poor. And the small group needs the parish to avoid becoming sectarian, narrow, or lost in personality and trendiness. They must regulate, balance and challenge one another.

from Why Be Catholic?

The Risk God Takes

Forgiveness is most profoundly experienced when people can own their darkness and *concretely* allow another human being to offer freedom and healing to them. Heavenly transactions need to become tangible human experiences. That's what sacraments are.

Do you really know how to receive forgiveness? If you can't receive it from another specific human being, I sincerely doubt whether you really know how to receive it from God.

Unmediated grace is a fantasy. Grace is always mediated through human persons and events. What a risk God takes! And God asks that we risk in turn. By seeing Christ in one another we find the mediation points that make the gospel credible, immediate and historical.

from *Why Be Catholic?*

Martyrs

Most of the martyrs were not killed simply for religious reasons. Throughout Christian history there's always been plenty of overlap between Church and state, politics and prayer. It was true with the English martyrs of the Reformation, with the Japanese martyrs; it was true with the early Roman martyrs.

We easily forget that truth. Now when we see, for example,

the martyrs of the poor Church of El Salvador, people say, "I'm not sure they were really martyrs for Christ. They were making waves with the state." But it has always been that way.

True religion, precisely because it is so holistic, is a threat to the system. The system can't tolerate free people who don't bow before the idols of the system, whatever they might be.

The martyrs have always turned around and walked out the back of their own logical heads. They found a way to that greatest freedom, the only true freedom: freedom *from* the self and freedom *for* the Great Truth.

from Why Be Catholic?

Solemnity of the Sacred Heart of Jesus   Day 225

Freedom and Incarnation

For this reason, when he came into this world, he said: "Sacrifice and offering you did not desire, but a body you prepared for me; / holocausts and sin offerings you took no delight in. / Then I said, 'As is written of me in the scroll,/ Behold, I come to do your will, O God.' " (Hebrews 10:5-7, *NAB*)

Our Creator is patiently determined to put matter and spirit together, almost as if the one were not complete without the other. This Lord of life seems to desire a perfect but free unification between body and soul. God even appears to be willing to wait for the creatures to will and choose this unity themselves.

The Lord apparently loves freedom as much as incarnation.

And that is the rub of time and history, and of our interminable groanings. The sons and daughters of a God who always is waiting to appear are afraid of freedom and do not trust incarnation.

It took one who would say, "I have come to do your will, O God," to trust God's process instead of demanding God's conclusion. He is the perfectly incarnate Son. He is Jesus. He trusted the process—"a body you have prepared for me." And so, like no other traveler, Jesus was totally ready for God's conclusion.

There is a perfect continuum between the process and the conclusion, between incarnation and redemption, and between Jesus and those informed by the same Father's Spirit. The reason we have trouble with the full incarnation in Jesus probably is that we have not been able to recognize or admit our own limited incarnation. We must trust that God's process will give the conclusion.

from Sojourners, "Baptism of Joy"

Memorial of the Immaculate Heart of Mary   Day 226

A Feminine Face of God:
Our Lady of Guadalupe

Since the Guadalupe story is multi-layered and multi-dimensional, I would like to share just one of the many interpretations that has allowed her to convert and heal for over four hundred years. A young Mexican theologian told me that the Guadalupe story is a paradigm of the typical Mexican family.

Juan Diego is the archetypal Mexican self-image: small, unimportant, unworthy, conquered. Juan Zummaraga, the archbishop, is the classic father: *macho*, cold, unbelieving, disconnected from the real life of the family. And the Lady of Guadalupe is the eternal feminine, *madrecita*, the heart, hope and strength of all new life. In their interaction, every Mexican sees the pattern lived out again—but now with a healing and victorious ending.

The Mother believes in the little one, challenges him, yet makes him special and beloved in a converted love that he can understand. She empowers him to face again and again the distant father, finally revealing the inner and transcendent woman on his own chest—and the disbelieving father finally kneels at the boy's feet. The dream of family is at last complete. No logic is offered, nor theological subtleties; just December roses given and received. God knew all along what feminist theologians are saying only now: Sometimes God's face must be feminine. Maybe it is only "the Woman" who will be able to heal the wars, mistrust and status symbols that divide the children of God.

from *Radical Grace*, "Our Lady of Guadalupe"

Ninth Sunday in Ordinary Time   Day 227

Work and Prayer

By temperament, we are all inclined to be either doers or be-ers. This tends to determine what kind of religion we gravitate toward. Some people immediately want to move into a kind of over-passivity that we used to call quietism: "Well, the Lord will do it," they say. Others take their own hard work and professionalism far too seriously. The balance is otherwise: Pray as if it all depends on God; work as if it all depends on you. That saying has been attributed to at least twenty-five saints. I don't know who initially said it, but it doesn't surprise me that it's attributed to so many holy people. Although the converse is maybe even more true: Pray as if it all depends on *you* and work as if it all depends on God!

You have to be mistrustful of any language when it's too much on one side or the other. You can't just endlessly wait; you finally also have to *do*. And then in the doing, the Lord either opens or closes doors; things either happen or they don't. You must be ready to go back to prayer. And if you act before prayerful surrender, the action will be filled with self, manipulation and frenzy.

Contemplation and action are equally important in the balanced life. I don't know which comes first; they are two steps in the one essential dance.

from *Letting Go: A Spirituality of Subtraction*

Monday of the Ninth Week in Ordinary Time   Day 228

Human Sexuality

Many men can't trust female love and many women can't trust male love today. This situation is the most subtle, certain and total way of destroying a people. The vulnerable and trusting love of Jesus is the only sign of salvation: It can be raised up like a white flag in a cold war. The present antagonism and mistrust between the sexes has all the scary signs of total war.

One of the most hopeful signs in familial church communities is that these issues have a safe environment where they can be dealt with openly. It is OK to show affection, and it does not mean that we are leading up to a genital relationship. It is acceptable to feel emotions; you do not have to be afraid or ashamed. Of course, you are going to fall in love! That is the meaning of life. I hope it happens to you many, many times.

In community it can happen creatively, "in spirit and in truth," but not without greater pain. I am convinced that the problem with so much aberrant sexuality today is not that people feel too much desire or too much passion, but rather that they do not feel enough, because there is no safe container to hold our passionate lives together. Our local faith community should provide both permission and containment.

from *Sojourners*, "Reflections on Marriage and Celibacy"

Becoming All Eyes and Ears

Was it dread or desire that I was feeling? I was not sure which emotion dominated me as I left for the six-plus weeks of Lent in a Big Sur, California, hermitage. All I knew was that it was time to go again and "cleanse the doors of perception." When I returned to Albuquerque on Easter night, with full white beard, I knew that it had been a bit dreadful but much more worthy of desire, and in fact, a new tryst with Life.

After a while in solitude, I felt that my eyes were as wide as my shoulders and my ears as big as my head: God had a much better chance of getting through. The rich daily Eucharists and meditation on the Scriptures led me to a new encounter with Jesus as the Image of the Beloved that has most taught and guided my soul. The chewy bread and sensuous wine at the midday Feast brought back primal memories of first food, loving kisses and the Inner Communion we all seek. All the other paths are good and helpful and expansive, but the Jesus path is clearly my path and, I believe, the liberating path for the World.

from *Radical Grace*, "The Bliss Ninny"

Wednesday of the Ninth Week in Ordinary Time   Day 230

Franciscan Poverty

Franciscan spirituality has never been an abstraction. It is grounded in Jesus' specific instructions to his disciples; not in theology. Franciscanism does not easily move into ideology. Francis' living of the gospel was just that: life-style pure and simple. It was the incarnation continuing in space and time. It was the presence of the Spirit taken seriously. It was *being* Jesus more than simply worshipping him. At its best, Franciscanism is flesh—naked flesh—unable to deny its limitations, unable to cover its wounds. Francis called it poverty.

This pure vision of gospel life attracted thousands to a new freedom in the Church and in ministry in Francis' time. Religious communities had become more and more entangled with stipends, benefices and rich land holdings. Members lived individually simple lives but were corporately secure and even comfortable. The begging, or mendicant, orders were born to break that dangerous marriage between ministry and money.

Francis did not want his friars to preach salvation (although they did that, too) as much as he wanted them to *be* salvation. He wanted them to model and image the life of Jesus in the world, with all of the trusting and insecurity that would entail. Today we would be arrested as vagrants or bums, but he believed that Jesus meant what he said when he told the disciples to "eat whatever is set before you, for the laborer deserves his payment" (Luke 10:7). When Francis first heard Jesus' sermon in which he told his followers to "take nothing for your journey," he left Mass overjoyed and committed the whole passage to memory, saying: "This is what I want. This is what I long for. This is what I desire to do with all my heart."

from *Sojourners*, "A Life Pure and Simple"

Thursday of the Ninth Week in Ordinary Time   Day 231

Private Prayer / Community Prayer

If a husband does not give specific time to his wife, simply to show her love and concern, he is being unreal when he says that his work is his love for her, or his taking care of the house is his love for her or whatever else. The same applies for wives. There must be moments of focus, of exclusive human love.

It has been easy to say that you see Christ in your brother or sister, which is true. But be sure you know what you're saying. Be sure you know what Christ looks like, or how can you see Christ in your brother? Unless you personally know the voice of the Master, how can you recognize him and hear where he is speaking in your brother and sister?

Without a private prayer life, community prayer doesn't happen and community life doesn't work. We can continue it for a while, but then it becomes a pretense. So if you are *just* praying at your prayer meeting, I'll bet you're not praying. If you're *just* praying on Sunday morning, I'll bet you're not praying. If you don't think of the Lord until Sunday morning, you don't think of the Lord enough. How could you relate to your spouse that way? Ignore him or her for six days of the week and then routinely say, "I love you" once a week. That's not a true relationship. Lovers share their entire lives with one another. If you love God, you share your whole life with God.

Private prayer becomes the acid test. Those faithful to private prayer are the ones who grow by leaps and bounds. They find a regular time for prayer. Those who make that kind of decision for God are the ones who come to know God as a personal presence.

from *The Great Themes of Scripture*

Friday of the Ninth Week in Ordinary Time   Day 232

Powerful Word

In *Man of La Mancha* we perceive a constant conflict between what is normally called reality and what Don Quixote called reality. Others call his reality idealism. He sets out for his reality at all costs and refuses to accept their sad definition of reality. The men with the mirrors come up before him and try to force him to face up to what they call realism.

We find sometimes that what people call reality in fact blinds rather than illuminates. This is most perfectly summarized in Don Quixote's relationship with the prostitute Aldonza. She is quite obviously a prostitute, but he refuses to believe it. He says, "No, you are not Aldonza, you are Dulcinea!" And at first she treats him with disgust and scorn. "How stupid you are! I am a prostitute! I'm evil!" But he continues to call her Dulcinea. "No, you are beautiful! You are good!" And finally, *the power of his seeing* overcomes her, and she begins to believe it and finally to become what he calls her.

That's how it is with the word of God. The word of God names us daughters and sons of God, all evidence to the contrary. One day it sinks in, and what we thought was reality shatters in the mirror.

from *The Great Themes of Scripture*

Water of Life

Humanity must constantly receive this promise of God: "I will make you into a new creation. I will create in you and in your people the New Jerusalem. But you must let me love you and let me wipe away the tears from your eyes" (Revelation 21:4-5). How we resist that! We go around beating our breasts and feeling sinful, as if that were doing anything for God or humans! In truth it is a refusal to allow God to be merciful.

Chapter 22 of the Book of Revelation (the end of the Bible) eloquently expresses the mercy of God: These words are trustworthy and true! They are already fulfilled! I am the Alpha and the Omega, the Beginning and the End. To anyone who thirsts I will give drink without cost from the spring of life-giving water.

God will give water free! But humans always want to buy, earn or deserve. These are the final and climactic words of the Bible:

> Let the one who thirsts come forward, and the one who wants it receive the life-giving water—and have it free!... Come, Lord Jesus! (Revelation 22:17, 20, *NAB*)

from *The Great Themes of Scripture*

Tenth Sunday in Ordinary Time   Day 234

A Smaller Church

I pray that the Catholic Church is much smaller in twenty years—and happy to be so. I suspect this is the only way we can regain our integrity and effectiveness as proclaimer of the Kingdom: smaller numbers, smaller parishes (communities), smaller bank accounts, smaller programs, fewer clergy, less officialdom, smaller expectations of our capacity for success—a "mustard seed conspiracy" of sorts. I take seriously Jesus' teaching about "two or three gathered in my name." Two hundred or three hundred look good, but mean less and less—to one another and to the world.

I hope for more truth, more real edges and influence, more

energy for the inward journey, more prophecy, more right-brain intuition, more adoration, more real security, more spiritual and political hope for the human heart—just big enough and strong enough "for all the birds to come and shelter in its branches" (Matthew 13:19). But not so big that we forget, or do not need, or imagine that we are the only tree.

If we continue to emerge as the group that is most capable of evangelizing culture itself, if we continue to stand in that naked place of the gospel somewhere between and apart from liberal or conservative, if we continue to be walked on as a bridge, I have every hope that this oldest institution in Western civilization might be satisfied and secure as God's "immoral" minority. It takes two thousand years of history to grow up to that! Now our identity is firm enough to prefer discernment over law, pastoring over programming and the inherent wholeness and rhythm of the wisdom community. By the year 2000 we should be old enough for an adult marriage with Jesus in all of his parts and all of his pains.

from "A Church Unashamed to Be Leaven and Salt"

Marriage Under the Mystery

The Orthodox faith has preserved a beautiful wedding liturgy. First, the civil ceremony is celebrated in some public arena, perhaps out in the plaza in front of the church. Then there is the option for a second, sacramental ceremony. And you have to make a specific choice for the second. Do you want to walk into the church, stand before the altar and have that marriage, which is already a marriage, crowned by the wisdom, glory and meaning of the cross of Christ?

I don't know that we've ever associated marriage with really entering into that deep mystery of the cross, of the death and Resurrection of Jesus Christ. But I think outside of that mystery, spoken or unspoken, marriage ends up being destructive in the long run.

So many marriages are two people drawn together with unbelievably false expectations of one another and then frequently feeling the other has let them down or has hurt them. Some have no sense of themselves apart from the other. Some couples compete for self-worth at the expense of one another.

Sacramental marriage is not just marriage but precisely marriage "under the mystery" of the cross and Resurrection. It is inspiring to be near the rare couple who love sacramentally. I wish we would separate the legal and the sacramental as the Orthodox Churches do.

from *The Spiritual Family and the Natural Family*

Tuesday of the Tenth Week in Ordinary Time   Day 236

Egotism Between Two

Mary Magdalene wanted to hold on to Jesus, that one relationship that was so perfect and good. He had to say to her, Mary, do not hold on to me. I must go to my Father and your Father (John 20:17). This relationship is given to you to teach you the structure of right relationship: *union*, but not too much!

So many have found their total identity in their children or in one another. But you can't endlessly look at one another's eyes and hope to find eternity. Look together toward something you both believe and share in. That leads you out and beyond yourselves and into something new, wonderful and dangerous, into something that demands that you risk your love, that you risk—if I can say it—your marriage, to find out how much more life and how much more marriage God wants to give you. Each love opens us to what we really love. Each desire fulfilled helps us to seek further for what we are still desiring. Don't stop! Each love relationship is seducing us into *the* Relationship.

from *The Spiritual Family and the Natural Family*

The Navajo Rug

In a Navajo rug there is always an imperfection woven into the corner. And interestingly enough, it's where "the Spirit moves in and out of the rug." The pattern is perfect and then there's one part of it that clearly looks like a mistake. The Semitic mind, the Eastern mind (which, by the way, Jesus would have been much closer to) understands perfection in precisely that way.

Perfection is not the elimination of imperfection. That's our Western either/or, need-to-control thinking. Perfection, rather, is the ability to incorporate imperfection! There's no other way to live: You either incorporate imperfection, or you fall into denial. That's how the Spirit moves in *or* out of our lives.

from *Breathing Under Water: Spirituality and the 12 Steps*

A Web of Grace

During my Lenten hermitage at Big Sur, I discovered I had to find once again what it is that supports me. Who is it that names and loves me, and who is this naked man behind all his public words? The Camaldolese monks were kind enough to offer me a hermitage where I could engage in protected solitude and daily mass and lunch with the community if I wished. So I tried to balance my day between Spirit, soul, mind and body.

I took two hours hiking in the California mountains and exercised each day, plus a bit of fasting and a vegetarian diet. I must say I felt limber, trim and embodied in a way that might be able to honor Spirit. I tried to do some heavier reading each day to challenge my mind and stretch my perspectives, mainly in the areas of theology, philosophy and history. "Soul" work included the whole area of poetry, symbol, dreams, contemplative sitting and some extensive reading in sacred psychology and mythology.

When we live realigned with our bodies and the natural world, when we have time for soul, mind and Spirit, it becomes very hard to believe in a merely random universe. Things are not just planned or accidental anymore, but a web of grace seems to unite all things into a symbiosis and synchronicity. It felt like forty-seven days of "coincidences"! It reaffirmed for me my long-standing belief in Providence.

from *Radical Grace*, "The Bliss Ninny"

Friday of the Tenth Week in Ordinary Time   Day 239

Graces of the Flesh

We are only now daring to believe, after two thousand years of revelation of the mystery of Christ, what Satan discovered at the crucifixion. The Evil One knows that the place to attack us is in the area where we are most subject to shame, where we are most weak and truly "out of character": our bodiliness. Satan knows that is the last place where we will expect or look for God. And God knows that only forgiven sinners and spiritual searchers will find God there.

So evil has found the breach in the wall and attacked each one of us there with "a thorn in the flesh, an angel of Satan" (2 Corinthians 12:7). Unfortunately, it worked! Much of Christian tradition has been negatively and uselessly trapped in guilt and preoccupation with the body, while the great issues of justice, gospel and grace have gone unheeded. The result has been rigidity and repression—much of it called "holiness." This response has been Evil's greatest triumph over gospel freedom. It has horribly entrapped the positive power of human affection.

Christ will have his harvest, though. It will be through weak flesh, that least-suspected place, that health and growth will be revealed.

from *Sojourners*, "Pure Passion"

Fishing for People Is Hard Work

As he was walking by the Sea of Galilee, he saw two brothers, Simon who is called Peter, and his brother Andrew casting a net in the lake; they were fishermen. He said to them, "Follow me and I will make you fishers of men." (Matthew 4:18-19)

Brothers and sisters, you have no idea how hard, discouraging and frustrating it is to be a "fisher of men." Sometimes I feel that I'd much sooner be an ordinary fisherman. Because then I'd at least have fish to show for my work. I could hold them up and say, see, I caught three fish. But for a fisher of humanity, it's sort of vague. You don't know when they're growing, when you have them, when they believe, when they've let go of their life. And so

I know why Paul said, We apostles are at the end of the parade, the scum of the earth, the off-scouring of the universe (1 Corinthians 4:9-13).

We're laughed at by the practical ones of this world. They ask, What do you have to show for your work? We're fishing around. We're out enticing hearts and calling them into love. Ours is a catch hard to measure, and the product is never completed by the five o'clock whistle.

from *The Spiritual Family and the Natural Family*

Eleventh Sunday in Ordinary Time   Day 241

Live in This Moment

Allow the Lord, by his love and grace, to let you live in this moment. Right now. This moment is as perfect as it can be. And God's call, the needs of the world, will make itself very apparent. Just respond to the need that presents itself right in front of you, today, tomorrow.

I think many parents become very good and holy people because children literally demand love. You can't legislate the times in which they can make demands on you. They literally pull life and death out of you and call you forth into a *now* that you would never have chosen or recognized as Christ.

from *Letting Go: A Spirituality of Subtraction*

Get Together by Getting Together

The only way that I know how to get people together is to start getting people together. When they start dealing with each other, they start learning who they are. They start getting feelings and resentments. They start getting hurts. They say, Brother, why are you getting hurt right now? What's hurting you? What need isn't being met? What are you afraid of? OK, let's deal with that. Don't run from it. Unless you've made some commitments, unless you understand loyalty, that's the point where you're going to move out. That's why there are and must be marriage vows. Who of you in the second year of marriage wouldn't have run away? The Lord gives you that pledge, that promise to hold you in there.

It's the same way in the Church: We've laid our lives down for one another. I'm not free to pull back on my love commitment to my brothers and sisters. Where you see unity, trust it. Now you might think I'm going to say the converse of that: Where you see disunity, distrust it. No. Where you see disunity, lay down your life until there is unity. What else would the cross be? What else will redeem the broken world?

Did you ever notice that God had to *lock* Noah and all the wild and creeping things in the ark? God knew they would try to escape from their own salvation (see Genesis 7:16).

from *The Spiritual Family and the Natural Family*

Romance

We have come to think of romance as that exciting and emotional—sometimes dramatic, sometimes gushy—thing that happens between two lovers. And of course we say it only happens once except for those lucky people who create affairs again along through their life. But for many it just happens once, and once it's gone it's gone and we all know it wasn't real. But that's a false definition of romance.

Romance, it seems to me, is the risk and the adventure—the tremendous sense of daring and gift—that comes into one's life when one is seeking something larger than oneself. The knightly tradition of courtly love in the twelfth century produced the very word *romance*. It referred to a pure love for a woman that never sought consummation! It referred to men testing their ideals and their singlemindedness. That is why many of our fathers consider World War II their great "romance" with life.

Romance isn't necessarily the gushy feelings between a man and a woman. I meet many religious sisters and brothers who clearly see their life and ministry as their "affair" with God. Romance is that sense of adventure and daring and surrender that comes into our life when we have a vision worth living and dying for. The "Great Romance" with life itself probably makes the smaller romances a lifelong occurrence.

from *The Spiritual Family and the Natural Family*

I *Trust* Unity

I trust those who have achieved in their relationships, by God's grace, a deep personal unity. I trust unity (with allowance for plenty of human sinfulness). That is why forgiveness and reconciliation are the primary gospel gifts. I think people who live in unity have the power of life and love. They alone can be trusted to bear good news. By their life together they have necessarily shown that they are capable of surrender, sacrifice, forgiveness, generosity—and compassion.

Those brothers and sisters are the ones I'll take with me into the front lines. I know they're not going to back out when it gets hard. I know they're not on a head trip. The brothers and sisters who are capable of membership in the Body—not roles and functions and titles and gifts and habits, but membership. That's why we say you've got to first be a brother or sister in the Body before you can talk about being a father or mother in the Body. I don't trust ministers in the Church who are not also satisfied to be *members.*

Among the people of unity I see the possibility of a healed humanity. And therefore I can realistically hope for some coming of the Kingdom from amongst them. Jesus thus gives great authority to those gathered in his name whom he sends forth "two by two." He tells them in the apostolic discourse, in words that are harsh and strange to our ears, that as they enter a house they are to greet it. And if the house deserves it, their peace will descend upon it. And if it does not, their peace will return to them. If anyone does not welcome you or listen to what you have to say, walk out of the house, shake the dust from your feet (see Matthew 10:12-14). The new family of God is not to apologize for itself. God has created unity between them, deep faith, hope and love.

The greatest weapon that the world holds against this unity is its own disunity, its own antagonistic hearts which arise from sin, self-hatred and vested interests. If we sell out to that disunity, if we are in any way taken in to their displeasure and their self-hatred, we have lost our gift.

We must confront the world with its inability to share in peace and enjoy brotherhood and sisterhood. We cannot at any step of the way deny or defend our unity simply because they have not shared in it yet. Our unity is God's love, and it's all we really have. It is all we have to offer to the enslaved world. It is a life that we can invite others into. It is the font from which our own life continues to proceed.

When we have lost our unity, we have just plain lost.

from *The Spiritual Family and the Natural Family*

Thursday of the Eleventh Week in Ordinary Time   Day 245

Hospitality

Shared life is a way of being present to another person so that another person can be present to you. It's a quality of being, of living. A sharing attitude makes room inside of you so that others can crawl in and you can crawl out into them. You become touched and touchable, supporting and supportable.

A Christian home is one with the doors open, and a Christian community of any form has doors open and swinging both ways. There's life moving in and life moving out. I could summarize Jesus' most radical teaching as a call to "universal table fellowship" (see with whom he eats, whom he invites to the banquet, and then you will know why they killed him!).

Don't tell people to come to our church or to come to hear Father preach. Ask them to come over for supper. That's more real and natural. Talk to them over the back fence. We hope our life is good news. When our neighbors see our unity and our good news, maybe then they'll say, I'd like to come celebrate and worship with you.

from *The Spiritual Family and the Natural Family*

Friday of the Eleventh Week in Ordinary Time   Day 246

Authority and Submission

There has to be authority in the family if it is to be a place where people can be called forth and challenged, where truth can be spoken to them. True authority is not simply proclaiming the male as head of the family, but instead, as St. Paul teaches, by the husband laying down his life for his wife (Colossians 3:19 and Ephesians 5:28-33) and the wife submitting her life to her husband (Colossians 3:18 and Ephesians 5:22-24). Those are equal demands and don't denote hierarchy. This is clear in Ephesians 5:21: "Give way to one another in obedience to Christ." The goal is partnership and mutuality, in which each can submit to the other.

The best way to understand the word *submission*, because it has such a negative connotation for us Americans, is simply the word *support*. To submit in Latin is to be sent under, to stand under—to *under-stand*. To submit to another is to understand another. When we call members of our community to submit to authority, we're saying, support authority, be free to say yes before you dare to say no. Until you're free to say yes, to be discipled and taught, led and loved by another, you're not free. The same applies for husbands and wives.

God's people have always been a hard-hearted and rebellious people, if you believe Genesis and the Old Testament. We don't give authority to anyone very easily. But I believe authority means precisely the power to author another person. That can't be proclaimed from on high; it must be given over. Real authority is either having the power or giving someone the power to author another, to call another forth, to challenge another and speak truth to another.

You have to bind yourself somehow in that relationship. If you're free to pull in and out when you don't like what you hear, you're not going to grow. Who are the only people we're going to entrust ourselves to? People whose lives are laid down for us. That's the enduring value of vows, commitments, loyalties and faithfulness. That kind of wisdom will never go out of style.

from *The Spiritual Family and the Natural Family*

Saturday of the Eleventh Week in Ordinary Time   Day 247

Community:
The Foundation of Authority

The good news that Jesus communicated to his brothers and sisters is the good news of a life-style, a life together. I believe the authority of the Church comes from a life shared and lived together. Out of that come our answers, our roles, functions. Out of that experience of the risen Jesus freeing us and giving us his victory come the teachings of the Church.

Unfortunately we in the Church are trying to teach a morality apart from the experience of the risen Jesus freeing his people. Yet the most compelling moral responses come from the ambiguities of real life—not from textbook answers that are prefabricated and so-called pure.

That's why any renewal of the Church that is not a return to some type of community, loyal relationships, family, isn't renewal. We do not think ourselves into a new way of living; we *live* our way into a new way of thinking. Educators and prelates seem to have a hard time understanding that.

from *The Spiritual Family and the Natural Family*

Twelfth Sunday in Ordinary Time   Day 248

The Need for Silence

We don't know how to take joy in simple things anymore because, frankly, we are sated. You and I have had so much thrown at us! Unless we choose to deliberately under-stimulate ourselves, I don't think we can reasonably talk about spirituality. We don't really taste, suffer, enjoy, feel the images that come our way.

Westerners have a mania for experience. Descartes said, "I think, therefore I am." For us, it is "I experience, therefore I am." But I'm pretty much convinced experiences don't change people; *realization* does. I think of all the powerful experiences that I've had. But only when I taste my experiences enough so they become realizations, do I change. That takes time and space. Put time and space together and you have a new definition of silence.

We've got to create some kind of space so our images can become realizations. Unless we choose silence, I don't think a lot of this is going to happen. I don't think we're going to become willing people. We become, instead, willful people, trying to make the world fit our needs. Will triumphs instead of the Spirit.

Silence alone is spacious enough to allow Spirit and to let go of will-fullness. Silence makes us willing instead of willful.

from *Letting Go: A Spirituality of Subtraction*

Monday of the Twelfth Week in Ordinary Time   Day 249

Five Great Gifts: Apostleship

St. Paul enumerates five great gifts. I like to picture these as a fence. If the five great gifts are operative, the rodeo is able to go on in the middle. The growth of the people of God is protected. The first is apostleship. An apostle is one who is sent. In Paul's sense an apostle is one who has the vision of the whole, of how all the gifts operate together. Apostles know the risen Lord. On this ground, Mary Magdalene is the first apostle and the one sent by Jesus to convince the other twelve. She can rightly be called the "apostle to the apostles."

Apostles are rooted in the Lord and tied into the whole tradition. The apostle speaks for the whole. Apostles aren't unaccountable; they're under authority. So apostles can be sent away from their community, almost appearing to be lone rangers, and because they're under authority, they can go out and call other people under authority.

We have today a lot of roving evangelists and prophets who are in no way accountable. They're not being sent from any spot. The private self decides everything. No community sends them; they just "go." But an apostle is always sent. Apostles are free to go because they are not their own center; the gospel is.

from The Price of Peoplehood

Five Great Gifts: Prophethood

The prophet is the one who speaks with an immediacy, an authority, an insight that is often seen as foresight into the plan of God. The prophet speaks with a special kind of non-institutional authority and tends to be in healthy tension with the apostle. If the apostle is in any sense an institutionalist, the prophet is the iconoclast. In the whole biblical tradition we always see that healthy tension between the priests and the prophets. It is the necessary and ultimately creative tension between David and Nathan (2 Samuel 12:7) and between Peter and Paul (Galatians 2:11). It is essential, yet most rare, that priests and prophets honor and remain in dialogue with one another's gifts. They need one another, today perhaps more than ever.

The prophet could be compared to the court jester who keeps the king honest and on course. The prophet is the passion, the justice, the truth-speaker of God, especially to all forms of institutional idolatry. They are set up for conflict and rejection (see Matthew 23:34ff.).

from *The Price of Peoplehood*

Wednesday of the Twelfth Week in Ordinary Time   Day 251

Five Great Gifts: Evangelism

I suppose many of us still think of *evangelism* as a Protestant term. But it's a biblical term. The evangelist is the one who gives Good News. The evangelist has the specific charism of being able to welcome, to invite, to announce Jesus and the Kingdom with excitement. The evangelist is the door opener. Catholics have been, historically, very weak on this charism, since most Catholics were baptized as infants.

Evangelism is what our pope and bishops are saying we need so much now. I find myself these days being much more a teacher, but I was called for some time a Catholic evangelist. I remember when I was first introduced as that, it sounded like a strange phrase. We don't expect the Catholic Church to have evangelists. We have often falsely assumed that because people were members, they already had a conversion experience and were basing their life on the gospel of Jesus.

Yet the Church desperately needs a new evangelism. And many of us need to be re-evangelized—or perhaps hear the Good News for the first time.

from *The Price of Peoplehood*

6-24-10

Five Great Gifts: Pastoring

The fourth gift is pastoring. What does St. Paul understand by pastor? It's not the same as an administrator, which is another charism (see 1 Corinthians 12:28). Our pastors today are forced to be managers of huge plants and often aren't really free to pastor.

I find that the biggest shortage in the Church today is pastoral wisdom, pastoral authority, pastoral knowledge, spiritual direction. Our priests haven't had the time to be formed as spiritual directors and pastoral leaders. But that's primarily what St. Paul is talking about.

A pastor is one who feeds and guides the people. I guess if I had to associate one word with pastor, it would be growth. A pastor is one who understands how to grow people. A pastor must understand human relationships, family, communication—in short, what makes people tick and how they tick well *together*.

from *The Price of Peoplehood*

6-25-10

Five Great Gifts: Teaching

The fifth gift, one we've confused, is teaching. The diocesan priests come out better here than we in the religious orders. We trained many kinds of our men to be teachers. But very often it meant teaching secular subjects like chemistry or mathematics, which is not bad or unnecessary, but it is not, as such, the biblical charism of teaching. And I know many religious priests who have never been in pastoral ministry. There has been a tremendous confusion between the ministry of secular education and the ministry of Christian teaching, which would include catechesis, adult religious education, theology and homiletics.

Teaching, as St. Paul seems to see it, is precisely that charism of good and consistent thinking to keep the Body of Christ in touch with its own Spirit. Ours is not an irrational or whimsical faith subject to trends and passing cultures. There is a Great Tradition that we must listen to and Scriptures that we need to study. Without good theological teaching, faith becomes passing on feel-good ideas. Intellect is not to be rejected.

from *The Price of Peoplehood*

Saturday of the Twelfth Week in Ordinary Time   Day 254

Church Divisions

A lot of the pretenses of institutional religion I don't take seriously. Sometimes the Roman Church takes for granted that it speaks for God without acknowledging that what it says is often politically motivated and culturally conditioned (for example, questions of expedience being preeminent to questions of truth). That's dangerous. I think we are entering a post-denominational period. I know my mother Church is Catholic. I am grateful for the great riches of my Catholic Church. But tradition is a runway, a takeoff point, a clear direction. Catholicism has not been a prison for me but a home "with many rooms" (John 14:2), which Jesus called his "Father's house."

Because of the Tradition, I feel a natural communion with many non-Catholics who share our same gospel values in life-style, practicing the two great commandments and asking similar questions of life. The historical European problems that divided us are a bore, frankly. Why do we have to continue to carry the baggage of the denominational issues we divided over?

If I cannot trust and work together with other Christians, what hope is there for any ecumenism with Judaism, Islam, Buddhism, Hinduism? What hope is there for the world? Especially when we can see the historical accidents, the cultural blindness, the self-interest on both sides of every schism and reform. Why should we need to defend that? I have too much baggage to carry already.

Often I feel like a juggler in this Church, trying to hold many truths together. I can't make the great issues of the Reformation key in my life. Especially when I see that so many of the questions were asked entirely by comfortable, white male clerics (on both sides) and, usually, were questions of power and righteousness! If we had to divide, why couldn't we divide over who was doing a better job of feeding widows and orphans?

from *The Other Side*, "Poverty and Surrender"

Rediscovering the Rosary

I've recently rediscovered the rosary, a prayer form I haven't used for many years. In this stage of my life I find it powerful. With the rosary, I don't worry so much about praying. I just let those beads go through my fingers and say the phrases over and over again, and for some reason that stops the racing of my mind. It allows me to live in the center, in the present—not in the past or the future.

This started for me on the Feast of Our Lady of Guadalupe. The person of Mary became very present and very real to me as guide and fellow traveler, as friend who loves me.

After I started praying the rosary, all sorts of things fell into place, and my dream of a Center for Action and Contemplation became a reality. I'm not trying to say there's a magical way to get God to do what you want to do. That would be a misunderstanding of the power of prayer. But I do know the rosary was the prayer form given to me to help get myself out of the way.

With the rosary I could listen. I could surrender and trust so I could be some kind of instrument, as Francis would have said, some kind of channel of whatever it was that God wanted to do. And I think that's the purpose of all of our prayer: not to prove ourselves to God or bend the arm of God but, quite simply, to be able to listen anew.

The only way we can listen to truth is to get ourselves out of the way: our feelings, needs, compulsions, responses and everything else. God needs nothing, God asks and demands nothing. We pray only so that we may know God.

from *Letting Go: A Spirituality of Subtraction*

Pilgrimage

(Recorded at the Shrine of Our Lady of Lourdes) We are always looking to the next moment to be more perfect. We're a people always rushing into the future because we're not experiencing a wholeness in the present. Yet, this moment is as perfect as it can be. When we haven't grasped the present, we always live under the illusion—and it is an illusion—that the next moment is going to be better: when I get around this corner, when I see this church, when I get to Jerusalem, when I get to the hotel, whatever it might be. Everything we do is for the sake of something else, a means toward some nebulous end.

That attitude is essentially wrong. As long as we think happiness is around the corner, we have not grasped happiness. Happiness is given in *this* moment. Everything is right here, right now, the total mystery of Christ; totally hidden and yet perfectly revealed.

Though pilgrimages are good for the spirit, if you can't find Jesus in your hometown, you probably aren't going to find him in Jerusalem. If you haven't already entered into a relationship with Mary before, you probably won't find her at Lourdes. We go on pilgrimage so we can go back home and know that we never need to go on pilgrimage again. Pilgrimage has achieved its purpose when we can see God in our everyday and ordinary lives.

from *On Pilgrimage With Father Richard Rohr*

Pilgrims, Not Tourists

(Recorded at Lourdes) We must pray for a deepening of faith. Pray for freedom from cynicism and judgments. On pilgrimage to a foreign land, you're going to see people who act and talk differently, and if you move into your sophistication, you will take offense. You will lose the childlike spirit that the gospel asks of us.

A pilgrim must be a child who can approach everything with an attitude of wonder, awe and faith. Pray for wonder, awe, desire. Ask God to take away your sophistication and cynicism. Ask God to take away the restless, anxious heart of the tourist, which always needs to find the new, the more, the curious. Recognize yourself as a pilgrim, as one who has already been found by God.

As we look upon a holy place like Lourdes and wonder about what we see, we can let it speak to us. It isn't our country, perhaps. It isn't our way of saying it. But it's a holy place. It has drawn thousands of holy people from throughout the world for a hundred years. Just listen and wait.

from *On Pilgrimage With Father Richard Rohr*

Faith Requires Faith

(Recorded at Lourdes) Faith is never going to be anything other than faith, and it's never going to be easy. I'm sure many people come to Lourdes thinking that the presence will be so obvious that faith will be unnecessary. That will never be the case. Bernadette, this little girl who herself saw Mary, lived a life of unbelievable faith. Mary told her, "Bernadette, you're never going to be happy on this earth. But I promise you happiness forever in heaven."

We see people, unbelievably crippled on the exterior, being wheeled up to the shrine, into the grotto. Our hearts ache for them, and we feel so lucky to have bodies that allow us to walk around.

We are forced to ask the question after the blessing with the sick, after the dipping in the water, Well, why aren't they healed? And if you and I are asking that, imagine how *they* are asking that. And yet, can you believe the joy, although it must be tinged with disappointment, that we see on so many of their faces?

The miracle of Lourdes is a miracle of faith. It's a miracle that is not immediately visible: People are not always healed. And yet we have to believe something deeply life-giving is happening here, and that's God's work. God is creating life on earth. Just hold on to that. It happens in a thousand different ways, and the most important ways are in the heart.

If, by coming to this place surrounded by holiness, prayer and faith, we see people who are more deeply able to enter into the mystery, more easily able to say yes, to smile, to trust—that is the miracle of faith. But it is still faith. For some of you the act of faith here is to believe why these people aren't healed. Sometimes it's almost harder for us than it appears to be for them.

from *On Pilgrimage With Father Richard Rohr*

The Obedient Person

The healing that God effects in us, even at a place like Lourdes, is an increased ability to be obedient and an increased ability, therefore, to listen. Obedience means listening. Don't be afraid to be silent and alone, to guard the quality of your speech, to write a spiritual journal. Watch your judgments and your cynicisms. Keep a childlike, simple heart.

The wonder of children is they see new things and beautiful things and take them in. The Lord wants you to take as much in as you can, but to take it in a way that it's going to be there a year from now, not just for the moment. Those are the healings that are going to last, because in a few days this journey is going to be memory.

Already Lourdes is largely a memory for us on this pilgrimage. Most of us will probably never be back here the rest of our lives. And the important thing is that we've experienced it in such a way that, even though we leave, it will still be able to teach us. We're on an interior journey. The exterior journey is only a symbol.

from On Pilgrimage With Father Richard Rohr

They Still Need Fixing

After twenty years of counseling, pastoring and clumsy attempts at helping other people, I am coming to a not-so-obvious but compelling conclusion: Much of our helping is like hoping for first-class accommodations on the Titanic. It feels good at the moment, but it is going nowhere. The big tear in the hull is not addressed, and we are surprised when people drown, complain or resort to lifeboats. Most of the people I have tried to fix still need fixing. The situation changed, but the core was never touched.

What is the core? And how do we touch it? What does it mean to essentially *help* another person? If we can find the answer to these questions, we are coming close to what the world religions mean by true ministry. It is absolutely unlike any other form of helping. It has many counterfeits and disguises. What Jesus, Buddha, Confucius, the saints and prophets are talking about is the *Absolute Help*, which alone is worthy of the name—the radical help that none of us can give to another. We can only point to it and promise that it is there. That is the first and final work of all true religion; all else is secondary.

Call it grace, enlightenment, peak experience, baptism in the Spirit, revelation, consciousness, growth or surrender; but until such a threshold is walked through, people are never helped in any true, lasting sense.

from *Radical Grace*, "How Do We Help?"

On the Temple Threshold

Salvation comes from the word *salus*, which means healing. It is not dependent on feeling or any person's response to me. It is not a theory believed, a theology proclaimed or a group that gives one identity. It is an inner clarity that forever allows one to recognize bogus authority and pseudo-surrender. This salvation cannot be acquired by a simple process of self-examination or new insight or ego possession. It is a gift *received* when the will has given up control and we are standing in that threshold place which allows us to see anew. Suffering, failure, rejection and loss can lead to this same threshold.

When we stand at the threshold, we stand before sacred signs. The true helper will get out of the way and encourage us to get out of the way so we can see them. *Grace* then walks us into the temple.

from *Radical Grace*, "How Do We Help?"

Live a Life of Charity

If you're still breathing, there's more conversion and more life that the Lord wants to offer you. That's what John the Evangelist means when he writes, You will know that the Spirit is within you "because I live and because you will live" (John 14:19).

Why do we feel the call to this kind of charity, this kind of love? It's not a tactic or a strategy in order to get into heaven. It's simply because that's who God is: God pours forth life in our hearts and calls us to be who God is.

It's the only thing that makes sense: When you know that your parent is love, then the only thing you want to be is love. The only thing that comes logically, naturally, to you is love. Nothing else makes sense after awhile.

There is a given-ness to God. God is not withheld; God is the one who is handed over. That's what we mean when we say that God is love. But it's not like our love. When we love, we wait and we see something good out there. If it's attractive enough, if it's good enough, we give ourselves to it. God simply gives. We find that kind of love very hard to understand because we're not able to love that way.

from *The Price of Peoplehood*

Monday of the Fourteenth Week of Ordinary Time   Day 263

Poverty Defined: Poverty As Sin

There are four descriptions of poverty in the Scriptures. First, there's poverty as sin, emptiness, the poverty of people who are dead inside. That obviously is not the poverty that Scripture idealizes. And yet it does play a part in the whole pattern of salvation. Sin and grace are related. In a certain sense the only way we really understand salvation, grace, freedom, is by understanding their opposites. That's why the great saints are, invariably, converted sinners.

When you finally have to eat and taste your own hard-heartedness, your own emptiness, selfishness and all the rest, then you open up to grace. That is the pattern in all our lives. That's why it was such a grace in my hermitage year when I was able, at last—even as a male and a German—to weep over my sins and to feel tremendous sadness at my own silliness and stupidity.

I think all of us have to confront ourselves as poor people in that way. And that's why many of our greatest moments of grace follow upon, sometimes, our greatest sins. We are hard-hearted and closed-minded for years. Then comes the moment of vulnerability and mercy. We break down and break through.

from *Letting Go: A Spirituality of Subtraction*

Tuesday of the Fourteenth Week of Ordinary Time   Day 264

Poverty Defined: Poverty as Destitution

A second way the Scriptures describe poverty is as destitution and dehumanization. Such poverty is the result of injustice, oppression or racism. When we talk about the glories of poverty, we're not talking about the oppressed human being on this earth who has never had a chance to take in cultural, social, emotional, familial values.

Oft-times work with the poor in more developed countries is very discouraging. In the United States we have people who have been familially destitute, culturally destitute, spiritually destitute. Although they're physically poor, they in fact have middle- and upper-class values through television and advertisements. They want the same things that you and I want. The trouble is, they can't get them. That's the worst of both worlds. They are trapped inside and outside. It is a state of sin—one which we must work to change.

We really need the wisdom of God to know how to break in to some of the subcultures of affluent countries. In great part, I think many of these brothers and sisters are going to have to do it themselves because that's the only way they're ever going to experience *their own empowerment* and God's presence and life within *them*. The best we can do, perhaps, is to stand there with them and not hold them down, not give them any more negative voices than they've already been given by society. Our evangelization is perhaps to believe in them, support them from the side and at least not give them bad news. That's *our* poverty: that we can't do more.

from *Letting Go: A Spirituality of Subtraction*

Wednesday of the Fourteenth Week of Ordinary Time   Day 265

Poverty Defined: Poverty as Simplicity

The third biblical description of poverty is simplicity. People poor in this way are centered in chosen values instead of possessions. And because their life is so centered in clear values—usually God, family and work—they normally don't need to compensate by spending their afternoons in shopping malls, buying more things, or filling up their boredom with distractions.

I was recently in a California shopping mall. Walking through this entire place, there wasn't a single shop that sold a single thing that was *necessary*. We have leisure time and the money to produce endless luxury items. Then it's considered patriotic to buy them! The people I saw, all with their shopping bags, were feverishly walking around to get these things that no one needs but feeling good about it "because it helps the economy." Now that's a trap! It's certainly the opposite of poverty as the simple and uncluttered life.

Few things are needed or desired by the one who lives simply because life is centered on another level of value. And maybe it isn't always specifically religious; maybe it's music, art, nature, or even work for a great ideal.

St. Teresa of Avila put it, "When they serve me partridge, I'll eat partridge; when they serve me porridge, I'll eat porridge." So when the nice dress comes along, you're not going to sneer at it in the name of simplicity. No, it's a nice dress, it's pretty, and you'd probably feel great wearing it. But you don't *need* it. That's the difference, and the simple person knows the difference.

from *Letting Go: A Spirituality of Subtraction*

Poverty Defined:
The Poverty of Being Human

The fourth and final poverty described in the Bible is the poverty of being human. This is the ideal poverty of Scripture. Jesus became human yet never sinned because he never rejected this level of poverty. He never rejected the limitations of the human scene, never fought or railed against it. He was happy to "empty himself...and become as humans are" (Philippians 2:7).

It's a gift to joyfully recognize and accept our own smallness. That's my best definition of Christian maturity. It's very hard for an affluent culture to accept a limited world, and that's why Jesus said the rich person cannot easily enter into the Kingdom of God (Matthew 19:23, Mark 10:23, Luke 18:24).

I meet many holy priests who are recovering alcoholics. I can almost pick them out by now; there's a kind of littleness from the very beginning, a kind of vulnerability, a relaxed-ness with themselves and with one another. They're not living in their heads anymore. They had to face, at one point in their lives, their littleness, their poverty. They had to wake up one day and say, I'm an alcoholic. They are some of the greatest priests I meet.

Humility and *human* come from the Latin word, *humus*, dirt. A human being is someone, as we are reminded on Ash Wednesday, taken out of the dirt. A humble person is one who recognizes that and even rejoices in it!

When Carl Jung was toward the end of his life, a student who was reading the classic book *The Pilgrim's Progress* asked him what his pilgrim's progress had been. Jung said, "I have had to climb down ten thousand ladders so that at the end of my life I can reach out the hand of friendship to this little clod of earth that I am." That's the poverty of spirit that Jesus chose and that he calls "blessed." It's his very first statement in his Great Sermon and his very last action on the cross.

from *Letting Go: A Spirituality of Subtraction*

Happy Fault

We don't think ourselves into a new way of living; we live ourselves into a new way of thinking. The journeys around the edges of sin lead us to long for a deeper life at the center of ourselves.

Ruthless ambition can lead one to the very failure and emptiness that is the point of conversion. Is the ambition therefore good or is it evil? Do we really have to sin to know salvation? Call me a "sin mystic," but that is exactly what I see happening in *all* my pastoral experience: Darkness leads us to light.

That does not mean that we should set out intentionally to sin. We only see the pattern after the fact. Blessed Julian of Norwich put it perfectly: "Commonly, first we fall and later we see it—and both are the Mercy of God." How did we ever lose that? It got hidden away in that least celebrated but absolutely central Easter Vigil service when the deacon sings to the Church about a *felix culpa*, the happy fault that precedes and necessitates the eternal Christ. Like all great mysteries of faith, it is hidden except to those who keep vigil and listen.

from *Radical Grace*, "Center and Circumference"

Standing In-between

Thanks be to God, the Catholic Church has produced more martyrs in the last twenty years than we did in the first two hundred years of the Church. Wherever I go on this earth, there are the Catholic missionaries, standing between left and right, standing between communism and capitalism, simply trying to be faithful to Jesus and the gospel. They spill their blood, invariably, because both the right and the left hate them. They're not playing either side's games. They are building bridges, but you can't build a bridge from the middle. You have to start on one side, and for Christians that starting place is on the side of the poor and powerless. That pleases no one, really—not even liberals.

That's the position we're in today. I call it the naked position of the gospel: where you don't please the liberals or conservatives, you simply are faithful to the gospel. It is asking more of our minds and our hearts than any of us are prepared for.

from *Letting Go: A Spirituality of Subtraction*

God Isn't a Twosome Off in a Corner

A relationship between two people, a true giving and receiving, becomes something that almost stands apart from the persons themselves. They can talk about their relationship. They can let other people in on their relationship and give their relationship to other people. That's precisely what a mother and father should do for their child. Children who receive that gift are the healthiest and most secure children.

I tell young people who are considering life together, I want you not to hoard your relationship. Give it to the community. Draw others into that space between you, into the way you relate, the enjoyment you have, the experiences you have. Don't always just be a twosome off in the corner.

God isn't a twosome off in the corner. There is enough space between the giving of the Creator and the Redeemer to let all of the cosmos in between, and that's us, the Church. The Church is what's created in the give and take between the Father and the Son. That's the first creed of the Church: The Spirit proceeds from the Father and the Son. The Spirit *is* the relationship between the Father and the Son, and we exist in the passion of that exchange. Think about that—forever.

from *The Price of Peoplehood*

Our Identity in Christ

You have died, and now the life you have is hidden with Christ in God. But when Christ is revealed—and he is your life—you too will be revealed in all your glory with him. (Colossians 3:3-4, JB)

Can you move below the surface to who you are objectively? That's what our Baptism was meant to announce to us: our identity in Christ. We are called to move back to that place of our identity in Christ—who we really are—whether we've done a single thing right our whole life. We hear about it in the story of the good thief. He had done everything wrong with his life. But at the moment of encounter with Christ, he was able to affirm a place of union and a place of identity, a place of trust. The Lord says, "Because you're living out of that place, you're already in paradise." What a challenge to our notions of holiness!

Right behavior does not necessarily lead to true identity, but true identity will eventually produce right behavior. The first *looks* like holiness; the second *is*.

from *Preparing for Christmas With Richard Rohr*

The Flotsam of Feelings

The life of prayer is the primary school of the Spirit. What we're doing in prayer is not creating successes; we're waiting upon the Lord. We're tuning into the stream of life and waiting to let that stream unburden itself of distractions and baggage. If you don't keep jumping on those ships that cross our minds during prayer, if you don't overidentify with the flotsam bobbing down the stream, they stop returning.

Try it. If you've identified all your life with your feelings and your opinions, that flotsam will keep coming by and expect you to jump on it. Stop doing that for awhile. It'll come by a second time and say, "Maybe you didn't see me the first time. Here I am. I am the relationship you always get angry about. I want you to get angry again so you can waste the rest of your morning." And this time you look at it and say, "I don't need you. Float on by."

Don't fight it. That's very important. We were trained to fight distraction. Yet there is no such thing as a distraction; everything is data. Look at it and then see if you can stay on the bank of the stream and name the feeling, feel the feeling and let it go by.

It'll probably come by even a third time, maybe even a fourth or a fifth, if you've indulged this feeling for years. But after a while you notice that it stops floating by in the stream of consciousness. "I'm not going to get anywhere with him! I'm not going to get anywhere with her. She's not going to feed me." And then you'll get to the holy place, beyond feelings, beyond opinions, beyond the passing world: the place where all things are One.

from *Preparing for Christmas With Richard Rohr*

The Four Stages of a Man's Life

People in India recognize four stages of male life. The first stage is student, where one is a learner and takes in life. The second stage is the householder, where he marries, raises children and learns to love and be faithful to his wife.

We Westerners for some strange reason consider this second stage to be the whole deal and the end of all life. People spend the remainder of their life fixing up the house, waiting for their children and then grandchildren to come home and visit them.

The third stage is called the seeker, or forest dweller. This is one who, after raising a family, takes them and moves beyond the nuclear family to a bigger world picture.

The question for most Americans today is, Who is going to get me a job next week? Who can keep the economy going next month? That's how farsighted we are, that's how big of a global consciousness we have. We're not connected to the rest of the world; we're not connected to anything except next week. It's hedonistic, it's a-historical, it's spiritually blind, and it keeps all of us from the fourth stage: the wise man, who puts the inner life together with the outer life, the small family together with the big family. Mahatma Gandhi personified this male journey. The sage, or wise man, thinks globally but lives and acts locally.

from A Man's Approach to God

Mellow Seventy-Year-Olds

I hope you have met a man who has become one of those mellow seventy-year-olds. I've met a few, not enough really. It's a shame we expect people in their seventies to be crotchety and set in their ways; it should be just the opposite.

When you have met him, you know you have met a great person. He's the real image of the grandfather or wise man, who can sit on the edge of the family and offer it security and caution. He doesn't stifle others with closedness and rigidity, dogmatic political opinions, or an Archie Bunker worldview. Rather, he offers a worldview in which we will feel both *safe* and *adventurous*.

Because most fathers don't have that kind of grandfather around, they bear the whole burden of life alone. They end up eventually becoming crotchety grandfathers themselves, and move to a better climate to find the sunshine.

We have to change this whole cycle. There has to be a different way. No civilization has survived spiritually unless the elders saw it as their *central task* to pass on wisdom to the young.

from *A Man's Approach to God*

Masculine Energy

The deep masculine is love for the truth like the love of John the
Baptist. You love the truth no matter what the price of it is, no
matter how many you displease. You stand by your principles
even if you don't get promoted or rewarded, applauded or
hugged, even if you are a lone voice crying in the wilderness. John
is shouting the truth in the desert, frankly because no one in civil
society will listen to him. It's how a lot of people felt during the
Persian Gulf War.

   If we don't have a lot of truth-speakers in our country, or in
our Church, I think it can in part be explained by the lack of
masculine energy—this lack of determination to go with what
you have got to go with, pay the price for it and let the cards fall
where they may. Many more women than men have this energy,
especially in the Church.

from A Man's Approach to God

Acting Versus Reacting

Most people I've known in my lifetime react, they do not act. They
spend their whole life reacting to circumstances and always
consider themselves the victim of circumstances. Seldom do you
see anybody choosing: This is what I want my life to be, and this

is the ten-year plan to where the family is going to go.

It was so inspiring to me when some of our young families of the New Jerusalem Community did just that: They decided to hold their level of consumerism in their family at their 1975 salary or whatever it might have been. They decided that was enough to live a comfortable life and any raises that came after that would just be icing. They wouldn't add to their consumption; they would find more ways to be generous and give it away. Now those are people with direction, with purpose, who are living out of real gospel values, not reacting but acting, choosing, deciding.

from *A Man's Approach to God*

Sixteenth Sunday of Ordinary Time   Day 276

Centered People

The greatest gift of centered and surrendered people is that they know themselves as part of a larger history, a larger self. In that sense, centered people are profoundly conservative, knowing that they only stand on the shoulders of their ancestors and will be shoulders for the generation to come. Yet they are, paradoxically, open and reformist because they have no private agendas or self-interest to protect.

People who have learned to live from their center know which boundaries are worth maintaining and which can be surrendered. Both reflect an obedience. If you want a litmus test for truly centered people, that's it: They are always free to obey reality, to respond to what is.

from *Radical Grace*, "Center and Circumference"

The Church in America

The overriding gift of the Catholic Church in America is that it is honestly in search of authentic spiritual authority. That may seem rather strange for a people who want to consider themselves free-thinking, self-determined and highly democratic people. And yet that is probably the very reason we are on such a desperate search. Our very individualism has given us a profound need for Someone else to trust. Our self-centered life-styles drive us back to a center that is in fact the Center. Our freedom from kings, popes and dictators leaves us free to desire a worthy Lordship.

Maybe we say it differently than the past tradition would have, but we would not fuss and bother with all of these miters and tiaras if we did not deeply desire a true spiritual authority that could truly unite us around common values, virtues and a common good. Obviously and rightly it is a longing for God. Our fierce independence and healthy mistrust of authority for its own sake put our American Church into a position to help the universal Church uncover and trust real spiritual authority. That authority is based in inherent truth and radical gospel—instead of limited appeals to right, power, philosophy and parental put-downs like, "Because I said so, that's why!"

The spiritual authority that the Church in America seeks is pragmatic authority that achieves its purpose. We cannot trust authority that claims to speak for God but does not achieve spiritual ends: Does it heal, forgive, reconcile, mend, restore, renew, enliven, awaken, integrate and validate the deepest human intuitions? Does it renew marriage relationships, does it reconcile countries, does it fill people with real hope and tangible joy? Is it an authority that is capable of self-criticism and seeking Kingdom values beyond self-congratulation and self-preservation? If not, I see no reason why I should trust it or surrender my only life to it.

As Jesus clearly taught us, we could distinguish the true and false prophets by one simple criterion: their fruits. The American Catholic is too independent, honest and commonsense to bow before ascribed and acquired authority when it is not also real authority.

And what is real authority? Leadership (and I do believe in the right and necessity of leadership!) and membership both owe one another holiness. That is the full authority of the Body of Christ.

from "The Future of the American Church"

Tuesday of the Sixteenth Week of Ordinary Time   Day 278

Reclaiming Authority

I believe the Catholic Church in America has the gift and the potential to redeem the intuitive Catholic respect for authority and to rediscover its base and power. There is no evidence in the Scriptures or in the founding and renewing of religious orders that God works outside or against the function of authoritative leadership. In fact, the recent histories of religious life say that there are no examples whatever of religious orders being founded or refounded by chapters, votes, groups, discussions, mission statements or anything other than individuals with an intrinsically authoritative vision and call. We call them charisms. I suggest that we refine and educate our awareness of charism, particularly the charism of leadership.

from "The Future of the American Church"

Wax Wings

Our shadow is somehow the other side of our gift. If Mercury is our gift-image, I guess I would have to say that Icarus is our shadow-image. As you may remember, Icarus is the other mythological son with wings, but his inflated self-image leads him to fly too close to the sun, revealing and melting the wax that holds his wings together. His pride, his non-listening, his false self-assurance are shown forth as he crashes into the sea.

In our case, Icarus is the American Catholic Church that is more American than Catholic, more individualistic than communitarian, more anti-authoritarian than authoritative, more psychological than radically gospel, more into freedom of choice than the real and disciplined freedom of the children of God. The wax of such wings is sure to melt because it is not gospel. Our shadowy tendencies are very difficult to describe and very hard not to be defensive about. I ask you to pray for the grace and gift of ego-detachment, so we can all move to a wider and wiser place where the future of the American Catholic Church can reveal itself.

from "The Future of the American Church"

The Rise of Fundamentalism

The foundation of fundamentalism is fear. When people feel distance from the Father, they may feel they can't trust him because he is hard and out to get them. When they believe they can't please the Father, they get into what the Church has so often gotten into, in almost every denomination, the merit/demerit system. They need to make sure they are right with the distant Father.

In Catholicism it takes the form of legalism and near idolatry of the institution. In Protestantism, at least today, it takes the form of fundamentalism. Fundamentalism creates a system of words, bible quotes and techniques for salvation that are supposedly certain, so you can always know the ground on which you stand and keep the feared Father on your side. It's very popular today in America, and wherever else the family system is collapsing and fathers are absent or abusive.

I would say that people who are attracted to fundamentalism are suffering from a lack of masculine energy, a lack of union with the Father. When you are in union with the Father, you don't need petty certitudes to overcome your fear. You can relax with God; you can even feel free to make mistakes. You resonate with the words of the Father, "This is my beloved son, in whom I am well pleased," and such perfect love casts out all fear (1 John 4:18).

from *A Man's Approach to God*

Father's Day Cards

When I was giving priests' retreats in Peru, a sister working in the main prison in Lima told me a story I have never forgotten. She said as Mother's Day was approaching, the prisoners kept asking for Mother's Day cards. She brought card after card so they could write to Mama. As Father's Day approached she decided to be better prepared. She brought in an entire case of Father's Day cards, so she could give them to the prisoners when they asked. She told me that case is still sitting in her office because no one asked for a Father's Day card. She couldn't *give* them away.

My friend looked at me with tears in her eyes because she understood the source of so much suffering. She realized so many of the men were in prison because they had never been told who they were, they had never been believed in by a man. So they moved into a violent and false masculinity, the destructive masculinity that occurs when one's manhood is not affirmed by other men.

I wonder if the jails and prisons of the world would not be much emptier if young boys had true mentors, guides and fathers to bless them and initiate them into manhood.

from *A Man's Approach to God*

The Price of Greatness

Ira Progoff says historically, culturally, he can prove that the only people who really achieved any greatness have been people who have agreed to live with a certain degree of stress in their lives. Now we have made stress somewhat of a bad word in recent years. We have stress workshops, and we all know you go to a certain point and stress isn't good. But in fact, lack of stress isn't good either. Our culture allows us constantly to coddle ourselves. We're always getting away from one thing or another because we need to relax. The price we may pay for that is greatness. Masculinity seems instinctively to sense this need for a certain hardness, obstruction and necessary stress. You see it in men's myths, their sports, their attitude toward childrearing. It's half of the truth, although largely rejected by contemporary liberal thinking. Masculinity senses that criticism, trial and non-affirmation are also a way of testing the mettle and thus affirming the one tested.

Masculine human nature needs to have a certain goad, an irritant that it's butting itself up against to fashion a creative tension. There is a direct correlation between the degree of imagination and the degree of creative stress in someone's life. We now have a positive word for this experience: *eustress.*

The peace of God is not the comfortable avoidance of all stress. True peace has room enough for all kinds of difficulties.

from *A Man's Approach to God*

To Be Biblical

To be biblical is not simply to quote the Bible. We need to tell that to the fundamentalists. To be biblical is not to quote Moses; it's to do what Moses did. To be biblical is to do what Abraham did; it's not to quote the Abraham story. It's to do what Jesus did; it's not simply to quote Jesus. Christians are to be in touch with the same God Jesus was in touch with, the same wisdom tradition Jesus drew insight from. We are to be building that same unity and creating the same life that Jesus was creating and building. That's what it means to be biblical.

I don't see Moses quoting the Bible. I don't see Jesus quoting the Bible as much as pointing to reality. That's exactly why the people said, "He's not like the scribes and Pharisees" (Mark 1:22). He "teaches with authority" (Mark 1:27). But he didn't do that by justifying everything he said with a Bible quote, which proves only a lack of authority, the inner authority of truth.

The Bible is that two thousand-year graph of "listening history" that helps us guide ourselves into the future. It reveals and names the patterns that connect all things, the rhythms and seasons of faith. Jesus read reality, listened to God, gathered the tradition and then spoke truth. Now if we're truly Catholic, it seems to me that's what we've got to aim for: to be biblical by gathering the wisdom of the ages. I'm not trying to take away the authority of this book but to ground it. Its reference point is outside itself.

from *The Price of Peoplehood*

The Holy Land Looks a Lot Like Home

(Recorded at Nazareth) The Gospel stories take on a new and beautiful significance as we stand and we celebrate in the very spot in which Mary lived and said yes to God. It was within three hundred yards of this spot that Mary and Joseph came to the life of faith that we now have come to participate in. I'm sure as you drive today across these very ordinary-looking hills, these very ordinary-looking villages and people, it must strike you, How could Mary, Joseph, anybody, have thought they were special?

We've idealized this land all our lives. And perhaps one of the great graces of a journey to the Holy Land is in fact to see that it's not only ordinary but perhaps not as pretty as many parts of the world. What makes it beautiful to our eyes is what happened here. As you see these little boys running around Nazareth, as you see young girls walking through these streets and young men in working clothes, it probably was no different in Jesus' time. And yet that woman Mary, that man Joseph, had to believe that they were the special ones of God. And that little boy Jesus who grew up in this town somehow had to dare to believe that he was God's son.

The word that comes to me at this place of the incarnation, this place where Mary said yes and the word became flesh, this place where they grew up in such ordinary circumstances, is a word of extraordinary faith. If they could believe, perhaps we can believe in our very ordinary-looking lives that God could somehow be taking flesh in us.

from On Pilgrimage With Father Richard Rohr

In the Land of Francis

(Recorded at Assisi) St. Francis, at the end of his life, said if he had to do one thing over, he would treat Brother Ass, which is what he called his body, a little better. But what characterizes all saints is a sort of fanaticism, a single-mindedness. They know one thing is important, and they hold onto that with a kind of feverish urgency and concern. Being in Assisi helps us to see St. Francis as a real person. He had to walk back to that piazza in the clothes of a dropout and have his old friends laugh at him. He had to walk through these streets and not be received, even by most of the established Church here who thought he was a nut. A fool, they called him. And he called himself that after awhile, the "idiot of God."

After awhile he moved outside the walls. He rebuilt a little church at San Damiano and there he heard Jesus speak to him. He lived outside the city a little, at Rivotorto and at the Portiuncula because the people here thought he was useless and disrespectful of his father and the proven economic system. Little did they think that eight hundred years later they would still be living off of him, as tourists from all over the world buy pictures and statues of Francis of Assisi.

from *On Pilgrimage With Father Richard Rohr*

Francis Stands for Love Emptying Itself

History eventually turns itself upside down. In the moment, the saint is never understood. So we had best be careful whom we name saint and devil. We had best listen because sometimes saints come in ways we are not prepared for.

Francis wanted one thing above everything else: the poor Jesus. So he went to the caves, dressed in the ragged tunic and let the people call him foolish. Even in his age he saw the importance of being poor. He saw how the Church was being destroyed by its own riches.

Above all else Francis stands for love, but love that empties itself, love that is so secure that it can be poor. It can let go of its reputation, securities, money. Francis in every age will be called the little poor man. He was free enough to be poor. He named his community "the brothers of the lower class" (friars minor). He changed sides intentionally. Today we call that taking a "preferential option for the poor."

We Americans stand for the upper class on this earth. Let us ask for ourselves and for our country the gift of poverty, the freedom to be poor. If we have not heard that, we have not heard Francis. All the rest is sentimentality—"birdbath Franciscanism."

from On Pilgrimage With Father Richard Rohr

Lepers and Wolves

It's wonderful news, brothers and sisters, that we come to God not by our perfection but by our imperfection. Because that gives all of us the only chance we'll ever have. And it allows us to walk, instead of a sometimes-journey of repression or denial, a journey into truth, into ever-deeper sympathy with what's going on inside of us. Deep within each of us live a leper and a wolf. Those are the two images that have caught the imagination of the world about Francis. We've pictured them but never internalized them. We always pictured meetings out there: Francis meeting the leper on the road, Francis taming the wolf in Gubbio. The stories did happen historically, but first they operate in the soul.

It is on the inside that lepers and wolves are first to be found. If we haven't been able to kiss many lepers, if we haven't been able to tame many wolves, it's probably because we haven't made friends with our leper and wolf within. Name your poor leper within, today. Nurse and tend her wounds. Name your inner wolf. Tame him by gentle forgiveness.

from *Embracing Christ As Francis Did: In the Church of the Poor*

The First Franciscan Community

(Recorded at the Portiuncula) There are many romantic pictures of Franciscans loving one another, praying together and lifting their hands to God. But I'm sure in this place, around this little chapel where their huts first stood, there were many days of complete doubt and disillusionment; feelings of dislike—maybe even of hatred—toward one another; doubt of their vocation in the Lord; feelings of anger; temptations of desire, lust, passion and fear—all the temptations that human beings experience.

The first Franciscans were no different from any of us. But somehow, they remembered the one commandment that the Lord gave us, which is to love one another. How can we more deeply love one another? The first Franciscans put their lives together, and they remained together. They said we're gonna stick with it until we become one. We're gonna remain together until we can walk through these barriers to love.

That will come up in every marriage, in every attempt at union and every attempt at community. We begin to see the dark parts of one another, those parts that we do not like. The way we learn to love is by walking *through* those: not around by avoidance, not underneath by spiritualizing, not over by denial—but through by incarnation.

from *On Pilgrimage With Father Richard Rohr*

Women-Stuff

"Women-stuff" is the hidden energy behind almost all of the justice issues. The movement toward nonviolence and disarmament, the movement against homelessness and refugee problems, the raping of the earth and its resources, sexual and physical abuse, the idolatry of profit and the corporation, the rejection of the poor—none of these will move beyond the present impasse until the underlying issues of power, prestige and possessions are exposed for the lie that they are.

Humanity's capacity to disguise its own darkness seems endless. Patriarchal logic is only logic in favor of the system and the status quo—which is proudly called the "real world." Believe me, because I always hear it quoted to me after my sermons, usually from polite men in three-piece suits: "That was an interesting talk there 'Father,' but you know in the real world...." The fathers of the system hate nothing more than another father who refuses the rules of the game. That is precisely our role in proclaiming the new system that Jesus called the Reign of God.

from Radical Grace, "Is This 'Women-Stuff' Important?"

Woman: Half of God's Work of Art

All this "women-stuff" is not only important, it is half of conversion, half of salvation, half of wholeness, half of God's work of art. I believe this mystery is imaged in the Woman of the twelfth chapter of the Apocalypse: "pregnant, and in labor, crying aloud in the pangs of childbirth...and finally escaping into the desert until her time" (12:1-6).

Could this be the time? It is always the time! The world is tired of Pentagons and pyramids, empires and corporations that only abort God's child. This women-stuff is very important, and it's always been important: more than this white male priest ever imagined or desired! My God was too small and too male. Much that the feminists are saying is very prophetic and necessary for the Church and the world. It is time for the woman to come out of her desert refuge and for the men to welcome her.

from *Radical Grace*, "Is This 'Women-Stuff' Important?"

We Are Deeply Hurt People

If there's one teaching of the Church that I've grown to appreciate, it's the concept of Original Sin. I have less and less doubt that all of us are infected with some kind of tragic flaw, that all of us are deeply wounded at the core.

I never really used to think that way. I came out of the very optimistic, Chardinian worldview. Now, after seven years building community, I've seen too many jolly, fine, together people come on the scene and think they were perfect people. After three months, I'd see they're just like all the rest of us. There hasn't been an exception in seven years.

We all are deeply hurt people, and we've all been infected. People are not whole and yet they constantly long for holiness, for wholeness. That's why Jesus' call to holiness is paralleled by the healing ministry. In fact, you could say that's almost all Jesus does: preach and heal, preach and heal, preach and heal. For the mature ones, the preaching is already healing and the healing is its own sermon.

from *The Price of Peoplehood*

Real Vacations

There are two types of passivity. First, there's laziness. That is largely avoidance, an aimless kind of moving around and saying, "I gotta rest." Why is it that so much recreation we take is not really re-creation? It does not really renew our spirit. A lot that people call a vacation is simply diversion, or distraction from a life that is already one big distraction. It's finding another kind of stimulation than the usual stimulation we have. We say, I'm not gonna do anything, I'm on vacation. But that isn't the true recreation that re-creates, the true vacation that vacates the overstuffed apartment.

A real vacation should encourage real inner passivity. True leisure, true emptiness, is, in fact, a vigilance, a listening, a waiting. It's a strong inner activity. And the irony is, this kind of passivity is the most disciplined activity. Thus the contemplatives were often the greatest activists.

Freedom comes when you can be and let be. Then you appear to be passive, but in fact you're operating out of a strong inner activity. On the other hand, some people who are really moving and achieving are not really active people at all. They're extremely passive people, following the collective herd of trends and dictated fashions, deaf and dumb inside.

from *The Price of Peoplehood*

Positive Passion

We live a long time in order to become lovers. God is like a good parent, refusing to do our homework for us. We must learn through trial and error. We have to do our homework ourselves, the homework of suffering, desiring, winning and losing, hundreds of times.

Loss is one of the greatest occasions of passionate feeling, and it's one that is socially acceptable. When we lose a beloved friend, wife, husband, child, parent, or maybe a possession or a job, we feel OK to be passionate. But we must broaden that. We've got to get to a passion that is also experienced when we *have* it, not just when we're losing it. And we have it all the time. Don't wait for loss to feel, suffer, enjoy deeply.

from *The Passion of God and the Passion Within*

Render Unto Rome...

Don't give Rome more authority than it was ever intended to have. Jesus told Peter to preserve the brothers in *faith* (see Luke 22:31-32). Jesus didn't say anything to Peter about preserving them in love or hope. The role of the bishop of Rome is to keep us united in the tradition of *faith*. We are preserved in love by the example of the suffering people of the world. Hope is given to us by prophets—prophetic movements and communities. When we put all of that on Rome we ask to be disappointed.

Once I was able to accept Rome's central, visible and important gift, while also realizing Rome does not have all the gifts, I didn't need to get so angry and disappointed with the Vatican. I go ahead with my Christian life. I hope I'm free to say yes and give them a due hearing. However, I also have my own prayer life. I have my conscience; I have my own study of the Scripture that I've done together with my Franciscan community, scholars and my lay community. I have to trust these hearings. I have to trust my inner authority as a complement to that outer authority. As Cardinal Newman put it, "I toast the pope, but I toast human conscience first."

My prayer is that they overlap as much as possible. But when they don't, I have to go back to prayer and back to other wise people. That's why we need wise and authentically obedient people like Charles Curran, Dorothy Day and Archbishop Hunthausen—to help us form our consciences. The *first* principle of traditional Catholic morality is that "one must follow one's conscience."

from *Catholic Agitator*, "Creative Dissent"

Friday of the Eighteenth Week of Ordinary Time   Day 295

Freedom Versus Fear

You can never bring about the Kingdom of God by means of fear (see Romans 14:16-17). It is not the Kingdom of God if it is brought about by fear or coercion. God allows and respects the freedom of creatures, even to the point of rebellion and blasphemy! The realm of freedom is a prerequisite of virtue, just as it is of sin. It is God's great risk.

The freedom to fall is also the freedom to rise. It's precisely in our failure, our experience of poverty, weakness, emptiness that we come to experience God's restoration and healing love. You can say, Oh, that's dangerous, it sounds like you're justifying sin. But I'm just trying to be the ultimate realist. Salvation is sin overturned and outdone, as God expands and educates our true freedom. Free will and freedom of conscience are at the heart of the doctrine of grace and at the center of Christian morality.

from *The Price of Peoplehood*

Weeds and Wheat

The servants came to the owner of the field, and said, "Where did the weeds come from?" "An enemy has done this to us," he answered. And the servant said, "Do you want us to go and weed it out?" But he said, "No, because if you pull out the weeds, you will pull out the wheat with it. Let them both grow until the harvest, and at harvest time I will separate the two." (Matthew 13:28-30)

This passage has to be one of the most overlooked, least influential, yet most needed of Jesus' direct teachings. It presents the ambiguous character of reality in a way that we were not ready for, it seems. The image of the weeds and the wheat has had almost no effect on the development of our moral theology, our self-understanding, or our patience with all institutions and with one another. Folks now chase after the yin and yang of Eastern religions as if they are a new, honest teaching. As usual, Jesus already said it: We just didn't hear.

We did, at least, speak of the "Paschal Mystery" as *the* mystery of faith, and the new liturgy proclaims, "Christ has died, Christ is risen, Christ will come again." But even there, we don't often translate mythic language into the human patterns that myths point to. Maybe it never computed into "Half will be dark, half will be light, again and again." Or, "No matter where, when or what, life will be both agony and ecstasy."

The field contains both weeds and wheat, and we must let them grow together. How much time I have wasted in trying to pull out my weeds! You cannot really pull them out, but don't ever doubt they are there! Thus, the Sacrament of Penance is not the sacrament of the annihilation of sin, or even getting rid of sin. It is more *reconciliation with* and *forgiveness of* those dang weeds in the field.

from unpublished sermon notes

Nineteenth Sunday of Ordinary Time   Day 297

Prayer Advice

In order to discover the right rhythm of prayer for us, the prayer that works with our temperament, we must listen to the ways that God speaks to us. How do you best slow down and enter into the dialogue of revelation and response? It's different for each of us.

You may need a holy spot, perhaps a place where God has spoken to you before. Maybe it's out in nature, maybe it's a certain chair or before the Blessed Sacrament. Maybe it's in the last pew in church. It's that place where you can return to and sort of settle back and seek God's face. That's the simplest form of prayer: Each day simply seek, for a moment, if possible, the face of God. Know that you've looked at God eyeball to eyeball, and you've let God look at you.

If you're more the thinking type, ideas will lead you into that revelation-and-faith dialogue. Use a book, if that's your style. But don't think that reading the book is itself the dialogue. You've got to end by talking to God from your heart, person-to-person, with ordinary words like you'd talk to everybody else. Speak out of what you're really feeling, not what you think you're supposed to be feeling. If you're feeling depression, failure, competition, that's what you bring to God. Everything is data. There are no such things as distractions.

from *The Price of Peoplehood*

Monday of the Nineteenth Week of Ordinary Time   Day 298

A Week of Prayers: Teach Us to Pray

Loving God, give us the gift of prayer. We want you to find us, and we want to find you. Teach us how to pray, Holy Spirit, and how not to be afraid of prayer. Give us the courage to reveal ourselves, because, Lord, you have not been afraid to reveal yourself. We need and want to expose our deepest heart to you, just as you have exposed your heart to us.

Free us from our fears. Put your arms around us and call us each by name. Call us daughter and son. Call us to yourself. Tell us it's OK, because we're so afraid, and we feel so bad about who we are. We long to be found out, Lord. Discover us, Lord. We want to reveal ourselves to you. And we want you to take us into your embrace. We pray together as your sons and daughters and we pray in Jesus' name. Amen.

from The Price of Peoplehood

Tuesday of the Nineteenth Week of Ordinary Time   Day 299

A Week of Prayers:
Help Us to Be Universal

Loving Creator, we want to be your people. We want to be your universal people, your catholic people. We want to be brothers and sisters to all of our brothers and sisters who eat of the same bread and drink of the same cup that we enjoy. Teach us how, Holy Spirit. Help us not to get in the way of this always-bigger thing that you are doing. Help us, teach us how to be ready to be Catholic. We trust in you, Lord Christ, that you are the Lord of our history and the Lord of our lives. We pray, trusting that you are both hearing and creating this prayer. We pray in the name of Jesus, whose Body we are. Amen.

from Letting Go: A Spirituality of Subtraction

A Week of Prayers: You Are Lord

Lord Christ, we salute you. We salute the love we do not understand. We wait for a love that we do not yet know. Help us, Lord, to stand under the cross and finally to understand. Give us, Lord, through the experiences of human life, the hearts to understand. We praise you. You are the loving Lord of history, and our knees will bend at your name, for you have created us out of nothing, loved us and saved us.

from *Days of Renewal*

A Week of Prayers: Make Us Signs of Hope

Spirit of God, Lord, again we come as sons and we need you; we come as daughters and we ask for your life. You are our God. You are our creator. You have made us something out of nothing. Free us so we no longer complain about what is not given. We know, God, what is given and we can no longer deny it. Make us signs of hope, Jesus, for this world, so that the world will not destroy itself. Give us faith to believe, Father, not in just some new, happy life, not in some good fortune in the future, but give us faith in the now that seems so empty.

Give us hope that you are what we suspect you should be:

love as we understand it. Mother, perhaps there is something else going on here. We dare to want to see it and want to believe it. Perhaps there is graciousness here. All we know is that we who were once nothing are now something, and you, God of life, have made it so. We are so grateful.

from *Days of Renewal*

Friday of the Nineteenth Week of Ordinary Time   Day 302

A Week of Prayers:
Prayer Over the Earth

Great Spirit God, you hovered over your creation from the very beginning. You also made a great gamble when you asked human beings to be stewards of this earth. You have withheld your hand as we have continued to misuse, overuse and pollute our Mother Earth. You have continued to create us and love us even though we have not always loved ourselves, our brothers and sisters, the many animals you have asked us to share this planet with, the plants, the water, the air. We ask your forgiveness, patient God, for our abuse of your many gifts. We ask that you give us eyes of love again for all living things, eyes of reverence for that which we did not create, eyes of healing for that which we have destroyed and overlooked.

As little Brother Francis tried to teach us, we praise you for Brother Sun, Sister Moon and all the stars. We praise you because of Brother Wind and Sister Air and the lovely clouds. We praise and thank you through Sister Water and Brother Fire. We praise you, God, Lover of all lives, for our sister, Mother Earth, who produces all our food, our medicine, our beautiful flowers. We live in constant thankfulness for all of Nature, which "bears the likeness of You, Most High."

We will start again, Holy Spirit, to re-create all things in beauty. Be with us—with your Eternal Beauty. Amen.

prayer at the 1991 conference on Francis and ecology

Saturday of the Nineteenth Week of Ordinary Time   Day 303

A Week of Prayers: Jesus Is Our Love

God of life, bless our days. Keep us alive and in love. Keep us listening. Keep us growing, Mother-God. Keep drawing us closer to you. Help our words, Father-God, not get in the way of your Spirit. Help the words we use not become too many or too confusing. Our faith, Holy One, is in *you* and not in any words or in any teaching. We just want these words to open us up to you and to your Spirit among us.

Help us not to be afraid of Jesus, the companion you have given us for our journey toward you. As St. Bernard prayed, "Jesus, our Lord, you are honey in our mouth. You are music in our ear. You are a leap of joy in our heart."

from *The Price of Peoplehood* and *Days of Renewal*

Your Name-place

God gives you two names: yours and God's. Listen for that place deep within where God has given you God's own name, that name lovers reveal to one another in intimate moments, where God has told you who God is for you. Who is God for you? It's unlike anybody else. You reflect a part of God that no one else will ever reflect. You reflect back to God a part of the mystery that no one else will understand.

Where God has given you God's intimate name, you also have been given your own name. It takes awhile; it takes some listening, some silence, some suffering, probably. It takes some waiting, desiring; it takes some hoping. But finally we discover that place where we know who we are; we know what God said.

That place-where-the-names-are-One, God's name and your name, that's the place of inner authority. That's the place where the Spirit is able to be heard and received. It's the only place big enough and grand enough to be able to believe the daring gospel of Christ.

I hope someone has given you freedom and permission to trust your own experience, to listen, and believe *your name*. It speaks and evokes you and no one else.

from *The Passion of God and the Passion Within*

Transformation and Change

There is a difference between change and transformation. Change happens when something old dies and something new begins. I am told that planned change is as troublesome to the psyche as unplanned change, often more so. We feel manipulated, forced, and impute it to some evil authorities, the change agents! But change might or might not be accompanied by transformation of soul. I'm afraid it usually is not. If change does not invite personal transformation, we lose our souls. Such is the modern malaise. We mass-produce neurotics and narcissists because there are so few medicine men and healing women and Spirit guides to walk us through transformation.

At times of change, the agents of transformation must work overtime, even though few will hear them. The ego would sooner play victim or too-quick victor than take the ambiguous road of transformation. We change-agents need a simple virtue: faith. It still is the rarest of commodities because it feels like *nothing*, at least nothing that satisfies our need to know, to fix, to manage, to understand. Faith goes against the grain.

Transformation in times of change is the exception, but it is also the norm. Deutero-Isaiah was written in exile; Francis of Assisi emerged as the first clocks turned time into money; and the martyrs of El Salvador spilled their blood during the last gasps of colonial and economic oppression. Nothing new seems to happen except when the old dies. But the old does not die gracefully: It always takes hostages. These have the potential of building bridges to the next coming of Christ.

from *Radical Grace*, "A Transitional Generation"

Child of the 60's

I do not know if it was an advantage or disadvantage to grow up in the 60's. Vision, hope, optimism and positive social change were the mood of the times. It was easy to believe that the Age of Aquarius was indeed upon us with its apex being a Vatican II Church and an enlightened America that would surely be the threshold of the coming Kingdom. Idealism seemed almost unchecked, open-ended and wonderful. All we had to do was get everyone educated and converted, and that was just a matter of time.

Now in 1992, the five hundredth anniversary of the European invasion of the Americas, things look different. It is hard to believe that the world could appear so changed in one lifetime. The values that we thought were roundly accepted are now roundly denied: racism is chic, war is a substitute for worship, materialism is the watertight myth, the poor are blamed for their condition, and religion, largely, is unimportant.

Were we wrong, or is this the price that one pays for false innocence? Is there such a thing as social progress? Must we take two steps back for each step forward? As you probably suspect, I now answer each of these with a humble yes. But I am very happy that I was formed in the lens-opening 60's, especially when I see the later alternatives. These alternatives threaten to close that lens through cynicism, discouragement, anger and darkness.

from *Radical Grace*, "A Transitional Generation"

The Divine Pickpocket

We can only dare to let go of evil in the presence of a perfect love. Don Quixote steals the shame of Aldonza by his continual respect for her. Love makes sin unnecessary and takes it away.

What do you think happens when God forgives your sin? Is it God changing suddenly, reassessing you? Is it God deciding to waive some eternal and required punishment? No! Nothing happens in God. God is a perfect given-ness, totally and always given, literally *fore-given*: ahead of time, before our act of faith.

God does not change; we change. Here is what's happening in the experience of forgiveness: When God's arms are tight enough around you, when for a moment you can believe in love, when you let God gaze into your eyes deeply enough and are ready to believe it, then you're able to let God rob you of your sin. God pulls it out of your pocket while holding you in her gaze!

from *Days of Renewal*

The First Temptation of Christ (Success)

I believe that all would-be ministers must face the same three temptations as Jesus before they really can minister. The first temptation of Christ, to turn stones into bread (Matthew 4:3), is the need to be effective, successful, relevant, to make things happen. You've done something and people say, "Wow! Good job! You did it right. You're OK." When the crowds approve, it's hard not to believe that we have done a good thing, and probably God's will.

Usually when you buy into that too quickly, you're feeding the false self and the system, which tells you what it immediately wants and seldom knows what it really needs. You can be a very popular and successful minister operating at that level. That is why Jesus has to face that temptation first, to move us beyond what we want to what we really *need*. In refusing to be relevant, in refusing to respond to people's immediate requests, Jesus says, Go deeper. What's the real question? What are you really after? What does the heart really hunger for? What do you really desire? "It's not by bread alone that we live" (Matthew 4:4).

from Preparing for Christmas With Richard Rohr

Friday of the Twentieth Week of Ordinary Time   Day 309

The Second Temptation of Christ (Righteousness)

The second temptation of Jesus: Satan takes him up to the pinnacle of the Temple, symbolizing the religious world, and tells him to play righteousness games with God. "Throw yourself off and he'll catch you" (Matthew 4:6). It's the only time when the devil quotes Scripture. The second temptation is the need to be right and to think of the self as saved, superior, the moral elite standing on God and religion, and quoting arguable Scriptures for your own purpose.

More evil has come into the world by people of righteous ignorance than by people who've intentionally sinned: Being convinced that one has the whole truth and has God wrapped up in my denomination, my dogmas and my right response (I am baptized, I made a personal decision for Jesus, I go to church).

It's not wrong to be "right." Once in a while if something works out, that's sure nice. The spiritual problem is the *need* to be right. We are called to do the truth and then let go of the consequences. One stops asking the question of spiritual success, which is the egocentrism of the rich young man: "What must *I* do to inherit eternal life?" (Mark 10:17). Jesus refused to answer him because it is the wrong question. It is again "the devil" quoting Scripture and not really wanting an answer, only affirmation.

As Mother Teresa loves to say, "We were not created to be successful [even spiritually successful!] but to be obedient." True obedience to God won't always make us look or feel right. Faith is dangerous business!

from *Preparing for Christmas With Richard Rohr*

Saturday of the Twentieth Week of Ordinary Time   Day 310

The Third Temptation of Christ (Control)

After the need to be successful and the need to think well of the self, the third human addiction is the need for control or power. So the devil tells Jesus to bow down before the systems of this world: "All of them you can have" (Matthew 4:8). Just buy them.

Believe in them. Jesus refuses to bow down before the little kingdoms of this world, the corporations and the nation-states, the security systems, the idols of militarism. The price of this love of power is to "fall at Satan's feet and worship him!" (Matthew 4:9). That's a very heavy judgment on "all the kingdoms of the world." In all these systems, self-interest *has* to dominate. For Kingdom people, self-interest *cannot* dominate.

Simply put, the third temptation is the need to be in control, to be aligned with power and money. The three temptations that Jesus faces, in a certain sense, all become one: the addictive system, the great lie, the untouchable mythology, "the sin of the world" (John 1:29) that must be unmasked and dethroned. And I know nothing strong enough to break the mythology—not ideology, not liberalism, not conservatism—except the upside-down gospel of Jesus. You must refound your life on a new foundation, the foundation of your experienced union with God.

Jesus tells Satan, " 'You must worship the Lord your God, and serve God alone.' And then the devil left him" (Matthew 4:10-11). When you have faced these three "biggies," Satan doesn't have a chance.

from *Preparing for Christmas With Richard Rohr*

The Baths at Lourdes

(Recorded at Lourdes) Being lowered into the baths at Lourdes is an act of humiliation and trust, an act of faith. Your mind wants to say, Why do this? What does this mean? What is this going to do? It seems everything in our life has to have an immediate, visible effect, or it hasn't "worked."

That attitude is a terrible enemy of faith because faith is not in the realm of the practical; faith means entering into the world of mystery, where deeper energies are at work, where transformation takes place even though nothing appears to change.

If we can enter into a deeper surrender in faith, like a child who can rejoice entertaining itself before its mother, then we can truly experience prayer together. We have to let go of our working ideas to play before the Lord, and in this shrine of Lourdes, to play before Mary. Only our humble, goal-less inner child can understand that.

[In fact, I was healed of seven years of severe hypoglycemia at Lourdes the day this was recorded, October 2, 1980. God is good!]

from *On Pilgrimage With Father Richard Rohr*

Respecting Our American Experience

The cultural experience of each country has to be respected and listened to, for God has spoken through the minds and hearts of each people. Each, I believe, holds different parts of the Great Mystery in special awareness.

If we're going to listen to the experience of our brothers and sisters in the Third World, I think, in fairness, we have to grant the same privilege to ourselves. We have to respect and listen to the only experience that we Americans have had. We have to trust it; we have to say, somehow there's some truth in it.

We must recognize the good in our society before we can eliminate the bad because good and evil are two sides of one coin. You can't recognize evil without recognizing good. You can't accept the one without, to some degree, accepting or at least understanding the other.

What is the American experience? What is our experience of life, for good and for ill? It's the only experience you and I have. I would list the essentially good values of American culture as: personalism, freedom and self-determination, pluralism, up-front honesty, democratic self-criticism, a not-so-bad emphasis on productivity and practical effect, and a natural egalitarianism that disdains caste systems in any form. These are all potentially gospel and part of the cosmic mystery of the Body of Christ.

The American experience has formed our psyche. God is willing to use these values. We must be willing to work with them, too, recognizing both their gift and their temptation.

from *Letting Go: A Spirituality of Subtraction*

Too Much Access

With so many time-saving devices, it doesn't make sense that people are so rushed. People seem to have so little time to do what they want. We've created tremendous accessibility to one another through the telephone, the car, mass transit, telegrams, postal service.

When I moved to Albuquerque, I got a phone-answering machine because I'm gone so much. I said, I must be crazy to be doing this! Now I'll go home and everybody I was able to get away from now will still be able to get at me. Earlier generations didn't—and other cultures still don't—have that access to one another. Sometimes, within the same day, I am speaking in two different parts of the world that in any former age would have required weeks to travel between them. It must be taking a toll on the psyche, on what is real, on our spiritual home. It is friendship and wisdom that seem to suffer.

Material affluence, ironically, creates scarcity of non-material things. Pope John Paul II said that very well when he first spoke to the United Nations. In a culture of affluence, he said, you will predictably see a decrease of spiritual values: time, knowledge, wisdom, love and friendship. Those decrease almost in mathematical proportion as you move toward materialism.

from *Letting Go: A Spirituality of Subtraction*

Checkbook Storytime

There is a couple I know who earn very good money, and yet they live simply, without any status symbols or luxuries, with money set aside for charity. It's a trimmed-down life for them and their six children.

Every month the mother gathers the six children around the checkbook. For each check that she writes to whomever it might be, to whatever cause or charity, she tells them a story: "This is why these people need it more than we need it." And so those kids actually know where the family money is going and that it isn't there in the bank account for them to buy a new toy.

The parents themselves are making choices not to have always new, better, more things. When the parents share those choices, the children are more willing to buy into them. They begin a process of solidarity (not without struggle, however!). At this point they are some of the most mature and responsible—and yet alive and real—children I'm aware of in their community.

I think the mother's check-writing process is probably the best form of religious education. The rubber has met the road. It's not highly metaphysical and spiritual; it's "Jesus means this. Commitment means this. Love means this." That's religious education.

Our checkbooks are probably our best theological statement about our real values. Jesus said, similarly, "Where your treasure is, there your heart will be also" (Matthew 6:21, JB).

from *Letting Go: A Spirituality of Subtraction*

Sharing the Pig

I had an experience in Guatemala similar to many others I've had in other Third World countries: As soon as you come to the village, in a very short time you will hear the squeal of a pig or the squawk of a chicken. They're killing it for you. They've been saving it for you. And sometimes you find out afterward that it was the last pig or chicken. The poor are so generous.

Hoarding traps you in a kind of scarcity mentality. But when you have little, for some reason you're willing to give it away and make a day of it. Saving and preserving is not your way of life. "This is it, the last pig. But Father came to town and we're going to celebrate," the people say. So they kill the pig, and then you sit there in that house for hours while they're cleaning and cooking the pig.

After you're finished eating with the people who were originally invited to the meal, there's lots left over. What would we do in our country? We have Tupperware and refrigerators. To save it would be a good, responsible thing to do: Don't waste food is our commandment. And we have the technology to do just that.

Here's a perfect example of how technology has a good side and a bad side. What have we lost by our refrigerators and freezers? Guatemalans immediately have to share the pig, the chicken with other people. Bringing food from one house to the next, which creates family, is a daily experience. It creates community and interdependence.

We North Americans don't need to do that because we can store it for ourselves. So it keeps us more and more inside our houses where everything is mine, and it needs to be protected from you. Our politics of scarcity and individual responsibility leads us to become more and more isolated, independent and competitive. The poor have an amazing politics of abundance precisely because they can rely upon the group and are not as tempted to securing for the future. Our biases see this as irresponsibility, but the poor actually are closer to faith, community and the Kingdom of God.

from *Letting Go: A Spirituality of Subtraction*

Announce the Gospel

There is an unbelievable vitality in the Church in parts of Central America and Asia. There's such excitement about faith that I felt like staying there when I visited. When I said, "Maybe I should stay here," people, without exception, said, "No, go back to America. It's America that has to be converted and really recognize the gospel."

"We don't need you down here in Central America," as they'd jokingly say. "We're actually doing better without so many priests. You go back and preach the gospel in North America."

We're First World. We are a people who have been graced unbelievably on many levels. And there's no point in feeling guilty about that, but ours is the large middle-class Church, and the mentality that goes with that must be challenged by the gospel. Our center in New Mexico has taken this as its task. Until the middle-class Church sees life from the Jesus side (the underside), much of the world will continue to live as our de facto slaves, subsidizing our life-style and our illusions.

from *Letting Go: A Spirituality of Subtraction*

Beatitudes People

How blessed are the poor in spirit:
the kingdom of heaven is theirs.
Blessed are the gentle:
they shall have the earth as inheritance.
Blessed are those who mourn:
they shall be comforted.
Blessed are those who hunger and thirst for uprightness:
they shall have their fill.
Blessed are the merciful:
they shall have mercy shown them.
Blessed are the pure in heart:
they shall see God.
Blessed are the peacemakers:
they shall be recognized as children of God.
Blessed are those who are persecuted in the cause of
uprightness:
the kingdom of heaven is theirs.

Blessed are you when people abuse you and persecute you and
speak all kinds of calumny against you falsely on my account.
Rejoice and be glad, for your reward will be great in heaven; this
is how they persecuted the prophets before you. (Matthew
5:3-12, NJB)

(Recorded at Lourdes) Something is happening at Lourdes. And
God wants to give us the eyes to see it and the ground to receive
it. What are all these crippled and handicapped people telling us?
What is the witness of all these nurses and life-bearers? It seems
God wants us to live a vulnerable life, a life dependent on other
people, a life that is unafraid to cry.

"Happy are those who hunger and thirst for justice," Jesus
says.

The little ones are able to see what is happening. These are
the ones who, when there is something more, will be ready.

Because the numb do not notice. The sophisticated will not suffer. The comfortable need not complain. But Jesus teaches us, in effect, how to suffer graciously. He actually *increases* our capacity for pain. This is the central message of the eight Beatitudes.

What kind of God is this? It is a God who increases our capacity to feel the pain of being human, a God who allows deformities and tragedies so we can all be bound together in a sisterhood of need, a brotherhood of desire.

from *On Pilgrimage With Father Richard Rohr*

Twenty-Second Sunday of Ordinary Time   Day 318

What God Has to Work With

The Lord cares, despite all of our silliness. We are the kind of being God loves. God's love doesn't depend on our doing nice or right things. Yet it's an illusion to think that any of us would operate totally beyond self-interest. Realistically, every action of our life is filled with self. That's human nature, and it's probably OK as long as we're honest about it.

For example, I have become tired of giving talks. As it does for everyone, my gift has become my curse. But at the same time I'd be lying if I didn't say that I gain some kind of ego satisfaction: I stand in front of crowds, and it makes me feel good. That's OK as long as I recognize my mixed motives and self-interest. That's the only way God gets anyone to do anything! It's legitimate and probably necessary self-interest.

What concerns me is when we say we're doing it *all* for Jesus, or purely for love, or for our spouse or children, or for the

Church. That's usually a delusion. We're doing it in part for ourselves, and God, in great love and humility, says, "That's what I work with. That's *all* I work with!" It's the mustard seed with which God does great things. Thank God!

True recognition of our basic egotism is a humbling experience, but a liberating one, too.

from *Letting Go: A Spirituality of Subtraction*

Monday of the Twenty-Second Week of Ordinary Time   Day 319

The Liberation of Men

Our liberation as men is different from feminine liberation. What our sisters are fighting—patriarchal culture—has oppressed women in so many ways, but men didn't realize it because we were on top. We must stand at our sisters' side to begin to understand their struggle. Yet men have their own liberation agenda, too.

Western men need liberation from the whole set of expectations that culture puts upon us and we put upon ourselves: to be overachievers, competitive, focused and necessarily unfeeling, successful, hard-and-strong cannon fodder for wars. That pressure is instilled from boyhood, both by women and other men. Both men and women profit from it; both men and women suffer from it.

Our liberation is to recognize and counter these voices inside us that give us false definitions of success. That may be even a more difficult form of liberation than women's. I think that is why men are behind in the process of liberation. One is more trapped at the top. At least that's what the gospel says.

In family after family, the woman has moved in her masculine journey farther than most of us men have moved into our feminine journey. A lot of men intuitively recognize that their wife is stronger in many ways than they are. In many families she knows how to organize life or get things done better than her husband. That becomes the pattern of the family. She becomes an androgynous person, really in her own way much more liberated than the man. The man stands on the side, earning money to support the whole system and losing the respect of his children, his wife, and often himself.

It has been much harder, culturally, for men to journey into their feminine side than for women to integrate their masculine. We need our sisters to recognize our entrapment.

from *A Man's Approach to God*

Tuesday of the Twenty-Second Week of Ordinary Time   Day 320

Love Unfolds in Solidarity

We had a refugee in our community once—Fernando from El Salvador—and many of us heard his story. It's just unbelievable that any human being could endure the suffering and torture that he has experienced from his own government—which we support with U.S. funds.

There is a possibility that, down the line, he could be sent back home. Members of the community have said to me that if they felt the government was going to try to take him back to almost certain death, they know they would have to stand in solidarity with him, even against U.S. law. They said they would gather down in the worship space and stand around him: "If they are going to take him, they will have to take us too!" They know the bond, understanding, friendship that they have with him. There would be no human alternative.

There is no big ideology in that. There is no leftist or rightist politics. It's finally just compassion and solidarity with friends and victims, and a willingness to pay the price for that friendship. Maybe we just need to build relationships beyond racial and class lines. Justice would soon follow.

from *A Man's Approach to God*

Grandfather Energy

A man of deep male energy is a truster of life. To be trusting is not to be naive; it is to make judgments, recognizing what is life and what is death. Once you clarify what is life and what is death, you will be able to trust both of them. People who can't distinguish between death and life can't trust reality.

Trust is not making a virtuous decision; it's not a leap of faith without any evidence. It's recognizing that every human situation is a mixture of both life and death, that the big truths usually are complicated truths. We are a mixture of darkness and light, life and death. Every action we perform has some quality of life to it, yet some quality of fear and self-protection. When we can accept that there is no perfect anything, we can find peace in this world. As Jesus put it, "God alone is good" (Mark 10:18).

It takes a monumental act of courage and a tremendous humility to accept a paradoxical world. I think that is what "grand" fathers (and "grand" mothers!) can do. You probably don't come to this full balance much before fifty years of age.

from *A Man's Approach to God*

Gandhi's Place

If you want to smell the aroma of Christianity, you must copy the rose. The rose irresistibly draws people to itself, and the scent remains with them. Even so, the aroma of Christianity is subtler even than that of the rose and should, therefore, be imparted in an even quieter and more imperceptible manner, if possible.—Mahatma Gandhi

Gandhi's rose is a magnificent image. The quiet and imperceptible authority of the rose comes from its beauty and lovely fragrance. It does not need to prove itself or convert you to its side. It knows it is a rose, and it knows it is beautiful.

If you have a nose and an eye for beauty, you will recognize the inherent authority of the rose. In fact, its inner authority might well be so pressing and demanding that you might say to the rose, as did St. Francis de Sales, "Stop shouting!"

If Christianity relied on its inner authority, the weight of its truth and the sheer power of genuine goodness, the world would also say to Christians, "I hear you—stop shouting!" And we would not have preached a sermon or spoken a single word.

The powers of the world, who are always fighting deadlines,

management goals and profit scales, do not expect to be motivated from within. They must produce, fix and accomplish, and that is one helpful *part* of life.

What about us? The author of life bids us share in divine freedom and authority. This will take longer, but it will also last longer, and this God seems to be building for the long haul. God waits, as only God can wait, because God knows the whole picture. Those with true authority can believe because they know that they know. And the rose can both blossom and die because she knows that she is a rose.

from *Sojourners*, "Authors of Life Together"

Friday of the Twenty-Second Week of Ordinary Time   Day 323

The Message of Job

Job, from the Hebrew Scriptures, can be for Christians a beautiful symbol of the Calvary that each of us will go through. In the story's first chapter Job is presented as the innocent man, confronted with evil and suffering. He has obeyed the law of God, he has been faithful. Satan comes before God and says: "Sure, he's been faithful. You have blessed him. Take everything away from him and see if he still praises you" (1:9-11).

Very well, says Yahweh. So Yahweh takes everything away from him, and still Job says: "Naked I came from my mother's womb, naked I shall return. Yahweh gave, Yahweh has taken back. Blessed be the name of Yahweh" (1:21, JB).

So Satan goes again before Yahweh and says: "You took away just the external things. But destroy his bone and flesh. Make his body suffer, then see if Job will still not curse you" (2:4-5). So Yahweh gives Job ulcers and diseases of the skin. But still Job refuses to curse Yahweh. Now the stage is set for the drama. Job is tempted to curse his life. He struggles with the absurdity and the meaninglessness of life but finally says, "If we take happiness from God's hand, must we not take sorrow too?" (2:10, JB).

Brothers and sisters, if you're seeking to lead a good life, sooner or later every one of you is going to be led to that point. Every one of us is led, sooner or later, to the ashpit with Job "picking at our own sores" (2:8). At that time you will hear many voices (symbolized by the various advice-giving friends of Job). Pray that you know which friends to listen to and which are being "reasonable" at the price of faith.

The Book of Job probably represents the greatest moral dialogue ever written. The final response of Job does not come from logical moral reasoning but from graced personal experience.

from *The Great Themes of Scripture*

An Incarnation Analogy

We need signs of salvation. We who are well off have been given signs of the cross among us like the poor and the handicapped. We have to enter their world on their terms to love them. And the beautiful thing we discover is that we become free. We come at last to know who we are by looking in their eyes.

There was a television show called *Son Rise* about a couple who had an autistic child. They wanted their son to change and enter into their space. And they did everything they could to get that child to enter into their world and to be like them, the normal people. And then one day they realized they would have to enter *his* world.

It was nonsensical and grueling to do so. The mother entered into the child's world on his terms, day after day sitting on the floor, playing seemingly silly, goal-less games with this child, waving her hands and entering his world.

After years, many days and thousands of hours of this, her son spoke to her! There's the incarnation. That's the pattern of redemption. That's the price that God paid. God entered our world on our terms to feel the grief of being human—so we could speak back to a God who would understand.

Jesus is the suffering of God. Jesus is the pain of God, the pity of God. He is the revelation of the heart of God. Somehow our own feelings, somehow our own pain and our own pleasure is a participation in who God is. God is in agony and delightful expectation until the end of time.

from *Days of Renewal*

Parents' Prayer, Everyone's Prayer: 'Be Done Unto Me'

A family came out to visit me in Albuquerque a few weeks ago, with three little ones sick with croup. The house sounded like barking dogs for three days! I did five full loads of laundry—they had vomited on everything in the house. I couldn't believe life could be that hard. You couldn't have one conversation or one meal undisturbed. And I thought we religious had the harder life. It's not even in the same ballpark! What parents go through to raise children is above and beyond the call of duty. Yet they rise to the occasion, more often than not.

I can see why God ordered the continuation of the human race through parenting: God had to find a way for all of us to get out of ourselves. We need reality checks that are simply *there*, like a brick wall, that demand a response, with no room for choice or "discernment." That's the best way to become holy. It's not what you do, it's what you allow to be done to you.

Seeking God and holiness becomes too self-conscious unless you allow it to lead you farther than you intended. Holiness comes from what you allow to be done to you by the circumstances of life, by the people who are there right in front of you. We don't convert ourselves; we are converted.

from *Letting Go: A Spirituality of Subtraction*

Saint Bill W.

Saint Bill W.? Consider the spiritual fruit that his "Twelve Steps of Alcoholics Anonymous" is now bearing throughout the world. In 1939 Bill Wilson codified his program for recovery from alcoholism. It has been so successful that it is now used by overeaters, gamblers, neurotics and those addicted to religion, drugs, sex, money, shopping, relationships and worry. Beneficiaries of these programs are some of the most spiritually open and religiously mature people you will meet.

While denominations haggle over metaphysics and belief systems, argue about who is saved and righteous with God, defend their sacramental and scriptural turf, Bill Wilson and his followers have moved forward with a humble realism that is both rare and convincing. They begin at an honest place and end at the same without arguing, proving, defending or spouting religious jargon. They come together not as a gathering of the saved but wearing their "scarlet letter" for all to see. They don't have to be talked into a salvation theory or a need for God out there.

Their broken and powerless humanity is all that they are sure of—like parched and weary earth waiting for rain. God is a felt need, no Sugar-Daddy-Answer-Giver but the very ground of their being. To be redeemed—"brought back"—is a daily gut and heart experience, not a liberal or conservative theology.

People in Twelve-Step programs, without knowing or intending it, have every likelihood of renewing the meaning of gospel in our time. The very word "Christian" has been so cheapened that probably the only way God could re-found the Churches was from the outside. But as Scripture says, "Who can know the mind of God or who can teach the Lord?" (Wisdom 9:13).

from *Radical Grace*, "The Twelve Steps: An Amazing Gift of the Spirit"

The Power at the Bottom

The spirituality behind the Twelve Steps and the Twelve Traditions is very similar to the phenomenon of the base communities in Latin America. It is a "low Church" approach to evangelization and healing that is probably our only hope in a suffering world of five-and-a-half billion people. Do we really need to verify belief in atonement doctrines and the Immaculate Conception when most of God's physical, animal and human world is on the verge of mass suicide and extinction?

The Twelve-Step meetings are probably the First World answer to Third World base communities. *Our* suffering is psychological, relational and addictive: the suffering of people who are comfortable on the outside but oppressed and empty within. It is a crisis of meaninglessness and the false self, which had tried to find meaning in possessions, prestige and power. It doesn't work. So we turn to ingesting and buying to fill our empty souls.

The Twelve Steps walk us back out of our addictive society. Like all steps toward truth, they lead downward.

Bill Wilson and his A.A. movement have *shown* us that the real power is when we no longer seek, need or abuse power. Real power is not at the top but at the bottom. Those who admit they are powerless have the only power that matters in the world or in the Church. Saint Bill W., pray for us.

from *Radical Grace*, "The Twelve Steps: An Amazing Gift of the Spirit"

Sorry, Boys!

It is no accident that we Catholics had a psychological need to exalt Mary to the role of a goddess. I am not sure if it was an inherent need to balance ourselves, a disguise for the patriarchy underneath, a love affair with the denied woman within or just a work of the Spirit, but it is an overwhelming example of instinct winning out over logic and theory. So much so, in fact, that the only two infallible statements of this Roman patriarchal Church are, ironically, the Assumption of the physical body of Mary into heaven and her privileged choice and protection by God, the Immaculate Conception.

We even celebrate her "Coronation as Queen of Heaven and Earth." I'm really all for it, but none of these are found in Scripture or public revelation. It's amazing how this male Church was in some ways always feminist—and unwittingly ready to bend all the rules to say so! That healthy instinct has now come to our service. I call it "women-stuff." Sorry, boys, we Catholics have always been there. Proud and orthodox in public, but Mama's boys whenever we could find an excuse for it. Feminism is not new or liberal or dangerous; it's very old, quite conservative, and as traditional as Mary and the eight Beatitudes.

from *Radical Grace*, "Is This 'Women-Stuff' Important?"

Faces of Faith

Western Christianity has been largely in the head, although the masses never were inspired that way. Institutional Christianity is mistrustful of enthusiasm, although *enthusiasm* literally means "in God." Conviction, passion, excitement changes lives much more than logic or theo-logic. If the salvation that we see in our Sunday-morning communities or congregations were the best that God could do, then we don't have much of a God. If those bored, sad, tired faces that we priests look out at on Sunday—those who rush in late and leave early—if those are the message, then the Good News isn't very good. Somehow it seems salvation should show in our faces, our lives; in our fire, conviction and zeal. Some kind of Pentecost is still the best way to begin, and the enthusiastic Churches will probably continue to evangelize, heal and gather commitment and resources much better than contemporary Catholicism.

from *The Great Themes of Scripture*

Tradition

We are called to know God personally, but we are essentially social beings. We only come to know who we are in the context of other people, in the context of living in a family, in a community. Would we be so arrogant to say that all the preceding centuries of Christians and Jews have not also known, listened to and followed the Lord? Did Christian history begin in America? With my conversion? Or in Waco, Texas, around 1962?

That is why the tradition of the Church is so important: We stand on the shoulders of all the wise persons and saints of the past. This is the true Tradition. Some historical accidents have been facilely passed on as universal tradition, yet are not the consistent coherent pattern. So we need the Body to keep us beyond cultural arrogance and tied to *all* the ancestors. We can't each start from zero.

So many modern groups—street preachers, "Jesus" people—have lacked a sense of the Body, a sense of standing on the shoulders of the past. They have their God moment, and they try to move forward simply based on their private experience alone and on the "Book." Often a small group of followers become so like-minded that they lose that sense of the larger wisdom, of histories and cultures of the centuries. They can be expected to support the local government over and against the universal good. We call it civil religion, where Christ becomes a tribal god and the Church a mere echo chamber of the state.

Both Catholics and Protestants have been guilty of this fundamentalism, but you would think Catholics would have known better by now.

from *The Great Themes of Scripture*

Why the Apocalyptic?

The apocalyptic style emerges to free prophets from taking themselves or their role in history too seriously. It says that after all is said and done (the work of the prophet), give history back to God and be at peace in the transcendent truth. Don't try so hard that you become part of the bigger problem. The prophet might appear to be saying, "Work as if it all depends on you." The apocalyptic figure says, "Pray and trust as if it all depends on God." At the end of the day, cool it; forget it, and give history back to the Holy One who is going to achieve the victory anyway.

The apocalyptic prophet has two simultaneous and self-correcting messages: (1) Everything matters immensely; (2) It doesn't really matter at all. How many people do you know who can live out their lives on that pure and narrow path? I don't know very many at all. It seems that some are called to take the strongly apocalyptic position and all of the accompanying criticism in order to free the rest of us from our over-engagement with and idolatry of "the way things are."

Probably the most visible and effective witnesses to this position in our time are Dorothy Day, with her "holy anarchy," and Thomas Merton, who left it all to sit in a hermitage in the hills of Kentucky. They will always be criticized for not doing more, but their absolute stance, as we have clearly seen, is the home and school for the emergence of true prophets.

Without the apocalyptic "No," prophets are no more than high-energy and idealistic activists, often working out of their own denied anger or denied self-interest. Apocalypticists are willing to be seen as fanatic, anti-American, anti-anything so that the rest of us can rediscover the Absolute. They are bothered and bored by our relativities and rationalization. They demand an objective ground from which all else is judged and will not be nudged from their uncompromising stance.

I believe one has to be a true and lasting contemplative to maintain apocalyptic firmness and freedom, and to keep from becoming a righteous and defeated prophet.

from *Radical Grace*, "Christ Against Culture or Christ
the Transformer of Culture?"

Twenty-Fourth Sunday of Ordinary Time   Day 332

Action, Please

If the Bible is anything, it's the word of God's involvement in the *action* of history. A great image of this is Mary's Visitation, as recorded in the first chapter of Luke. Last year I gave a retreat in the Holy Land to the Franciscans in Ain Karem, the town of John the Baptist. Right across the valley is the Church of the Visitation. Every night after I'd talk to the friars all day, I'd walk across the valley and sit on a beautiful wall and look over the area and try to picture Mary coming from Nazareth (which is quite a walk, by the way, and would have certainly taken some days) up through this valley and to this place where she met Elizabeth.

As I read this story, I was struck by how different her response was to what my response probably would have been. If I found out I was to be the mother of God, the first thing I would plan would be a thirty-day retreat or something. I'd say to myself, "I gotta go into solitude and get it together and purify my motives and work this out theologically." I would go inside my head.

Yet read the passage. She is out of herself; she is free of her need to get it together. Immediately she set out for the hill country of Judea to help her cousin, whom she heard was pregnant, too (Luke 1:36-39).

Marian images are so simple that we can listen. They're so right on; they're so clear-cut and defined. And here it is, the primacy of action. God can teach me in my taking care of my pregnant cousin, in moving toward the world as it is. I think when we respond to need as it is right in front of us, usually we are not as susceptible to our egos. Life in front of us pulls us out of ourselves and we have to do it because it's there. That's how I see people being purified. That kind of spirituality I can trust.

If your life is not moving toward practical action in this real, living world, with other people, with the not-me, don't trust your spirituality. But your engagement must happen in tandem with contemplation, the inner disengagement with ego and openness to God. Contemplation is the Divine therapy that purifies our work and involvement.

Action and contemplation are the two polarities that regulate and balance the faith-filled life. It saddens me that most Christianity is right in the middle. It's neither radical interiority nor radical engagement. You don't learn much in the mediocre middle, and you don't have much to give.

from *Letting Go: A Spirituality of Subtraction*

Risk All for Love

The Pharisee is one who demands a sign (Mark 8:11). The poor person is one who believes "that the promise made her by the Lord will be fulfilled" (Luke 1:45). The Pharisee is the one who takes pride in being virtuous (Luke 18:9); the poor person is the one who cries to God day and night, even when God delays to help (Luke 18:7). The beggar who continues to pester the Lord is more pleasing than the dutiful and self-sufficient servant.

Jesus has reversed our human scale of values. He would rather have us live in the insecurity of traded money (Matthew 25:14-30) while trusting in the Master, than to place our hope in the sure thing that we have hidden out of fear in the field. Risk all for love, Jesus tells us, even your own life. Give that to me and let me save it. People who seek to save their own lives, doing a good job of saving themselves, are saying that God's salvation is not needed. People who lose their lives for the sake of the Good News will find their lives. The healthy religious person is the one who allows *God* to save.

If this is the ideal Christian attitude toward God, then Mary is the ideal Christian of the Gospels. She sums up in herself the attitude of the poor one whom God is able to save. She is deeply aware of her own emptiness without God (Luke 1:52). She longs for the fulfillment of God's promise (1:54); she has left her self open, available for God's work (1:45, 49). And when the call comes, she makes a full personal surrender: "Let it be!" (1:38).

from *The Great Themes of Scripture*

The Virtue of Obedience

You can see all relationships and events in our Christian life as a training of the will, preparing it to say yes, to let go of itself. The utterly important thing is union, and this can only happen when the will is ready to let go of its ego boundaries. The virtue of obedience, and I use the word intentionally, is supremely important for the training of the will. All the great spiritual pastors, religious founders and mystics, without exception, spoke of the "virtue" of obedience. Now I don't mean blind obedience. I don't mean lying down and playing dead. But I do think that all Christians have to practice saying yes before they dare to say no.

In that sense the Church makes saints of us, although it's somewhat different from the way we expected! We exist in a creative tension with the Body of Christ which challenges us, stretches us, calls us, makes demands on us and forces us into conflicts of conscience. This refines our conscience, "kicking against the goad" (Acts 26:14) until we realize we don't need to kick. Church and obedience operate as a foil, against which *our own* Christian integrity is measured and too often found wanting.

Obedience is important. But I also believe in ways of listening for and hearing the Spirit beyond looking to the hierarchy or the Bible. No one else can do our homework for us.

from *Catholic Agitator*, "Creative Dissent"

Inculturation

I think Catholicism's numbers, its institutions and traditions, have sometimes given it a false sense of power. We think that just because we have the numbers we're influencing culture. Sometimes we're not at all; we're just reflecting the culture. There's a big difference between influencing culture and reflecting it. In many cases the Church tends to reflect the local prejudices and biases much more than influence and change them.

We think there are so many of us that we're having a great effect here, that we're really making a difference. But are we? Outsiders, underdogs, minorities and immigrants have an easier time protecting boundaries and their own identity—and dialoguing with a culture from that clear position. The Catholic lobby or vote was once a force to be reckoned with, I'm told. Now we have made it to the top and largely mirror the prejudices of party-line politicians. The Catholic ghetto was better than this!

from *Why Be Catholic?*

St. Therese

Saint Therese of Lisieux, toward the end of her life, had a beautiful image of salvation. It's not in her autobiography so many have not heard of it. She describes salvation thus: All of her life she is a little girl. She is proud and happy to be a little girl. Her heavenly Father is standing at the top of the great staircase, always beckoning her, "Come, Therese! Come! I ask more of you!" She lifts her little foot again and again by all the actions of her Catholic faith and religious life, trying to please God. She is trying to climb up to God.

God watches Therese and sees her desire to come. Then in one moment that we call grace, God rushes down the staircase, picks her up and takes her. She knows afterward by hindsight that God has done it, from beginning to end. But it was important for her to keep lifting up her little foot. Our struggle, our desire, our yes is significant and necessary. But in the end it is always grace that carries us up the staircase.

from The Great Themes of Scripture

Friday of the Twenty-Fourth Week of Ordinary Time   Day 337

Guadalupe: Evangelizing Woman

In 1531, exactly ten years after the Spanish conquest of the native peoples of Mexico, there was an unprecedented "constellation of signs" that came at once from the heavens of Catholic Spain and the mythologies of the indigenous Americans: We call it the apparition of Our Lady of Guadalupe. Like all ongoing revelation, it has taken us four hundred years to begin to unravel the depth of loving mystery that was revealed in this encounter between "a dear brown woman from heaven" (*La Morenita*) and Juan Diego, a poor Christianized Nahuatl Indian.

The oppressed Indians had lost everything: their land, their honor, their freedom, but most of all their gods. There was nothing left to do except die. But true to the biblical pattern, God's way is not just to punish or destroy the misguided oppressors, but to surprise and subvert their explanations by creating a new and better reality through which they themselves could be converted and transformed. As always, God seems to be an expert in beating people at their own game.

In this case, the Lord speaks through the "Mother of the true God through whom one lives," whom the Spanish call Mary. But she is dressed in the clothes of the Indians, speaks their Nahuatl language and uses Juan Diego, one of the poorest, to "repreach" the gospel back to the people who thought they had the gospel in the first place. It's a classic example of God taking unexpected sides to usher in a new civilization—just when the Nahuatl thought it was all over!

In one generation, under this mother symbol, almost all of the native peoples accept Christianity. A new *mestizo* people, and I might say a new mestizo Christianity, unfolds. We are slowly, hesitatingly learning that there is no other kind. Christ always takes on the face and features of each people he loves. In this case God knew that the face and features had to be feminine and compassionate. There was no other sign that could convert both the Spanish *machismo* and the matriarchal religion of the Indians at the same time.

from *Radical Grace*, "Our Lady of Guadalupe"

The Power of the Cross

The language of the cross may be illogical to those who are not on the way to salvation, but those of us who are on the way see it as God's power to save. (1 Corinthians 1:18, JB)

When Christianity loses the doctrine and power of the cross as its central strategy, it becomes a false and impotent religion. When this happens, as it has again and again, Jesus renews his people by calling them back—usually in spite of themselves—to the "way of the cross."

This is dramatically happening in our time in the Churches of the poor and persecuted, particularly those of Central and South America. Their lives and deaths appear to be a crisis and grace for the Churches of North America and Europe. Through their faith and forgiveness, Jesus is calling all of this Church back to the doctrine and power of his cross, "to tell us what God has guaranteed...only the knowledge of him as the crucified Christ" (1 Corinthians 2:1-2).

from Coalition for Public Sanctuary pamphlet
"The Cross of Jesus and Human Suffering"

We Need New Ways to Worship

As much as I love liturgy, it still reflects the pyramid structure of the Church. It suggests an official religious experience, from the pulpit to the people. There isn't much chance for the community to feed on itself, to enrich and nurture itself. The priest's religious experience becomes the only source. One result of this narrow sense of liturgy is a very limited view of the Scriptures. It is a celibate, male, clerical, sometimes academic reading of the Scriptures.

Part of the reason New Jerusalem Community grew strong is that we had formats for worshiping and praying other than priest-led liturgy. I think the Church of the future is going to have to discover these formats. You see the power of other prayer gatherings, for instance, in the *communidades de base*, or base communities, which began in Latin America. They have sharing of lay religious experience. They ask, What is Jesus saying to us through the Scriptures and our daily lives? There is an opportunity to share faith experiences. It's non-academic; it's non-male; it's non-clerical. It's much more homey and folksy; it's much more alive, even if it's also harder to control. But that shouldn't be our main concern, should it?

from *U.S. Catholic*, "Recipes of a Gourmet Pray-er"

Spiritual Fixes

So many people I met in Africa walk around with a calmness and a self-assurance and a sense of presence that many of our people no longer have. And you say, This doesn't make any sense. We've tried so hard to be OK, to affirm one another and give ourselves "positive personal regard." The self-esteem movement is a national business.

If what I'm seeing in the American Church is the fruit of all that stroking, I don't think it's working at all. In fact, it seems like these folks need a fix every few days. Many seem incapable of really grasping the good news, taking it into their hearts, standing with it and moving forward with it to lives of surrender, service or silence. Instead, it's a world of noise and weak identity, where we need constant reassurance, someone to be holding our hand all the time and telling us, "You're good. God loves you."

from Letting Go: A Spirituality of Subtraction

Stone Houses

Some people live without anything and have everything. The example that always comes to mind for me is in Africa, where I preached. This little old black African man and I prayed together after a long session. He prayed with such tenderness, he said, "O

Lord, help us never to move into stone houses." And everybody echoed, "Yes, Lord. Yes, Lord." Afterward I asked the missionaries what he had meant. "Well," a priest said, "look at the villages. They're all doorless thatch huts. And so as long as you live a simple life in a thatch hut with no doors, you don't know where your family ends and where the next family begins. You move in and out of one another's lives, and it's all really one family. And there's no possessing, there's no mine and thine; it's ours. It's a world of community.

"Once the first stone hut is built in a village," the missionary continued, "very quickly a door and locks are put on it. Immediately the world of mine and thine is created. The entire social worldview, the entire understanding of self, changes."

We've got to realize the world of stone huts is the only world you and I have ever known. We've paid a price for that inheritance. We can't reverse it. We're not going to live in thatch huts, and I'm not here to say we should. But we've got to know what we've given up by the so-called technological advances of this very sophisticated society. It's one reason why we are producing neurotic and psychotic people at such an unbelievable rate. Teen suicides, for example, *doubled* in the 1980's. Crime in general has increased 500 percent since 1960!

We've chosen security over solidarity in First World countries, in Western Europe and North America. Jesus said you can't serve God and mammon. I'd say you can't see God very well if you spend too much time inside your stone house.

from *Letting Go: A Spirituality of Subtraction*

Spiritual Spectators

Western civilization has had such victory in terms of science, technology—the outer world—because we are able to objectify everything. But the price we've paid is our state of alienation. We're over here apart from it. We analyze the world as an object over there.

Once consciousness surrenders to that subject/object split, quite frankly, prayer becomes very difficult, if not next to impossible. Prayer is unitive experience. Yet for us prayer has sometimes become confused with mere inner awarenesses, me analyzing my own inner states and feelings about God. Those of us who were raised in religious contexts, for example, are often inclined to give a value judgment to everything and to ourselves. That's the guilt middle-class folks have. We have it because we are alienated from our own souls. We're standing over here, apart from ourselves, analyzing: Is it good, better, best? Is it venial sin, is it mortal sin?

When you're in that stance of analyzing the self, you're a spectator and you're necessarily divided from your own soul. Maybe that's why Jesus said, "Do not judge and you will not be judged" (Matthew 7:1). Our judgments separate us, alienate us and, therefore, condemn us.

from Letting Go: A Spirituality of Subtraction

Self-respect

You cannot give yourself away until you have a self. That's why the gospel was meant primarily for adults. The most we can do with children is love them and touch them; cuddle, hug and believe in them. You can't preach a full-fledged, heavy gospel to children because everything in their psyche and soul is saying grow, experience, develop, run, prove myself, be ambitious. A child's psyche cannot understand the way of the cross.

Only adults are ready for the gospel. And, in fact, if we aren't ready for it around age thirty we haven't grown up. Thirty years should teach us that life is both merging and also separating, loving and letting go, yes and no. Both are sacred and necessary. It seems to me the people who have the best sense of self, who don't constantly need to have it affirmed or stroked, are people with self-respecting boundaries. They are always people who, in some way or another, know how to set limits to their lives and know, quite simply, how to say no to themselves. They have an appropriate sense of boundaries and an instinctive sense of their own center.

That is precisely the way the ego is formed: not by pandering to the self, but in fact by setting limits to its voracious appetites. That gives ego the boundaries and the center that it needs. You *are something*, it tells you, because there is something there you can say no to. The "sacred no" to the self, ironically, gives us a sense of self-respect. Continual yeses to the self are actually a humiliation to the ego.

from *Letting Go: A Spirituality of Subtraction*

St. John of the Cross

True spirituality is utterly countercultural because it's non-merchandisable, non-measurable, non-provable. It is precisely nothing. Who wants to be nothing in this world? This culture's goal is for us to be something, to be everything, to "win friends and influence people."

St. John of the Cross puts it this way: "In order to come to pleasure you have not, you must go by a way that you will enjoy not. To come to the knowledge that you have not, you must go by a way that you know not. To come to the possession that you have not, you must go by a way in which you possess not. To come to be what you are not, you must go by a way that you are not" (*Ascent of Mount Carmel*, I, 13, #10).

We fear nothingness, of course. That's why we fear death, too. I suspect that death is the shocking realization that everything I thought was *me*, everything I held onto so desperately, was precisely nothing. The nothingness we fear so much is, in fact, the treasure that we long for. We long for the space where there is nothing to prove and nothing to protect; where I am who I am, and it's enough. Spirituality teaches us how to get naked ahead of time, so God can make love to us as we really are.

from *Letting Go: A Spirituality of Subtraction*

Grin and Bear It

Real holiness doesn't feel like holiness; it just feels like you're dying. It feels like you're losing it. And yet, you're losing it from the center, from a place where all things are One, where you can joyously, graciously let go of it. You know God's doing it when you can smile, when you can trust the letting go.

I'm not suggesting stoic, teeth-gritting tolerance; I mean grin and bear it. Unless the grin is there, unless the joy is there, it isn't God's work.

Many of us were taught the no without the yes, the joy. We were trained just to put up with it, to take it on the chin. That destroyed a lot of people in the Church. Saying no to the self does not necessarily please God. When God, by love and freedom, can create a joyous yes inside of you—so much so that you can absorb the no's—then it's God's work.

from *Letting Go: A Spirituality of Subtraction*

Jesus Subverts All Domination

The twelve apostles as men were the entitled ones in their society. Jesus helped them to shed their entitlement, their sense of false empowerment. He undercuts every attempt at the domination of one group over another. When his own disciples try to take the high road of power or control, Jesus takes the low road to teach them his new "way."

Jesus undercuts their idea of the in-group against the out-group (Mark 9:38-40). He undercuts the domination of one over another (9:33-35), of adults over children (9:36-37 and 10:13-16) and of the rich over the poor (10:17-30).

In Mark 10:1-12 he undercuts the domination of men over women: "The Pharisees came to him and they asked him, 'Is it lawful for a man to put away his wife?' And he answered and said unto them, 'What did Moses say?' 'Moses suffered to write a bill of divorce, and to put her away.'"

This is not so much a teaching on the indissolubility of the marriage bond as a teaching on domination of men over women. Jesus refuses it. The divorce laws of his day were mainly laws to protect men by allowing them to keep moving ahead freely and to abandon women without penalty. Jesus refuses to buy into that. He says, "From the beginning of creation, God made them male *and* female." He sees them as brothers and sisters, as equals. "And so the two shall be one flesh." They shall not be two but one, preaching a word of equality, not of domination. This becomes clear in the final parallelism of verses 11-12: "He said to them, 'Whoever divorces his wife and marries another commits adultery against her; and if she divorces her husband and marries another, she commits adultery.' "

Why did we never see this? Partly because we didn't understand how women were oppressed in Jesus' time and partly because males have been doing most of the Bible interpretation, I suppose. You never read the gospel very well from the high road.

from *Kingdom Spirituality Is Global Spirituality*

If this is so, why no female priests? Why no married priests in the Latin rite?

- 335 -

Positive Sexuality

If I can fault Catholic tradition in one area, it's that there's never been a single century in two thousand years when we have had positive teaching on our sexuality, or on our emotional and bodily selves. Despite the Song of Songs and a few enlightened saints, there's never been general *positive* teaching on how to integrate our bodies, minds and feelings. So a lot of us, even the clergy, are emotional babies. We're reacting and over-reacting, feeling, not knowing how to feel, repressing feelings, and therefore getting lots of ulcers, alcoholism and depression. We had Logic 101 in seminary; we had Metaphysics 101. Where was Emotions 101?

Affection, intellect and will: All three of these must be open to God. God can speak to us through our affections, through our emotions, through our experience of our bodiliness. We've allowed ourselves continuously to name our bodily functions, our passions, as humanity's "fallen" part. Yet our emotions are no more fallen than intellect or will! Maybe we good Christians don't sleep around, but a lot of us—priests and lay—go to bed with power, greed and superiority. That keeps us just as far from God as any sin of the flesh.

from *The Price of Peoplehood*

New Eyes for Truth

"Stop judging, that you may not be judged. For as you judge,
so will you be judged, and the measure with which you
measure will be measured out to you. Why do you notice the
splinter in your brother's eye, but do not perceive the wooden
beam in your own eye? How can you say to your brother, ' Let
me remove that splinter from your eye?' You hypocrite, remove
the wooden beam from your eye first; then you will see clearly
to remove the splinter from your brother's eye." (Matthew
7:1-5, NAB)

Carl Jung, after many years as a psychologist, said this is how he'd
sum up everything he'd learned: Humanity tends to project its
inner world onto the outer world. If you're always seeing people
out there, let's say, as two-faced, then very likely you're two-faced.
If you're always seeing people as hard and demanding, I bet you're
hard and demanding on yourself and you believe God is hard and
demanding on you.

We see out there what's already in our minds. Yet the healing
ministry of Jesus was to give us new eyes so we could begin to live
in the truth and see the real. With the eyes of Christ we accept and
forgive our real self instead of hating it in others.

from *The Price of Peoplehood*

A Way to Happiness

(Recorded at the Mount of the Beatitudes) *Beatitude* means happiness. The Beatitudes could also be called the ways to happiness. But they are not prescriptions for happiness in the next world, as much as a daring *description* of happiness in this world. So notice that the first and last Beatitudes are in the present tense. He says for those who are poor in spirit, the Kingdom of Heaven is *now* (Matthew 5:3). For those of you who are persecuted in the cause of justice, the Kingdom of Heaven is *now* (5:10).

The people must have been sitting here on this very hillside with their mouths open. They say, well, that's not what they teach us. They teach us to be cunning and to be strong and to be self-assured. He says, oh yes, I'm telling you to be self-assured, but self-assured from within because of your awareness of who-you-are-in-God. Jesus knew that happiness is an inside job, to borrow a phrase. And then he points up to these trees and these birds that you hear chirping above you and he says, be like them. They're not worried, so "Stop all your worrying. Tomorrow will take care of itself" (Matthew 6:34). It sounds a lot like the advice for happiness from the recovery movement: "One day at a time."

from *On Pilgrimage With Father Richard Rohr*

We Need to Waste Time

I want to look at the experiences in your lives of people who've deeply touched you, who've deeply changed you. They're always people who are not afraid to be personal. Ideas really don't change people. People change people. Those who are truly bringing good news are people who know how to be in relationship, who know how to waste time with you.

We need to waste time with the Lord, too. This is the foundation of our prayer lives. You're not being unproductive when you wait for God, when you listen for and seek the Holy One. The Judeo-Christian tradition gives us the Sabbath, a sense of sacred time in which to be, to listen, to be personal and not to "work at it." The Sabbath idea is that at least one-seventh of your life needs to be fallow, useless, empty and expectant—person to person.

Cardinal Newman wrote, "So much sanctity is lost to the Church because brothers [sic] refuse to share the secrets of their hearts one with another." He put that in his coat of arms (*"cor ad cor loquitur"*), which doesn't sound like what a cardinal should put on his coat of arms. He's no sloppy sentimentalist, but a great intellectual. But it's obvious Newman was a man who put it together. He was speaking from an educated heart. He knew the power of sharing the personal. The *truly personal* is usually the *most universal*.

from *The Price of Peoplehood*

The Church and Civil Rights

Our people, by and large, haven't developed a sense of social conscience. It's amazing when we look at the 1960's. You know what attitudes were rather blandly accepted by all of us in the early 1960's, let's say, in regard to race relations. Here and there stood out a man or woman of obvious conscience, one who dealt with good and evil, with truth. But they were few and far between.

To our forever shame, it was by and large the movement of history, the movement of culture that raised our consciousness to the evil involved in denying people civil rights. Most of us didn't even know this stuff was going on! It was the Spirit in *history* (what the Germans call the *zeitgeist*), that for the most part formed our consciences. And the Church came along, caught the wind and said, Yeah, we believe in that too, that's right, that's the gospel! It is the same for militarism, slavery, human rights, sexism and respect for the earth. We have been "Peter-come-latelys" on all of these.

Notice in the twentieth chapter of John: Peter (the Church) gets to the tomb late (after the lover, John) and *finally* believes. It's always been that way, I guess. Simple love sees and believes even before the Church. But at least we finally get there and back it up!

from *The Price of Peoplehood*

The Harder Way

We're not freed *from* our humanity; we're freed *in* our humanity.
We're not freed *from* the flesh, which is what so many of us want;
we're freed *in* the flesh. It's a matter of integration, of synthesis.
That's how grace works: in the flesh, in our humanity. Don't try
to climb over it; don't try to deny it and tunnel underneath it;
don't try to run around it. Go through it. True, it's the harder way.
Both/and is for some reason much more demanding than
either/or. It is an easy litmus test to distinguish the beginners
from the more mature Christians.

from *The Price of Peoplehood*

The Sabbath: Be-ers or Do-ers?

The biblical tradition of personalism begins with the Sabbath, a
law that boggles our minds. We can't relate to such emphasis on
"non-doing" in a progress-oriented culture. The meaning of the
Sabbath is clear in the Bible, though: "The Sabbath is a sign
between myself and you, from generation to generation, to show
that it is I, Yahweh, who sanctify you" (Exodus 31:13, *JB*).

The Sabbath puts us in a relationship of truth with God,
telling us very clearly who is creating us. The Sabbath rest tells us,
on a gut level, there is more to life than what we put into it. The

future is not simply determined by our accomplishing and succeeding. We discover our future by discovering the abyss-like nature of today.

This idea developed for the Hebrews in their biblical concept of working the land. There were traditions of laying a field fallow every seventh year (Leviticus 25:2), and the erasure of debts twice a century during the Jubilee Year. What an excellent foundation this would have made for an earth spirituality: "Land must not be sold in perpetuity for the land belongs to me. And to me you are only strangers and guests" (Leviticus 25:23) [JB].

The Sabbath is God creating space. It forces the great distinction between being and having, whether we live for things or for people. God asks whether we're be-ers or do-ers. The Sabbath calls the Jewish people to be, first of all, be-ers: people who know how to listen, wait, hope, depend, trust.

It's amazing to me this was given up by Catholics so easily compared to other changes. Who complains about it? Middle-class Americans fought for a while about taking their hats off in church. But I've yet to hear a Catholic complain about being allowed to work or shop on Sunday. Our bias is not toward being; we're hooked on accomplishment and success. So we saw no problem in changing what was once a foundational commandment.

from *The Price of Peoplehood*

Forgiveness

Forgiveness is the beginning, the middle and the end of gospel life. It is the energy of being forgiven that first buoys us up. It is the experience of being forgiven (when we didn't even think we needed it) that renews our flagging spirit. It is profound forgiveness that becomes God's providence and mercy at the end.

Zechariah spoke well when he said that God would "give his people knowledge of salvation through the forgiveness of sin" (Luke 1:77). It is as important to give forgiveness as it is to receive it. On both sides of the equation, you know you are enjoying a life and power not your own. Forgiveness given (unearned) and forgiveness received (also unearned) are always the pure work of uncreated grace.

Forgiveness is the supreme work of God for the re-creation of all things: Nothing new happens without it.

from *Radical Grace*, "Risking Reconciliation: The Hope of Christian Unity"

Tuesday of the Twenty-Seventh Week of Ordinary Time   Day 355

Homophobia

A true spirituality *necessarily* is going to be involved with the issues of the world, with the issues of society, of the poor, of politics. When you cut off the human issues, the issues of suffering and society, in fact, you have cut off the soul. Human sues hold the key to your own shadow, what you are afraid of, what you deny and what you hate. The marginalized, those of other races, religions, ideologies and gender usually hold a gift for us. That's why homosexuality is so threatening to people. In many ways it is the last taboo.

In the homosexual person we have the image of masculine and feminine put together in one person. That's why we are terribly afraid of gays and lesbians. They are an image of what we all need to integrate, the contrasexual. We've all got to put the masculine and the feminine together within ourselves. We are so terrified by that wholeness that those who represent it are hated in most cultures based on domination and patriarchy.

Interestingly, more holistic cultures such as the Native Americans and some Asiatics have no taboo against the homosexual. These cultures recognize more easily the mystery and paradox of all things human.

from "Naming the Father Hunger" interview notes

Wednesday of the Twenty-Seventh Week of Ordinary Time Day 356

It's OK to Be Human

After the first couple months of living in community, many people fall apart. All of us have this skeleton in the closet, this bit of guilt, this big fear, this demon, whatever it might be, and in community we finally feel free to let it out. We finally feel free to yell and scream, to say, "I hate myself; I'm angry at God; I'm angry at the Church!" Or we might admit being restless in our marriage or other vows.

Now that's a messy way to live. If you're looking for a comfortable, neat, proper way to live, don't get involved in community. The great risk we have to take is the risk to be human, to realize it's OK to be human. A healthy community allows us and protects us while we "fall apart."

We've been trained to follow scriptural advice to become "perfect" (Matthew 5:48). [This passage must be seen as the conclusion to Jesus' teaching on the love of enemies, a seemingly impossible ideal.] So it's very hard to love and accept ourselves when we are imperfect, messy, broken, angry, or sad. Sometimes it's hard to accept one another.

You know what I think God's calling you to be? Simply a member of God's family. That's all. This is the training ground for heaven. Heaven is "forever-family" where God is father and mother, and we are brothers and sisters. God wants to know if you want family, and if you are willing to choose it now—and forever.

from *The Spiritual Family and the Natural Family*

A Church We Can Trust

If our Church is to be properly political and apolitical (and it must know how and when), then it must also be properly mystical—again and always seeking the contemplative center. That is the only Church we can trust, the only Church worth waiting for, the only Church that has a future created by God.

More than ever, this global village needs a Church that is

truly catholic (literally, "according to the whole"). And after naming our gifts and shadows, we must also say that this Catholic Church also needs the American charism, also more than ever. We might be Peter and we might be Paul, but we are also John Carroll, Elizabeth Seton, Flannery O'Connor, Junipero Serra, Katherine Drexel, Peter Maurin, Dorothy Day, John Courtney Murray, Kateri Tekakwitha, Raymond Hunthausen, Thomas Merton, Frank O'Malley, Maisie Ward and Robert Kennedy. We are the American face of Christ.

This gives me joy. I believe it gives Christ joy. Why should it not give joy and great hope to this universal Church? I have no doubt that it will.

from "The Future of the American Church"

Friday of the Twenty-Seventh Week of Ordinary Time   Day 358

Bastards and Orphans

When there's something right happening between two, it invites life into itself. That's what happens in the natural family. Just as a man and a woman can put two bodies together and bring a child into the world, that child can have a name but still be a bastard and an orphan if it is not loved. Likewise, we in the Church can gather people together and say because they had water poured over their heads, they are in the family of God. But there will be no spiritual life for them if no one is family, sponsor, spiritual friend, confessor, teacher or master for them.

Many of us have discovered we are bastards and orphans within the Church: We have been neither fathered nor mothered in Catholic and Christian faith. It's nobody's individual fault but the sin of all together; we have a Church that is largely formed by administrators and programs.

It's not all bad. It's just not enough. As many have said, "Faith is caught much more than it is taught."

from *The Spiritual Family and the Natural Family*

Longing for Wholeness

In the polarity between man and woman, God is able to speak to us powerfully. We don't know what's going to happen. But it's there, in what is opposite, hidden and scary for us: masculinity for the woman and femininity for the man. Contrary to popular opinion, men and women are not merely longing for warm bodies of the opposite sex; they're longing for wholeness. Faithful friendship and true partnership teach us more than a shallow sexual encounter.

As one minister told me after his many mistakes, "It took me a long time to admit that I can help people a lot more from my chair than by jumping in bed with them."

from *The Spiritual Family and the Natural Family*

A Transitional Generation

We are in a transitional time, a hopeful bridge-building generation. Maybe every age is. Most little people born onto this planet have known that they are first the children of their parents and the parents of their children. We *always* stand in-between. We hold hands tightly and gratefully and know that we must finally let go. That is the fate of all humans. It is humble, partial, a mere link in a universal chain of being. For most folks it has been enough, and it is amazing that we baby boomers ever thought it would be different for us.

All philosophy of progress, self-actualization and Yankee-can-do aside, we are overwhelmed by the amount of death and depression in our society. We are obviously mere tracings in a much larger history and a Mystery where only an Eternal God draws the final lines. That's not a copout; it's not denial. It's the most courageous yes a human being can offer. After Gulf Wars for oil, catastrophic worldwide poverty and Churches that themselves run from the gospel, it might be the only yes that we can utter—and the only yes that will finally make a difference.

Let's try. It's the only life that we have on this planet. I am content to build bridges that the next generation might possibly walk on. I am happy and even freed to be part of a merely transitional generation.

from Radical Grace, "A Transitional Generation"

Fear, the Enemy of Faith

(Recorded at the Mount of the Beatitudes) The greatest enemy of faith is not doubt; the greatest enemy of faith is fear. Most of the world is controlled by fear, petty and big. Petty fears control people; great fears control nations. We could feed all the people in this world if we would stop building arms, but we are afraid.

So the great peacemaker sat on this hill and preached to the world. In the Beatitudes he said those of you who make peace will be happy (Matthew 5:9). You will be God's own. Yet even we Christian people are preoccupied with fear and protecting ourselves because we don't believe what Jesus said here. We read the Beatitudes in church once a year on the Feast of All Saints. But we don't base our lives on it.

Jesus preached the Beatitudes here as the inaugural sermon of all of his teachings. Teachers know how crucial your first sentence is. What is Jesus' opener? "Happy the poor in spirit." We don't understand Jesus at all until we understand the absolute centrality of that line and the rest of the sermon he gave here. Yet I could make a strong case that the Sermon on the Mount has been and is the most neglected and rejected part of his teaching, even by the Church. The Sermon on the Mount is an antidote to fear. But we have never seen fear as the crucial issue, only "doubt."

from *On Pilgrimage With Father Richard Rohr*

Lady Poverty

In 313 Constantine made Christianity the established religion. He tried to do Roman civilization a favor. But today we're not sure he did us a favor at all. Because for seventeen hundred years Christianity has largely looked at history and at itself not from the bottom but from the top, from the position of the privileged rather than the oppressed.

At times we've moved toward the poor. Look at all of our founders, foundresses and saints: It's hard to find one who didn't dis-establish himself or herself and move toward the poor. And yet the Church, by and large, canonized these people after their deaths, idealizing the good things they had done but retaining its position of establishment, its position of looking at history and judging history from a position of power and wealth.

This doesn't mean the Spirit was not in the Church, but a great gift was lost to the Church, a great freedom, a great insight. The love of poverty is one of the deepest and most profound blessings of the gospel. Francis saw it. He was able to call that scary thing, poverty, a lady. Until we can call her a lady, I don't think we've made the discovery so apparent to those at the bottom and those on the edges.

All things considered, poverty has a better chance of getting at the truth. The poor woman, the poor man, has nothing to protect. The richer we are, the more we have to protect and the less free we are to hear anything new or really to understand the old.

How much do I have to protect? How much public image, self-image, possessions, security, comforts, future? These tell me how rich and how poor I am.

from *Embracing Christ As Francis Did: In the Church of the Poor*

We Will Never Be Poor

Middle-class Americans are, by the standards of the whole world, very rich people. That includes most Franciscans. We are trying as best we can, from our establishment position, but we know we can't be the Church of the poor. Because if we have even a high school education, we're rich people by reason of that. We can't be poor again.

Wherever we go, we're articulate. We know how to make connections, how to move in and out of systems, how to write forms, resumés and applications, or whatever else it might be. We will never be outside for long. We have some degree of self-confidence and know how to present ourselves to other people.

We can no longer be satisfied by simply being the Church *for* the poor from our position of establishment. Because we realize that sometimes that very generosity, that very attempt to be good to other people, has kept us in a position of paternalism or maternalism. We go home to our houses feeling good because we gave a thousand dollars to Bread for the World or helped a failing program from our largess. That's OK, and maybe even good, but we must never forget that we are still looking at the world and all issues from the side of power. I don't think that is the privileged vantage point of the Gospels. Somehow we must be *of* and *with* the poor.

from *Embracing Christ As Francis Did: In the Church of the Poor*

The Internal Oppression of Poverty

When people lack a sense of self, they will enter into victim behavior. People outside of their pain cannot understand that victim behavior. We label them and often "blame the victim."

Poverty is primarily a psychological state that people surrender to after repeatedly being assaulted by negative voices, from within or from without. Usually we get them from within because someone gave them to us from without. As children we are so little and vulnerable that we can't resist the negative voices of parents, "friends" and culture.

We've all seen marriages where one partner is constantly putting down the other. And it doesn't take very long for one to believe what the other says: I'm not much, I'm stupid; I'm ugly, I can't do anything right. Then the partner becomes victim. Soon they are oppressed, they cannot recognize—much less take advantage of—any opportunities that come their way. They have internalized their persecution.

Now, we folks who were loved as little children, who were believed in and given good news, we can do it. We have inner ego-strength. We know we can influence, we know we can change, we know we can rise above it. But brothers and sisters, much of the world doesn't know that. They don't know their power. No one gave them any good news. It often seems like this is the large majority of the earth's population.

from *Embracing Christ As Francis Did: In the Church of the Poor*

Outlaws and Outcasts

Why are we afraid of mentally and physically disabled people? What is it that happens in us when we're in front of the homeless? What is it that happens to us when we're close to people of another ethnic group who don't use our language or jargon? What is it that happens to us when we hear of refugees coming into our cities; when we're in the presence of an addicted person, a homosexual person, a prisoner, or any person who's failed in our social or economic success system? Why is it that we surround ourselves with other white, middle-class American Catholics? Why do all the others threaten us?

The Lord in his goodness offers us a blessing. And many are beginning to recognize it. I think the little ones of this world represent what we are most afraid of within ourselves. *We need* to embrace them even more than they need to be embraced. As Umberto Eco says in *The Name of the Rose*, "The people of God cannot be changed until the outcasts are restored to its body."

from *Embracing Christ As Francis Did: In the Church of the Poor*

Living Sacraments

We're learning how to embrace and cherish our inner brokenness and violence. So it's no accident that our Church is rising to the occasion and addressing the great global issues of social justice. Brokenness doesn't terrify us so much anymore. We see the disabled one as a sacrament. He or she is an icon and a mirror image of our own souls. When I look I see not only the person, but I see my self that I'm afraid of.

The retarded woman is not simply an accident of history over there but someone we must gather into our midst and let teach us. Our soul asks, Why would God create someone like you? You can't be educated the same way we can. What value are you? Why would God bother with you?

When we see the refugee, we recognize the terror in our own soul at not having a place to lay our head and not having a home. When we see the homosexual, we see the male and female parts of our selves that we are so afraid of. Yet these are the ones we push to the edge, whom we run from and call names. We lock them up in prisons where we can just assume that they are evil and bad and that we are good.

Humility is the only appropriate response once we take the inner journey. What do we have to boast about? Who are we? We are fragmented and fractured to the core. We rail against that and fight it every day because there's a very large part of us that wants the world to be right and wants the world to be perfect in a way it will never be. And maybe it doesn't need to be.

The only truth I find is the humiliating truth. The little ones are icons of our own souls. The outsiders are sacraments of the eternally rejected Christ.

from *Embracing Christ As Francis Did: In the Church of the Poor*

Carry Our Cross

St. Paul loved his people enough to ask a lot of them. He led them into the true source of power, he taught them how to die, how to carry the cross—and not in a death-dealing way.

We modern Christians have been told to carry the cross by just bowing our heads and putting up with it. Really, I don't think the individual has that power to carry the cross. I think only the Body of Christ can carry the cross, which is why the Twelve-Step movement has been so important. Our Western tradition has given us an individualistic private salvation, without a support system for us to believe in it, or for us finally to see the resurrected power that comes from it.

Take the example of a woman in an alcoholic marriage or a lone sister in a convent of broken, destructive women. They might ask, Are you asking me simply to stand in there and be destroyed? I'm saying, No. God never said you could do it by yourself. Immerse yourself in the love and the life of a supportive community. Find and discover the spiritual family of God. Together, confront the corporate evil of the world. That's what we're confronting in Twelve-Step groups. We do need some network of faith or "base community" to survive in this world and sometimes to survive in this Church. We're not confronting individual evil. We're confronting a complexity of factors that must be confronted with corporate good, the Body of Christ.

from *The Spiritual Family and the Natural Family*

A Negative Sacrament?

During my sabbatical retreat at the Gethsemani Trappist monastery in Kentucky, I spent a lot of time sitting on the front porch of the hermitage where Thomas Merton lived. I would ponder one thought for twenty minutes, and then for the next twenty minutes it was another thing. By the time I was to the third one or the fourth one, I didn't even remember the first one anymore. In the silence they were able to come and go because there was nothing I could do with them. There was no one I could yell at, or work out a problem with. I couldn't go write a nasty letter, I couldn't get on the phone and chew someone out or love someone, whatever it might be. I had to let it be. I couldn't attach myself to it.

Now if I were living in society, I would have probably acted upon my feelings, gossiping to someone else about a difficult situation. Gossip is a kind of negative sacrament. Remember our old definition of sacrament? We said sacraments, once you do them, *effect what they symbolize*. It's the same way with gossip. When you talk negatively you invest in your negativism. You justify it, and it becomes harder to avoid. The most nasty and irrational judgments I have received from people have often followed upon a negative bull-session.

For me the way to break it is silence. In silence I see my negative feelings passing before me like a mist. All of these paranoid and self-pitying feelings were not really justified by the situation *out there* as much as they were needed by myself. They were attachments that I created to define and validate myself. In the hermitage they meant nothing.

from *Letting Go: A Spirituality of Subtraction*

African Lessons

(Written in Africa) The missionaries here love to talk about their peoples. At every meal I inquire about the ways of the different cultures: the hard-working Kikuyu, the fascinating Masai, the exotic and primitive tribes of Turkana and others.

The more I travel, the more it becomes evident that it is culture which finally and firmly forms our attitudes—so deeply that we don't recognize them as chosen attitudes. It is an emotional seeing that is not easily challenged or overcome. How will God ever make unity out of our extraordinary diversity? Especially when each culture is so committed to its own pair of glasses.

My best memory from this trip to Africa is the young man who gave me two of his carvings in exchange for my watch. I got the bargain. He gave me himself, his art, and took away a tyrant from my wrist. All I really gave him was my address, since he wanted to write. The poor don't know how to lose.

from *St. Anthony Messenger*, "African Journal"

The Dreams of Youth

Hindus and Buddhists are way ahead of us Westerners in terms of what their young people idealize. They're led to idealize holiness, inner freedom, inner truth, rather than simply outer success. Our drive for outer success has given us tremendous advantages in terms of the scientific and industrial revolutions, but Asia and Africa are more able to triumph over the inner world. Wisdom is still idealized as the value that binds them together.

During my travels I was glad to see, in Africa especially, the almost universal puberty rites and initiation rites still in place. Basically they are intense, three-month "CCD programs" that work. The young people are taken apart by the wise men or women of the tribe and taught what wisdom is: "This is what holds us together as a people. This is what we stand for, this is who we are, these are our values." And when those young men and women return from those kind of groupings, they know who they are.

In our culture we're forever searching for our values, what we want to believe in, what we might want to commit ourselves to. Adolescence, the time of open options, now lasts until age thirty-two in the West! In some cultures adolescence really ends as early as sixteen and seventeen. You often see that in the self-assurance of young people who find their ground and meaning much earlier.

I suspect we actually are stunted and paralyzed by having too many options. We are no longer the developed world; we are the overdeveloped world.

from *Letting Go: A Spirituality of Subtraction*

Lazarus and the Rich Man

In a culture of affluence, people don't necessarily lose the desire to do good. It's worse than that. They don't even recognize the good anymore. They become spiritually blind. They wouldn't recognize true moral goodness if it were in front of them.

A terrible aristocratic mentality has taken over the United States in the 1980's. When I was being formed in the 1960's, you never could have talked the way some people talk today. Making racist and ethnic remarks, making fun of poor people, that's quite acceptable in the jet-set society of America today. That is spiritual blindness, and it's dead wrong. It means people aren't recognizing Christ anymore.

In the biblical story, the rich man didn't consciously persecute Lazarus (Luke 16:19-31). He didn't kick him out the door. The story doesn't even say he was the cause of Lazarus's poverty. The evil of the rich man, in that terrible story that Jesus tells, is simply that the rich man didn't even notice. He isn't ill-willed, villainous, or necessarily arrogant or mean—he just isn't aware.

The rich man in the story never notices Lazarus because his concern is for prestige, comfort and consumption. "He dressed in purple and fine linen and feasted well every day" (16:19). You wouldn't put a man in jail for that! He has done nothing "wrong," yet the story places him in "the torment of Hades." Why?

It's the strange character of greed: The more you have, the more you want. Ask rich people if they're ever satisfied. It's always, I need more. The level of sophistication in this country moves higher every decade. Our restaurants, hotels and cars get better and better, and we get used to it! It's difficult to go backward. And it's not simply the more we have, the more we want. The final clincher is (ironically but not surprisingly), the less it satisfies. The more you have, the more you want, and the less it satisfies. What a sophisticated and useless form of torture!

from *Letting Go: A Spirituality of Subtraction*

Friday of the Twenty-Ninth Week of Ordinary Time   Day 372

Our Global Village

On a timeline of history, ninety-five percent of human history could be called the tribal age, the age of little groupings that gathered together in extended families. It's only really in the last ten thousand years, which is no more than a drop in the bucket of time, that we speak of civilizations, great groupings gathering together in the beginnings of what would eventually become nations.

Nation-states came along during the last thousand years. And it's in great part during that time that much of our Christology has been formulated. Much of our theology became overidentified with particular nation-states and with Europe, a very small part of this whole planet. As the Church became closely identified with the Holy Roman Empire, we found a theology and an understanding of Christ to protect it (both the Church and the empire).

The world age is largely a product of the last forty years, beginning with the Second World War. At that time a large part of the world was still under European colonial control, something like forty percent of the world being controlled by four percent.

The social and political picture has changed immensely since then. But maybe we're not yet fully aware that it's radically changing our reading of the Gospels and our understanding of Church. The axis the world moves on is changing. It's not asking the same questions, and invariably it's not going to come up with the same answers.

At the beginning of this century, seventy percent of Catholics were in Europe and North America. In the year 2000, seventy percent will be in the Third World and the southern hemisphere.

The next papal conclave will, we hope, have a majority of Third World cardinals. It's very likely that within our lifetime we *Pope* might see a pope who's looking at the world from some other eyes *FRANCIS* than European eyes. (Apparently it was God's will for most of a thousand years that the bishop of the Universal Church always be an Italian!) That isn't to say that European perspectives are wrong (and nothing's wrong with Italians!); it's simply that the perspectives of a single continent are necessarily limited. They're one set of assumptions, one set of questions about the gospel. Through African, Asian and Latin American eyes, we're prepared now to ask also a different set of questions of the gospel. We are truly becoming a global village, and, we hope, a truly *catholic* Church.

from *Letting Go: A Spirituality of Subtraction*

Remember the Alamo

In chapters six and seven of the Letter to the Romans, St. Paul goes to great pains to describe sin. He describes it in some of these ways: It's a power; it's a pattern of predictable knowledge, a law of necessity. Sin might also be described as a culture of blindness, a pattern of agreed-upon lies. It's a system that people get trapped in: We all tell the same lie, and therefore, it isn't a lie anymore. Sin is when life freezes and truth hides out of fear. It's when self-interest tells us what to remember and what to forget.

The Bible is writing us a counter-history, an alternative narrative. Yet national history is always going to tell you that we are the heroes. Take U.S. history's reading of the Alamo, for example. We tell ourselves we were great there. We create a myth: Davy Crockett and Jim Bowie and all these other people were heroes. Yet you should hear that same story from the Mexican point of view. It's absolutely different. The Bible does that same thing for us. It puts our selfish interests aside and tells us a true history from God's point of view, which is usually from the side of the victims.

from *Letting Go: A Spirituality of Subtraction*

The Spiritual Family and the Natural Family

All in-depth renewal is somehow a return to family. We come into this world through a relationship called family. We come into the Kingdom through a set of relationships called Church or spiritual family. The same rules for the creation, the sharing and the destruction of life apply in both the natural (biological) family and the spiritual (Church) family, and therefore in our very relationship with God: The areas in our life where we cannot be shared are the very areas where God cannot touch us. The areas that we cannot let God touch will never be shared for the good of all.

The natural family and the spiritual family seem to need one another for correct image, focus and direction. The natural family without the spiritual family becomes isolated, insulated, inbred and without vision. The spiritual family (the Church) without the natural family has become cold, ideological, impersonal, task-oriented and unable to carry out its purposes.

from *Sojourners*, "Building Family: God's Strategy for the Reluctant Church"

Identity, Then Marriage

One of the big myths in our culture is that marriage is the answer to one's problems. Instead, I'm told, marriage *reveals* one's problems. The people who enjoy marriage are those who first have learned to live life itself. You can't create intimacy without identity.

Rather than being the save-all answer to problems, anyone who understands marriage knows it creates a whole set of new ones. It makes us aware of a need to grow, a need to forgive, to share, to die. Better to come into married commitment with some sense of those needs and an appreciation that their fulfillment is the work of a lifetime. Marriage won't always meet these needs; it puts the couple in a context for working together. In that context, we learn our issues and problems—and we are given a partner to walk with through those problems.

from *The Spiritual Family and the Natural Family*

Sexuality

We all are sexual. Sexuality simply means the attraction of oppositeness, the polarity of oppositeness, that longing for totality, completion—for wholeness. There are levels of intimate desire going on within all living things and between *all* living people: to reveal the desire for God, the need for the other. Whenever you see something that you are not, and you want to be that and take that into yourself and give yourself to it so that you can be whole, that's the search for God. It's not bad or shameful.

Our sexual drive is no morality test from God. It is God teaching us we're not whole within ourselves, that we *must* be in relationship. And God pulls us out of ourselves by every means possible. Without sexuality we would live private, antiseptic lives—and the world would be cold.

from The Spiritual Family and the Natural Family

Wednesday of the Thirtieth Week of Ordinary Time   Day 377

The Pure Person

Purity isn't simply being true to some kind of behavioral pattern. The pure person is the one who has a vision of the whole, who can see things uncluttered and unfiltered. The only completely pure one, therefore, is God.

Impurity is the partial vision, the ability to separate what should not be separated. It is the ability to create lies about yourself and other people.

God purifies us. How? Not by burning us in some kind of flames, but by gazing into us. (The "beatific vision" is perhaps God looking at *us* instead of our seeing God.) Just as the pure person purifies others by relating to them in a special way, by calling forth the goodness he or she sees in them, so God purifies us. God makes us pure by the way God looks at us. Purity is given by one who sees us purely.

How, then, do you become pure? By letting someone see and love the truth in you, by letting them see *all* of you. It's those who know you only partially who don't like you. I've never known anyone who really shared all of their story with me whom I could not love. When you know only the partial truth, you can see them as despicable. When you know the whole picture, people are always lovable, somehow, and purity is regained. One sees with the pure eyes of God, where all is transparent, understood and forgiven.

from *The Spiritual Family and the Natural Family*

Thursday of the Thirtieth Week of Ordinary Time   Day 378

God Is Poor

I hope you've dared somewhere along your journey to say "I love you" to someone. We're afraid to say it because we're not sure it will be accepted and given back. If we say "I love you" and don't hear it back, it's as if we've dropped our pants and exposed ourselves.

I use that shocking image because that's exactly the nakedness of God on the cross. God said "I love you" to the world. God took that great risk of looking stupid, and we didn't say it back. God hangs there naked and vulnerable before his enemies who will not believe in the love of God.

The fate of God, it seems, is to be poor, to be given and not received, to fail. We share as Christians in the eternal fate of God: not to succeed, to be poor and often to look foolish and defenseless. Once you say, "I love you," you stand foolish and exposed until the other says, "I love you, too." Such is the fate of God.

from *The Price of Peoplehood*

The Pain of Rejection

Love is a humbling experience, as we learn in our interactions with intimate friends. We must learn how to keep giving and dying and getting hurt and trying again and overcoming the obstacles—it's terribly humbling to love. That's why the proud person cannot love or grow.

There's no pain on this earth like the pain of rejection. Especially when we lay out our life, when we surrender ourself, when we let go of our heart and the other does not let go of his or hers. Rejection reveals the seemingly bottomless character of our need and our need to connect. Humanity has been rejecting God since the beginning. In the pain of being rejected, in the pain of non-union we come to know how God loves and therefore needs. Good theologians don't want to apply the word *need* to God. But I think that somehow God has created a world in which, in a certain sense, God *needs*.

from *The Spiritual Family and the Natural Family*

Love

Love is not a feeling or an infatuation. It's a decision to lay down your life. Unless you know that God has laid his life down for you, unless you know that she has surrendered herself for you, you cannot understand love as decision. Whenever you want to know how to love, or how not to love, simply ask the question: How does God love me? God's love is patient; it is not jealous; it endures; it does not take offense; it waits, believes, hopes, forgives (1 Corinthians 13:4-8). That's the way we must learn how to love one another. Love is a practical decision to *act on what is*—and *for* what is.

from *The Spiritual Family and the Natural Family*

New World Order

In order to understand the Sermon on the Mount, you must recognize that Jesus was preaching a message aimed directly at the heart of the Jewish culture he lived in. He preached a new world order.

There are many dimensions to Jesus' challenge, but Jesus' new world order is, first of all, utterly subverting the old world order. He doesn't even bother to fight it, and this is what makes the people so furious. He just ignores it. That is utterly subversive.

Why would anyone try to get rich, for example. *Why?* It doesn't make a bit of sense once you know the real. In effect, Jesus doesn't buy into any of the values of his culture that kept people out of union. He goes for the real, the Kingdom experience. That is the heart of Matthew's Gospel. It is the experience of the Absolute that all religion is about.

from *Sermon on the Mount*

Monday of the Thirty-First Week of Ordinary Time   Day 382

Leaving the Temple

In the twenty-fourth chapter of Matthew, in what is called the "Eschatological Discourse," we read, "Jesus left the Temple." That's the first verse. Now remember, everything is symbolic—there's not a phrase wasted. We're tempted to jump over that verse on our way to the central meaning of the text, but the first verse makes an important point. The Temple is the entire system personified in one big structure. He leaves it. "As he was going away, his disciples came up to him to draw his attention to the Temple building" (Matthew 24:1). Isn't that interesting! They always do this!

It's almost the end of the Gospel and they still haven't got the point. He's leaving the Temple and they are admiring its architecture! If we read this as sacred mythology, we see the message: The disciples are still rooted there. They still think the Temple is *it*, and he's done everything to tell them it isn't it. "He said to them in reply, 'You see all these? I'm telling you, not a single stone will be left on another. Everything will be destroyed' " (Matthew 24:2).

That's Jesus' big proclamation: It's all going to fall apart. Stop putting your trust in it. Jesus is preaching not only the end of the world but the end of worlds. If you've had a moment in your life when you finally get the point, when a world is let go of, then you understand this text. We cannot welcome the new world order until we let go of the old. The illusion is that we can have both.

from Sermon on the Mount

Tuesday of the Thirty-First Week of Ordinary Time   Day 383

Birthpangs

All this is only the beginning of the birthpangs. (Matthew 24:8, JB)

Birthpangs is an image of something painful that is bringing about something better. The price for bringing about something better is to go through the pain of birth. Male gods create by a flick of their creative finger. Female gods create by labor pains. Much of patriarchal Christian interpretation has been trying to avoid pain; it thought birthpangs were unnecessary. That's why we couldn't hear Jesus.

If we had an image of God as the great Mother who is birthing, I think birthpangs would have been preached about a lot more. And a woman—at least a woman who has had a child—understands something I will never understand: the connection between pain and life.

from Sermon on the Mount

Jesus' Shame-and-honor Society

Shame and honor are, in fact, moral values in the culture Jesus lived in. In other words, retaliation was the rule of Jewish culture. Not to retaliate would be immoral because you would not be maintaining your honor. You must be true to the honor of your village, your family, yourself to be a good first-century Jew.

For Jesus to walk into the midst of that and to say, "Do not retaliate" is to subvert the whole honor/shame system. People who heard this would wonder, "How do I find my self-image, my identity?" And all Jesus does is to point radically to God. Who you are in God is who you are. In that system there are no ups and downs, no dependence upon families and villages for self-esteem, upon wealth or good societal standing. Jesus puts identity on a solid foundation: life in God and not in passing definitions of honor and shame.

from *Sermon on the Mount*

Jump Off the Tower

It's important to realize that Jesus' message was being given, at the same time, to those on the top of society and to those on the bottom. To those on the top, he is always saying, "Come down. Give up your power, your righteousness, your explanations.

Jump off the tower." To those on the bottom, the little
Syrophoenican woman (Mark 7:26), the woman with the
hemorrhage (Mark 5:25), the lepers—all nobodies—he's always
saying, "Come up! You've got faith. Go show yourself to the
priests. You've got the power."

There's a gospel to the oppressors and a gospel to the
oppressed, reversing both of their self-evaluations. The reaction
of good, proper, churchgoing people to this Jesus is outrage and
scandal. And at the end of some passages they plot to kill him (see
Mark 3:6, 11:18). We don't like Jesus' new world order, especially
if we think we are on the top.

from *Sermon on the Mount*

Friday of the Thirty-First Week of Ordinary Time   Day 386

Feet in Both Camps

We have to learn to live both in the world-as-it-is and the
world-as-it-should-be. One is power; the other is love. Power and
love are conjugal partners. Power without love is brutality, but
love without power is soon mere sentimentality. We have to put
the two together in this world.

Power is not a bad word; it *has* to be a good word. We cannot
live in this world in the perfect kingdom of pure love, where it's
structured correctly, where everybody thinks like us, where
everybody celebrates liturgy like we think it should be celebrated.
We are pilgrims and strangers, walking on the road, like the
disciples, with a fragile possession, that we ourselves do not fully
possess or even understand.

At this time, which I do believe is a time of exile on the level of culture and Church, cynicism comes far too easily. It's the too easy response, for it requires no surrender, love, trust, virtue. Yet we are called to faith, to the place where we can trust and respect both worlds, the world as it is (power) and the world as it should be (love). To live patiently and humbly without cynicism is the gift of the gospel.

Jesus proclaimed the reign of God in a time of occupation, enslavement and corruption of religion. If he could say, "The kingdom of heaven is in your midst" right now, then how, brothers and sisters, can we do any differently? The genius of biblical faith is the grace to keep one foot firmly in both camps at the same time: the world as it is and the world as it should be

from *Sermon on the Mount*

Saturday of the Thirty-First Week of Ordinary Time   Day 387

Faith Can't Be Taught

Faith can't be taught; faith can only be caught. The environment where people are living a faith life, openly trusting in God and one another, is where real faith is tossed back and forth. Children who grow up in that kind of environment where faith is being tossed around, where a faith vision is being celebrated and the invisible is taken seriously, naturally receive the gift of faith.

Real faith is too real to ignore. If a person is teaching religion without offering some faith to catch, then teaching religion is largely a waste of time. It becomes an immunization against the real thing.

from *The Price of Peoplehood*

The Meek Shall Inherit the Earth

Possession is an illusion in light of the Kingdom! What do you possess? Wait a few years! We'll see how much we possess when we are six feet under.

Only the meek possess the land (Matthew 5:4). Meek is also translated as "lowly," "humble," and even the "nonviolent" or "powerless" ones. I am reminded, as a Franciscan, that Francis told us never to own anything because, as he said, then you own *everything*. When you get rid of this idea of ownership, you are free. Public museums and libraries are a good example. We don't have to buy art and bring it home to enjoy it. We must purge ourselves of the desire to possess, which is the clear teaching of the forgotten Tenth Commandment. When we need to bring everything into our homes to make it all "mine," then everything outside is "thine," and the life of covetousness begins.

from *Sermon on the Mount*

Happy Are Those Who Weep

Happy are those who weep. They shall be comforted. (Matthew 5:5)

On the men's retreats now we speak of "grief work." A very different kind of work for men! There is undoubtedly a therapeutic, healing meaning to tears. Is not weeping, in fact, necessary? To understand? To let go? To enter in? But Jesus is also describing the state of those who have something to weep about, who feel the pain of the world. He's saying, those who can grieve, who can cry, are those who will give comfort and compassion to the world.

The Syrian Fathers Ephraem and Simeon understood tears. The Greek Fathers of the Church tended to filter the gospel through the head. The Syrians, like today's feminist theologians, find the gospel much more localized in the body. The Syrian Fathers wanted tears, in effect, to be a sacrament in the Church. And St. Ephraem goes so far as to say, "Until you have cried, you don't know God." How different! We think we know God through ideas! But this is body theology: Weeping, wiping away the tears (Luke 7:38), anointing bodies for death (Mark 14:3-9), perhaps will allow you to know God much better than concepts and orthodox formulas.

Jesus claims the weeping class: The forgotten, the voiceless, the rejected will understand, he seems to say.

from *Sermon on the Mount*

Happy Are Those Who Thirst for Justice

Happy are those who hunger and thirst for justice. They shall be satisfied. (Matthew 5:6)

Most Bibles to this day will soften the word *justice* into "what is right," or *righteousness*. Those have a kind of "religious" feeling. But the word in Greek is clearly *justice*. This Beatitude is set right at the mid-point, and the word justice appears again at the end. It could be seen as a couplet saying, This is the full point. To live a just life in this world is to live a life identified with the little ones. As much as Matthew tries in vain to soften it for his middle-class audience, it's still radical, revolutionary and most extraordinary.

What Jesus is saying is, Make sure you're *not* satisfied. Keep yourself in a state of dissatisfaction. Contemplation and voluntary simplicity bring us to that state. Real prayer stirs holy desire (as do deprivation and injustice, when we take them to prayer). The unconscious bubbles up, and you find out what you really desire. (It isn't a new set of clothes, although if you move too quickly you really think it is.) Stay with it longer—a new set of clothes is not going to do it! What you really desire is always God.

The sad thing about those who try to avoid that state of longing and thirsting is that they can never be satisfied. Wealth never sees enough wealth; justice is satisfied with justice.

from *Sermon on the Mount*

Wednesday of the Thirty-Second Week of Ordinary Time   Day 391

A Center for Action and Contemplation

People have liked and affirmed our long name since the beginning. It was cumbersome, but also descriptive and up-front. We hoped it would keep us honest and force us toward balance and ongoing integration. No one could meaningfully disagree with the stated goal. It was classic and rather universal spirituality.

But after four years I have reason to believe that some might agree with the title for the wrong reasons. Activists can see it as an affirmation of their agenda and introverts can use it to affirm quiet time, not working, and leisure-class navel-gazing. Neither is the delicate balance and art that we are hoping for.

Action as we are using the word does not mean activism, busyness, or do-goodism. *Action* does mean a decisive commitment toward involvement and engagement in the social order. Issues will not be resolved by mere reflection, discussion or even prayer. God "works together with" all those who love (Romans 8:28).

By *contemplation* we mean the deliberate seeking of God through a willingness to detach from the passing self, the tyranny of emotions, the addiction to self-image and the false promises of this world. Contemplation is the "Divine therapy" and the perennial clearinghouse for the soul.

It is important that we continue to clarify and hold to these two pivots of our lives. Rightly sought, action and contemplation will always regulate, balance and convert one another. Separately, they are dead-ended and trapped in personality. The clear goal of our center is to meet people where-they-are and help them trust where-they-are-not. For all of us it is an endless rhythmic dance. The step changes now and then, but Someone Else always leads.

from *Radical Grace*, "Not the Center for Activism and Introspection"

The Catholic Family

The imagery of Catholicism is family imagery. The Church is headed by the papa, the holy father. We call our priests father. Our religious communities have mother superiors; men and women religious are called brother and sister. We constantly see the Church as some kind of family. And that's why it was so abhorrent to Catholicism to confront the schism and then the Reformation. The breaking of unity from the holy father and one another in Christendom was simply unthinkable to the Catholic mind. The great Catholic principle is unity.

The family naturally has place for a mother. If Church isn't family, Mary becomes, frankly, a bother, a theological irritant. When you understand the Church as incarnate family, then there's nothing wrong with hailing our older brothers and sisters, the saints, the ones who went ahead of us and did it first. The Catholic mind intuitively understands that.

It's amazing how those things don't need to be proven to the person who's internalized the Catholic myth. It's nonrational and it's highly powerful. But it works as a joke works: You either get it or you don't. That's Protestantism's problem with us, and it's a very understandable problem.

from *The Price of Peoplehood*

A L'*Arche* Conversion

I was privileged to be able to give a retreat to some of the North American leaders of L'Arche, Jean Vanier's community. Some twenty years ago Jean Vanier gave himself to a vision of the gospel where he intended to live the rest of his life with two mentally handicapped men. He didn't think anybody else was going to know about it except his immediate friends. He didn't know that twenty years later there'd be sixty communities all over the world trying to live the same vision.

I had a real eye-opener with the L'Arche folks. They enjoyed me and I enjoyed them, but after the meals everybody went their own direction. So I went mine. About the second day I realized that no one there seemed to need me. I was experiencing a loss of energy because I am energized by people needing me. As I was walking back to my room, it hit me: This group, probably like no other group, has the most simple and straightforward gospel.

They find Christ in the least of the brothers and sisters. Period. They meet the Lord in the mentally and physically handicapped. Stop. They wanted an outside preacher to come in and inspire them, but they would have been fine without me. They found their real sermons in the broken bodies, the simple hearts, the unfair and paradoxically free lives of those with whom they lived.

from *The Passion of God and the Passion Within*

The Good Samaritan Revisited

It's always the powerless one who gathers the community, the Church. I recently discovered a new way to read the story of the Good Samaritan. I had always assumed that the Good Samaritan was the Christ symbol—and that's certainly one way to understand the parable. But from another point of view the real Christ symbol is the man lying on the side of the road.

The man lying on the side of the road is the one doing all the converting. He is the one who forces a whole new agenda, who takes your head off, shakes it and turns it upside down, puts it back on and says, This is what reality means.

The things we can't do anything *with* (the useless) and the things we can't do anything about (the necessary) are always the things that connect us to the Real. We'd sooner just be Catholics; we don't want the Kingdom! We'd sooner just be Americans—we don't really want to be a global, universal people! We'd rather protect our boundaries here—we're not ready for the big boundaries that Jesus calls us to. I'd have to empty too much of myself and make space for the not me, the other, the enemy.

We cannot and will not learn—even to the point of going to war against Iraq. It's as if we cannot live without an enemy, as if America does not know who it is unless it has someone to focus its energy against. The Cold War is over, and we created a hot one because we needed one. We have become a militaristic people who cannot live without negative energy, who cannot live in the realm of peace that Jesus announces, because the price of peace is nondomination. The price of peace is justice. The price of peace is truth. And it is the people left for dead on the side of the road who teach us that.

from *Kingdom Spirituality Is Global Spirituality*

Our Promise of Heaven

What word of hope does the Church have to offer the world? The world is tired of our ideas and theologies. It's tired of our lazy church services. It's no longer going to believe ideas, but it will believe love. It will believe life that is given and received.

We are afraid to touch the flesh of God, even to touch the flesh of one another and understand what God is calling us into. Thomas the apostle symbolizes our temptation toward heady faith, so Jesus asks him to touch the wounds (John 20:27).

God is not calling us into our heads. Yet we've lived in our heads so long, the world no longer listens to us. I don't need your words, the world says to us. I don't need your sermons. I want life. And I want life more abundantly.

What word of hope do we have to offer to the millions of workers in the world who see no meaning in their life? What word of hope have we for all the women who bear children and, day after day, say, What is the meaning of this life?

For most people in the world the question is not, Is there a life on the other side of death? It is, rather, Is there life on this side of death? Until we Christians give evidence that there is life on this side of death, the world does not need to believe our dogmas and giant churches. It doesn't need our words of hell. It needs our promise of heaven.

from *Days of Renewal*

Sanctity

Then he made the disciples get into the boat and precede him
to the other side, while he dismissed the crowds. After doing so,
he went up onto the mountain by himself to pray. (Matthew
14:22-23, NAB)

Some may think that this was a waste of time. Jesus could have
been out healing lepers. There were many sick in Israel. What
kind of messiah is this? He spends the whole day out there
praying to his Father. Yet Matthew is trying to tell us about the
deeper wisdom.

Where is the source of your power? What is the basis for
power? It's union with God, not doing good things. So often we
make the basis for ministry professionalism and up-to-date-ism
instead of chosen union. Never will there be any basis for fruitful
Christianity except sanctity. Leon Bloy said it well: "There is only
one sadness in life, only one—*not* to be a saint."

from *The Great Themes of Scripture*

Brother Sun, Sister Moon

Jesus is Brother Sun, Mary is Sister Moon. The moon receives its
glory as a mirror: It has no glory except that it receives the
reflection of the sun. It perfectly reflects it so that it gives us light

in the darkness. That is the meaning of Mary. It is the meaning of the Church. As the poet Brother Antoninus said, "The soul is feminine to God, and hangs on impregnation, fertile influxing grace.... Annul in me my manhood."

Mary tells us about the difference between attainment and grace. Grace is everything and everywhere, as she proclaims in the Magnificat. Because God is everything to Mary, she is not afraid to boast of her own beauty and greatness.

Humanity is God's miracle by God's grace, not by our merit. Mary is the perfect yes to Jesus. Therefore she is totally fruitful and victorious, and bears Jesus to the world. Mary will always be the most orthodox image of how holiness works in humanity.

from *The Great Themes of Scripture*

Wednesday of the Thirty-Third Week of Ordinary Time   Day 398

Thrashing About

The deepest level of communication is communion. When we know and love someone we are simply happy to be near them. We feel power and energy passing between us. That is the power of prayer. That is what we must do to bask in the sunshine of God's love. The word to us is, "Don't just do something; *stand there!*"

Perhaps you've seen someone trying to learn how to swim. We tell the swimmer, one can float just by lying still in the water. But the swimmer thrashes around, throwing arms and legs about. That's just like us in prayer! We go down! Finally, little by little, the swimmer has a moment of quiet. We stop those limbs moving and, lo and behold, we are buoyed to the top—and we really float!

To receive the love of God is to recognize it is all around us, above us and beneath us; speaking to us through every person, every flower, every trial and situation. Stop knocking on the door: You're already inside!

from *The Great Themes of Scripture*

Thursday of the Thirty-Third Week of Ordinary Time   Day 399

Mother Teresa's Authority

> Jesus summoned them and said to them, "You know that those who are recognized as rulers over the Gentiles lord it over them, and their great ones make their authority over them felt. But it shall not be so among you. Rather, whoever wishes to become great among you will be your servant; whoever wishes to be first among you will be the slave of all. For the Son of Man did not come to be served but to serve and to give his life as a ransom for many." (Mark 10:42-45, *NAB*)

Why is it that Mother Teresa can stand up before crowds of thousands and simply repeat for the most part simple New Testament phrases? She's not complicated. Yet people sit on the edge of their chairs listening to her. She doesn't say anything new: "Jesus loves you," she assures you. "We're sons and daughters of God and we have to love Jesus' poor." Yet people walk out renewed, transformed and converted.

She's not a priest. She's not well educated. Her authority comes from her life-style. Her life has been given over and she stands on her life. There's a truth in her like a magnet. That's the power the saints have. And that's why Paul would teach that the Church is built on the authority of the apostles and the prophets, the evangelists and healers, the teachers, lovers and helpers, all together making unity in the work of service. Servanthood is the true basis of authority in the Church, much more than title or ordination.

from The Spiritual Family and the Natural Family

Politics

The First Letter of John says: "If you claim to be in the light but hate your brother or sister, you are in the darkness still" (1 John 2:9). He couldn't be much stronger. He goes on, "By this do we know that we have passed from death to life, if we love the brothers and sisters" (3:14). For John, the two great commandments (Love God and Love neighbor) have become one and the same.

In its better moments, Catholicism has taken that very seriously. We've taken history seriously and involvement with public life. That's why we're always getting involved in politics and social justice. There is only one history: God's history. Salvation history and secular history are not two different tracks that we can separate. Reality is unified.

People like to say today, "Oh, the Church has suddenly gotten involved in politics." Well, all you need to do is read medieval history. The Catholic Church has always been involved in politics; now we are just changing sides! Unfortunately, we were often on the side of the rich and the powerful instead of the side of the poor and the victimized that Jesus chose.

Politics can become corrupt, but the original meaning of politics is involvement in human affairs. We care about human history because God cares about human history. It's that simple.

from *Why Be Catholic?*

Saturday of the Thirty-Third Week of Ordinary Time   Day 401

Who Was Jesus?

In Mark we read that Jesus' own family does not understand him:

> He came home. Again [the] crowd gathered, making it impossible for them even to eat. When his relatives heard of this they set out to seize him, for they said, "He is out of his mind." (Mark 3:20-21, *NAB*)

Those words have never really been read in our churches. We probably are embarrassed by them. He must not have appeared as that very neat, proper, "normal" person we associate with religious people. Maybe that's telling us that our very concept of religiosity is on a wrong track. We've been influenced much more by Anglo-Saxon puritanism or stoicism than what Jesus tries to communicate.

Religion is not doing nice, right, ordinary things that humans expect. God's goodness strikes much deeper than that and demands much more. Who of us, for example, would be proud to accept John the Baptist into our house—that very wild-looking man, no doubt difficult to understand, whose harsh words would make us all squirm? Jesus, too, spoke to his contemporaries and he was not understood. He was outside the mainstream of expectation enough to be called "crazy."

Jesus was not that person we've often seen in pictures with the perfect masculine Caucasian face and the neatly combed hair. He was a man who at all costs sought to be true to God and to speak that truth to the world. The world did not want to hear it. He would be crucified again today, and maybe even by the Church.

from *The Great Themes of Scripture*

The Cosmic Christ

In the centuries of fighting over the humanity and the divinity of Christ, the Western Church has gradually lost touch with the larger and more universal message: "The image of the unseen God, the firstborn of all creation, for in him were created all things in heaven and on earth....and he holds all things in unity....because God wanted all perfection to be found in him and all things to be reconciled through him and for him" (Colossians 1:15-20).

This is not a problem-solving Christ, not a denominational or cultural Christ, not a Christ domesticated by the Churches. This Christ names in his life and person what *matters*, what *lasts*, and finally what *is*. He holds it all together in significance, reveals the redemptive pattern that we call the life and death of things and holds the meaning and value of our lives *outside of ourselves!*

Because we no longer worship such a Christ, we are condemned to worship smaller stories. We try to replace him with colorized myths of pilgrims, George Washington and General

Norman Schwarzkopf, but none of them are big enough or real enough to give universal order and meaning. We look to the private psyche, but it is just not big enough or connected enough to encompass human spiritual longing.

The Church's efforts at evangelization will remain trapped in culture and fundamentalism until we are ourselves large enough to proclaim a Cosmic Christ.

from *Sojourners*, "Why Does Psychology Always Win?"

Monday of the Thirty-Fourth Week of Ordinary Time   Day 403

Radical Grace

I used to say that if I ever wrote a book, its title would be *Nothing Truly Radical Happens After Age Six, Except Grace*. [Hence, the title of this book.] Grace, that experience of unconditional love, breaks through the whole system and can change anything.

All of Christian life could be described as an ever-deeper encounter between our wounded inner child and the wondrous world of grace. Grace can bring us back to the *radix*, our roots, and orient us toward the conversion Jesus called for. That's why we say grace is radical. Radical grace empowers us to shuck off the system and become children again: children of God, brothers and sisters to all of humanity.

from *The Spiritual Family and the Natural Family*

Unconditional Love

Most people think we repent and then we experience redemption. Actually it's exactly opposite in the Bible (read Ezekiel 16, the allegory of Israel, for example). You really repent, you truly turn again to the Lord for new life, *after* you've experienced redemption. First you experience God's saving love, and that's what gives you the power for true repentance: "Not our love for God, but God's love for us" (1 John 4:10).

Many people are incapable of true repentance because they are trying too hard. They get into breast beating and putting themselves down. It will never work, but only deaden and paralyze. That's never God's work. God enters into our sin and redeems it. God loves us first before we can do anything. And from that experience of unearned love, unprepared-for love, comes within us the power to begin again. We end up looking good and getting the credit, but we know better inside!

from *The Spiritual Family and the Natural Family*

Teach Your Children Well

We've got to teach the next generation the real meaning of generosity. Give *yourself* to your children, as opposed to just giving them things. You can't be with them all the time, but when you do have time, let them see you enjoy being with them. Let them see you value them simply for their own sakes.

Women have learned this better than men. Men have thought we could love our children simply by earning money for them. But we have to teach our children how to *care deeply*, and then they move toward caretaking. The only way we can do that is by being caring people ourselves. If you're constantly complaining about having to give too much, about how much is asked of you, don't be surprised if your children are petty and selfish and do not care about people, much less about things.

When they see a magnanimous, generous, fearless heart ready to make acts of faith, ready to serve, they are inspired to holiness. Teach your children that we don't own this earth, that "the earth is the Lord's and the fullness thereof" (Psalm 24:1). We are caretakers of this earth, and we must learn how to *care* before it is too late.

from The Spiritual Family and the Natural Family

Thursday of the Thirty-Fourth Week of Ordinary Time   Day 406

Between Myself and God, Give Me God

If I would have to choose between judging myself and being judged by God, I'll take God. Give me God, who sees the whole picture and who is my father and mother. God's going to say what parents say: "Don't bother me with the facts, this is my child!" We condemn ourselves with facts, but the facts don't mean very much in terms of relationships.

When your daughter keeps running toward you and calling

you Daddy, do you really care that much whether she stumbles a few times on the way? "If you then, who are evil, know how to give to your children what is good, how much more will your Father in heaven give good things to those who ask him!" (Matthew 7:11, JB).

from *The Spiritual Family and the Natural Family*

St. Francis' Prayer

Our father St. Francis passed on to us only prayers of praise. He went simply through his life finding new things for which to praise God at every turn: the little things, nature, the creatures, the animals, situations, his brothers—for whatever is happening, he praises God. Francis is never achieving God's love; he is celebrating it! He continually celebrates God's love in everything he sees and experiences. Mature prayer always breaks into gratitude.

Prayer is sitting in the silence until it silences us, choosing gratitude until we are grateful, praising God until we ourselves are an act of praise.

from *The Great Themes of Scripture*

Lord Jesus, I Love You

In the final appendix to the Gospel, the disciples are fishing. The Risen Jesus asks them from the seashore if they have caught anything. "You've fished all night and have caught nothing" are words he could say to the Church. "You've thrown out the net again and again and have borne little fruit. Trust me. Throw out the net once more at my word. Do it a different way. Throw to the other side." And on the word of Jesus they throw out the nets. There are 153 fish, symbolizing all known species, all the nations of the earth that they would bring if only they would believe and trust in him, and nothing less than him.

Then Peter in the boat recognizes Jesus on the shore. He forgets everything else, jumps into the sea and swims to Jesus. He was no doubt filled with fear because he knows that the last time he spoke with Jesus was when he denied him three times. Perhaps he's afraid that he will reprimand him, but he must return to him. He comes ashore and Jesus only says, "Simon, son of John, do you love me more than these?" "Yes, Lord," he said, "you know that I love you" (John 21:15).

And again, "Peter, do you love me?"

And with anguish, Peter replies, "Lord, you know that I love you." And a third time Jesus asks, "Peter, do you love me?" And Peter was upset that he asked him a third time. He said, "Lord, you know everything. You know that I love you" (21:17).

In this we see the gracious love of Jesus. He could not bear that for the rest of his life Peter would carry the guilt of those three denials. So three times he permits him to say publicly and proudly, "I love you. You know everything. You know that I love you." Peter has at last become a disciple. Now he is led to give everything away and follow the Lord.

The Lord calls us to that same public, proud act of faith, for yourself and for your brothers and sisters. Before the whole Christian community, let us say: Lord Jesus, I love you and I am proud to love you. You are my Lord and you are my God. I will leave all things to follow you. You are my teacher and my endless joy.

from The Great Themes of Scripture

Other works by Richard Rohr, O.F.M.
Available from St. Anthony Messenger Press

Books

From Wild Man to Wise Man: Reflections on Male Spirituality
with Joseph Martos

The Great Themes of Scripture: New Testament with
Joseph Martos

The Great Themes of Scripture: Old Testament with
Joseph Martos

*Hope Against Darkness: The Transforming Vision of Saint Francis
in an Age of Anxiety* with John Feister

Jesus' Plan for a New World: The Sermon on the Mount with
John Feister

Why Be Catholic? Understanding Our Experience and Tradition
with Joseph Martos

CDs and Cassettes

Authentic Religion: Membership or Transformation?

Breathing Under Water: Spirituality and the Twelve Steps

Catholicism: More Than a 'Head Trip'

Dying: You Need it For Life

Faith: Recovering the Language of Belief

Faith in Exile: Biblical Spirituality for Our Time

Fire From Heaven: A Retreat for Men

Gravity and Grace: Insights Into Christian Ministry

Great Themes of Paul: Life as Participation

Healing Our Violence through the Journey of Centering Prayer with Thomas Keating, O.C.S.O.

Hearing the Wisdom of Jesus

Jesus: Forgiving Victim, Transforming Savior

Letting Go: A Spirituality of Subtraction

Life-Changing Teachings of Richard Rohr, O.F.M.: An Introductory Set

'Love Your Enemy': The Gospel Call to Nonviolence

A Man's Approach to God: Four Talks on Male Spirituality

The Maternal Face of God

Men and Women: The Journey of Spiritual Transformation

New Great Themes of Scripture

The Parables: Letting Jesus Teach Us

Preparing for Christmas With Richard Rohr

The Quest for Holy Wisdom

Rebuild the Church: Richard Rohr's Challenge for the New Millennium

Sermon on the Mount

A Spirituality for the Two Halves of Life with Paula D'Arcy

The Spirituality of Imperfection

True Self / False Self

Liturgical Calendar

The following dates are provided to help the day-by-day reader who wishes to follow the liturgical year. If your parish bulletin or a missalette is not handy, locate the most recent date on this chart, go to that meditation and count forward until you reach today's meditation.

	2005	2006	2007
First Sunday of Advent (*Day 1*) *	Nov. 28	Nov. 27	Dec. 3
First Monday of Ordinary Time (*Day 53*)	Jan. 10	Jan. 9	Jan. 8
Sunday Before Ash Wednesday (*Day 108*)	Feb. 6	Feb. 26	Feb. 18
Easter (*Day 157*)	Mar. 27	Apr. 16	Apr. 8
Monday After Pentecost (*Day 207*)	May 16	June 5	May 28
Ninth Sunday of Ordinary Time (*Day 227*)	—	—	—
Tenth Sunday of Ordinary Time (*Day 234*)	June 5	—	—
Eleventh Sunday of Ordinary Time (*Day 241*)	June 12	—	June 17
Twelfth Sunday of Ordinary Time (*Day 248*)	June 19	June 25	June 24
Thirteenth Sunday of Ordinary Time (*Day 255*)	June 24	July 2	July 1
Fourteenth Sunday of Ordinary Time (*Day 262*)	July 1	July 9	July 8

* Date refers to prior year (e.g., 2004, 2005, etc.)

2008	2009	2010	2011	2012	2013	2014	2015
Dec. 2	Nov. 30	Nov. 29	Nov. 28	Nov. 27	Dec. 2	Dec. 1	Nov. 30
Jan. 14	Jan. 12	Jan. 11	Jan. 10	Jan. 9	Jan. 14	Jan. 13	Jan. 12
Feb. 3	Feb. 22	Feb. 14	Mar. 6	Feb. 19	Feb. 10	Mar. 2	Feb. 15
Mar. 23	Apr. 12	Apr. 4	Apr. 24	Apr. 8	Mar. 31	Apr. 20	Apr. 5
May 12	June 1	May 24	June 13	May 28	May 20	June 9	May 25
June 1	—	—	—	—	—	—	—
June 8	—	—	—	—	June 9	—	—
June 15	—	June 13	—	June 17	June 16	—	June 14
June 22	June 21	June 20	—	June 24	June 23	—	June 21
June 29	June 28	June 27	—	July 1	June 30	June 29	June 28
July 6	July 5	July 4	July 3	July 8	July 7	July 6	July 5

Index